# LAWRENCE AND NIETZSCHE

**AUP titles of related interest**

**THE MEANING OF FREEDOM**
*Philip Drew, Glasgow University*

**PHILOSOPHY AND FICTION**
**Essays in Literary Aesthetics**
*edited by Peter Lamarque, Stirling University*

**THE HISTORY OF SCOTTISH LITERATURE**
*general editor Cairns Craig*

Volume 1 Medieval and Renaissance
Volume 2 1660–1800
Volume 3 Nineteenth Century
Volume 4 Twentieth Century

# Lawrence *and* Nietzsche

*a study in influence*

## Colin Milton

ABERDEEN UNIVERSITY PRESS

First published 1987
Aberdeen University Press
A member of the Pergamon Group

© Colin Milton 1987

**British Library Cataloguing in Publication Data**

Milton, Colin
 Lawrence and Nietzsche: a study in
 influence.
 1. Lawrence, D H—Criticism and
 interpretation  2. Nietzsche, Friedrich
 —Influence—Lawrence, D H
 I. Title
 823'.912    PR6023.A93Z/

ISBN 0-08-035067-4

Printed in Great Britain
The University Press
Aberdeen

*to my wife*

# Contents

# Acknowledgements

I am grateful to Dr Malcolm Pittock who supervised my original research on D H Lawrence many years ago and to Professor Ronald Draper who took over from him; they put their knowledge of Lawrence freely at my disposal and provided much of the initial stimulus for this book. Over the years, many of my students and colleagues at the University of Aberdeen have found themselves helping—more or less willingly—in the development of many of the ideas in this book; I would like to thank them all for their interest and encouragement, particularly Dr Paul Schlicke.

Like all researchers I owe a great debt to the staffs of the various libraries I have used and I wish to thank especially the staff of Aberdeen University Library, Aberdeen Public Libraries and the British Library for being invariably helpful, courteous and efficient.

Mrs Anne Robertson of the Aberdeen University English Department typed the manuscript with impeccable accuracy and Miss Marjorie Leith of Aberdeen University Press gave me a great deal of help and advice in the final stages of preparation.

My greatest debt of all is to that peerless teacher, the late Walter Keir, who communicated his enthusiasm for modern literature to so many Aberdeen students. Without him, this book would never have been written.

University of Aberdeen
February, 1987

# A Note on Texts and Translations

I have used the Penguin editions of Lawrence's novels and short stories throughout and page references in the text are to these editions; in the case of *St Mawr*, references are to the text in the Penguin English Library volume of the complete short novels. For Jessie Chambers' memories of the young Lawrence, I have quoted from the second edition of her 'Personal Record' (PR), edited by J D Chambers (London, 1965).

Modern translations of Nietzsche are more reliable—and more readable—than those in the 1909–1913 Foulis edition, which is still the only edition of the Complete Works available in English. Where possible I have used the recent translations of individual works by Walter Kaufmann and R J Hollingdale; where such modern versions were unavailable at the time of writing, I have used the appropriate volume in the Foulis edition. Much of the material which was unpublished in Nietzsche's life-time is included in the standard German editions of the Works, but has not appeared in English. However, in his exposition of Nietzsche's philosophy, *What Nietzsche Means*, George Allen Morgan quotes extensively from this *Nachlass* and I have used his translations in cases where such material seemed to me more apt and illuminating than similar passages in the published works. Morgan's translations are taken from the twenty volume second edition of the Complete Works published in Leipzig between 1901 and 1926, the *Grossoctavausgabe*, in which Nietsche's *Nachlass* occupies volumes IX–XVI. Where I have used Morgan's translations from the *Nachlass*, I have given the volume and page number in the German edition, as well as indicating where the translation appears in *What Nietzsche Means*.

CHAPTER 1

# Nietzsche and Lawrence

The intellectual kinship between D H Lawrence and the nineteenth century German philosopher Friedrich Nietzsche has been widely recognised, but there has been no general agreement among those who have written on Lawrence's work about the precise nature and extent of the relationship between the two men. Opinions have ranged from Harry Steinhauer's confident assertion that Lawrence 'takes over the Nietzschean "system" in its entirety',[1] to John Carey's warning that if the novelist's ideas do resemble those of his contemporaries and near-contemporaries, Nietzsche among them, this is because 'he did not write in some cranky limbo, but was stirred by the same questions, and occasionally the same answers, as the rest of intellectual Europe at what we have come to think of as the end of the Christian era'.[2] Steinhauer's remark is made in a brief article which in itself can scarcely even begin to justify such a sweeping and confident conclusion and in the absence of a full and convincing demonstration of Lawrence's intellectual dependence on his German predecessor, those who think him an important and original writer are likely to find Carey's position the more appealing one. On the other hand, the relation between Nietzsche's 'system' and what Lawrence sometimes called his 'pseudo-philosophy' is so intimate and pervasive that even a common origin in a shared cultural climate and intellectual agenda scarcely seems sufficient to account for the resemblance. For what is involved is not so much a matter of several—or even many— particular similarities, themselves part of some general current of 'advanced' or 'post-Christian' speculation of the time, but the sharing of a whole organically related structure of ideas and one, furthermore, which is highly individual in character. And, as the investigations of David Thatcher[3] and Patrick Bridgwater[4] into the influence of Nietzsche on the allegedly insular intellectual life of these islands have shown, Nietzschean ideas had a powerful effect on certain sections of the British intelligensia during Lawrence's intellectually formative years—in the period, that is, from roughly the turn of the century to the outbreak of the Great War. It was Nietzsche above all who drafted the agenda for the advanced intellectuals of the time, who asked the most challenging and radical questions, who offered the most interesting and provocative answers and who, more than any other thinker, convinced his contemporaries that they were indeed living 'at the end of the Christian era'.

My aim in what follows is to identify and illustrate the most important of these resemblances; I shall argue that Lawrence and Nietzsche share essentially the same idea of the relation between character and environment, of the structure and dynamics of the human psyche, of the fundamental rhythms of human development and of the way in which continuing growth depends on confronting risk and challenge. And the view of human nature they share becomes, for both, the basis of a radical critique of the dominant cultural, moral and religious traditions of Western culture. Each believed that these traditions had brought Western man to a point of crisis where his continuing creativity and even his survival were at risk, and that if he were to regain his vitality he would have to emancipate himself from them without delay. As a result, both philosopher and novelist devote much of their energy to attacking, in their different ways, those things which they see as debilatating or corrupting elements in our culture and to defining and commending an alternative ethos which will enhance rather than diminish human vitality. Lawrence took over from Nietzsche a complex and ambivalent analysis of the main element in the psychological and moral formation of our civilisation—the Christian faith. While both men recognise and, indeed, celebrate what they see as the noble aspects of the Christian ideal and concede its historical importance in chanelling and disciplining psychic forces which might otherwise have proved anarchic and destructive, each also condemns Christianity as a religion created by the weak, incapable and inferior and used by them as an instrument of revenge against the vital and powerful.

Lawrence first came upon Nietzsche when he left his native Nottinghamshire in October 1908 to take up a teaching post in Croydon. In her memoir of the novelist's early life, Jessie Chambers records that it was in the public library there that he first came upon the works of the man who was to have such a powerful influence on his own vision:

> It was in the library at Croydon that Lawrence found Nietzsche. He never mentioned him directly to me, nor suggested that I should read him, but I began to hear about the 'Will to Power', and perceived that he had come upon something new and engrossing ...
>
> (PR p 120)

Lawrence had first developed a serious interest in philosophy during his second year at college in Nottingham in 1907–8 and from the beginning his philosophical explorations had an urgent and personal, rather than a merely abstract and intellectual character, because it was at this time that he began to feel the full impact of the new developments in science and of the rationalistic and materialistic outlook associated with them. To someone from Lawrence's provincial Non-Conformist background, scientific materialism was still a profound shock and challenge, even though nearly half a century had elapsed since the publication of Darwin's *Origin of Species*. Jessie's memoir makes clear just how deeply the encounter affected him:

> The Lawrence that came out of College at the end of two years was a different man from the Lawrence who entered. For one thing he had come up against the materialist attitude to life and religion and it seared his youthful freshness. We were still regular attenders at the Congregational chapel where our minister used to preach interesting sermons that were more lectures than sermons, and on the walk home we would discuss the sermon and religion in general ... Far more than in any dogma, Lawrence was interested in the question as to how the old religious ideas stood in relation to the scientific discoveries that were sweeping away the familiar landmarks.
>
> (**PR** p 33)

The result was that during his years at college, he 'completely outgrew the conception of life that chapel and all it stood for offered'. (**PR** p 85)

Like many of his contemporaries, Lawrence felt the crisis of values most acutely in the realm of morality. The scientific picture of the natural world as a kind of gladiatorial arena, the scene of an incessant struggle for survival among all living things, together with the complete assimilation of man to this violent natural order, cast serious doubt on the validity of the Christian ethic with its emphasis on altruism and non-violence. For many of those influenced by evolutionism, the genesis and subsequent influence of the Christian moral code—and of similar moral codes in other religious traditions—became problematic. How could such apparent aberrations, such seeming violations of evolutionary 'laws', have come into existence and how could the human conceptions of value they embodied be related to the scientific facts? One way of answering the question was to see Christian morality and its analogues as means by which—consciously or unconsciously—the true nature of human motives and impulses are concealed. Christianity could be seen, for instance, as a cynical political strategy devised or adopted by ruling groups to maintain their privileged position in the social order; for political radicals it was an ideological creation, designed to reconcile the poor to their present hard lot by promising them unending plenty and felicity in the life to come. Alternatively, it could be seen as an idealistic illusion with psychological rather than political roots, which works to deceive the believer in ways that he is not conscious of. This second kind of explanation sees Christianity and other similar belief-systems as inconsistent with the imperatives of the evolutionary process essentially because they are pathological growths, springing from and expressing declining and decadent life: by various means these 'decadent' values have become the dominant— though not the only—moral influence in our society, infecting the healthy as well, and so threatening the continuing vitality of our culture. It was Nietzsche who developed most fully and expressed most forcefully this diagnosis of Christianity as the product of 'declining, debilitated, weary, condemned life'[5] created by those too weak to affirm the difficulty, struggle and suffering inseparable from earthly existence, and he contrasted it with Buddhism, which has similar origins but employs different and less dangerous psychic strategies. Lawrence follows him in claiming that Christianity and Buddhism 'belong together as nihilistic religions' and his account of the historical origins of the Christian faith in Roman times is essentially the same:

> When men become poor in life they become anxious about their fortunes and frightened about their fate. By the time of Jesus, men had become so anxious about their fortunes and so frightened about their fates, that they put up the grand declaration that life was one long misery and you couldn't expect your fortune till you got to heaven; that is, till after you were dead. This was accepted by all men, and has been the creed until our day, Buddha and Jesus alike. It has provided us with a vast amount of thought-forms, and landed us in a sort of living death.[6]

During his college years, Lawrence became convinced that the discoveries made by contemporary science had created—in Nietzsche's phrase—a 'total contrast between value and fact': scientific understanding of both the physical world and of human nature had come to seem completely at variance with the moral and religious truths he had been brought up to believe. His philosophical reading was part of an urgent search for new life-values founded on the new knowledge offered by science. Jessie Chambers records that during this period of his life

> In all his reading he seemed to be groping for something that he could lay hold of as a guiding principle in his own life. There was never the least touch of the academic or scholastic in his approach. What he read was to be applied here and now; he seemed to consider all his philosophical reading from the angle of his own personal need.
>
> **(PR** p 112-3)

At first he tried to satisfy that need by turning to the attempts made by various followers of Darwin to apply evolutionary principles in the moral and social realms. It was at this time that, in Jessie's words,

> The materialistic philosophy came in full blast with T H Huxley's *Man's Place in Nature*, Darwin's *Origin of Species*, and Haeckel's *Riddle of the Universe*. This rationalistic teaching impressed Lawrence deeply. He came upon it at a time of spiritual fog, when the lights of orthodox religion and morality were proving wholly inadequate ... My feeling was that he tried to fill up a spiritual vacuum by swallowing materialism at a gulp. He would tell me with vehemence that nature is red in tooth and claw, with the implication that 'nature' included human nature. Yet when he heard the cry of a rabbit trapped by a weasel he would shiver with pain.
>
> **(PR** p 112)

Jessie's lack of sympathy for the kind of outlook which attracted Lawrence is evident in her suggestion that 'the materialistic philosophy' was a single intellectual tendency and, furthermore, one which implied that man was completely at the mercy of his egoistic and predatory animal impulses. As a result, she fails to discriminate between the very different positions taken up by the three writers she mentions. While there is evidence that, in private at least, Darwin himself came to adopt a materialist position, he consistently refused to be drawn into the intense public debate on the wider implications of evolutionism; in his published works at least, Darwin is not a spokesman for the 'materialistic philosophy' often linked with his name. T H Huxley, Darwin's main British ally and publicist, did explore the implications of evolutionism for moral and social questions, as did his fellow zoologist Ernst Haeckel, chief propagandist for Darwinism in Germany. However the work of these two prominent Darwinians demonstrates just how diverse and even contradictory a phenomenon 'Darwinism' was and just how difficult it is to derive unambiguous conclusions about how human beings ought to conduct themselves from a scientific hypothesis about the forces active in the natural world.

In the published version of his 1893 Romanes Lecture on 'Evolution and Ethics'[7] – his best known and most fully worked out attempt to derive a moral 'ought' from a scientific 'is', Huxley accepts that the 'laws of nature' as elucidated by Darwin are indeed in conflict with our ethical tradition, but he rejects the view that because of this we should radically revise or even abandon that tradition. Huxley was able to retain his belief in traditional moral values because, unlike many of those who tried to extend Darwinism to moral and social matters, he was always aware that 'fitness' in the evolutionary sense carries no moral suggestion and cannot be equated with 'higher' or 'more developed'. Success in the struggle for survival does not demonstrate the value of the successful form in any independent sense.

Huxley's distinguished German contemporary, Haeckel, on the other hand, strongly influenced by the teleological conception of evolution which nineteenth century German biologists inherited from the mystical *Natur-philosophie* of their Romantic predecessors, did interpret 'fitness' in a moral sense and as a result was 'haunted by what he believed to be man's blind rebellion against his biological origin and biological destiny'.[8] Haeckel felt that by adhering to moral codes—particularly Christianity—which were in conflict with the 'laws of nature', man had turned aside from the harsh but exemplary discipline of the natural order and put his vigour and even perhaps his survival as a species at risk—an apocalyptic view of the human predicament also shared by Nietzsche and Lawrence. And like them, Haeckel argued that in order to avert this racial disaster, the disappearance of humanity not with a bang but a whimper, a moral revolution was needed which would replace the Christian ethic with its over-emphasis on altruism by a more robust and 'natural' outlook. In his most widely read work, *The Riddle of the Universe*,[9] Haeckel urged a revival of paganism centering on the natural world and involving sun-worship, a suggestion which made a lasting impression on Lawrence's imagination as did the idea, outlined in the same work, that much of our extensive unconscious psychic activity is centered on our ganglionic cells. But despite these borrowings, Lawrence did not remain satisfied for long with this kind of rationalism and the major influences on his intellectual development are more substantial figures—Arthur Schopenhauer, Friedrich Nietzsche and William James.

Lawrence had become interested in Schopenhauer during his college years and for a time was very much under the influence of the great German pessimist. Jessie reports that during his second year at college

... he advised one of my brothers to give me Schopenhauer's *Essays* for my birthday, and read 'The Metaphysics of Love' aloud to us ... This essay made a deep impression on him ... Schopenhauer seemed to fit in with his mood. He thought he found there an explanation of his own divided attitude and he remained under the influence of this line of reasoning for some time.

**(PR p 111)**

But Lawrence was not interested in Schopenhauer only because of the light his ideas seemed to shed on his own personal dilemmas but also because of their relevance to the general question of how traditional beliefs stood in relation to contemporary scientific knowledge. Unlike the materialism of Huxley and Haeckel, Schopenhauer's philosophy was not a post-Darwinian creation—indeed his main work *The World as Will and Idea*, had been published as early as 1819 and although it was expanded and reissued twice in 1844 and 1859, Schopenhauer did not alter his philosophical position in any significant way in the later editions. Nevertheless it was only after the mid-century and especially when the influence of Darwinism began to be generally felt that he became widely known, and the first English translations of his works were made in the 1880s and 1890s. Schopenhauer saw life almost entirely in terms of conflict, cruelty and suffering, an emphasis which matched the gladiatorial view of existence characteristic of evolutionism, and his fundamental principle, the Will, seemed to offer an explanation of why the world is as it is. Schopenhauer borrowed the term from contemporary psychology, but his Will is both more fundamental and more pervasive than 'will' in the ordinary sense; a metaphysical rather than a psychological entity, Will is the ground of all being. It is a formless, non-rational, endlessly creative energy, a plenitude which, in constantly striving to realise itself, gives rise to the various and changing world we inhabit. Because it is not a rational, self-consistent or even intelligent force, but a sort of blind, incessant striving, the world the Will brings into being is far from being an orderly or harmonious one—it is characterised instead by pain and struggle and waste. Schopenhauer's view of how the phenomenal world of our ordinary experience is related to the ultimate reality which gives rise to it was profoundly influenced by eastern philosophy and represents a sharp break with—even an inversion of—the view which has been the dominant one in western metaphysics. While western philosophers have tended to locate 'true' reality in a figuratively 'higher' realm—a clearer, cleaner, more rational and intelligible world above the confusion, mess and transience of this world—Schopenhauer places his ultimate reality as it were *below* the sensible realm, so that the 'real' world is one in which the characteristics of our familiar world are intensified. The Schopenhauerian Will is a dynamic principle of unimaginable fullness and incessant struggle, the antithesis of the traditional picture of 'ultimate reality' as a world of clear and permanent forms. To many of those impressed by the discoveries of nineteenth century science, reality conceived in this way seemed a more plausible creative principle than the traditional Christian conception of a creating Godhead.

Schopenhauer is important in the history of western philosophy as the first philosopher to make the Will his fundamental principle and in doing so was Nietzsche's immediate predecessor in a particular philosophical tradition, but both his conception of the Will and his attitude to its activity differ from those of his successor. According to A R Orage, one of the earliest English interpreters of this tradition, 'Schopenhauer had traced the sources of life beyond the reason to the will' and 'it was characteristic of his doctrines that he should lay greatest stress upon the self-preservative aspect of the will'. Nietzsche, on the other hand, while accepting Schopenhauer's 'conception of the will as the essence of life ... substituted, or rather added, the significant definition: Life is the Will to Power'.[10] For Nietzsche, the Will is a more active and imperialistic principle than it was for Schopenhauer and its activity is something that should be affirmed; for his predecessor, the Will is essentially something which should be resisted and human virtue consists in denying its importunities.

Like Nietzsche and Lawrence, Schopenhauer lays great stress on the power of instinct, which he sees as the Will expressing its purposes in the individual life. Almost everything we do is determined at the instinctive, unconscious level although this fact is usually hidden from us by the concealments and disguises behind which the Will characteristically operates. Schopenhauer also shares with Nietzsche and Lawrence a profound scepticism about the reality and importance of 'exalted' human feelings and, in general, about the efficacy of all that is conscious and rational. Like them, he stresses the fact that most of our psychic life is unconscious and that the most powerful impulses in us, those that determine the direction of our lives, come from that unconscious area of being. It is a conception of the psyche which was in harmony with the theory that man had evolved from lower forms of life so that consciousness and rationality were comparatively late developments in his total history and the wide interest in Schopenhauer's work after the mid-century was largely due to the way in which his central philosophical conception seemed to fit in with 'the scientific discoveries that were sweeping away the familiar landmarks' of the time.

In the essay on 'The Metaphysics of Love' which impressed the young Lawrence so much, Schopenhauer argues that 'love', that apparently most intimate and individual of feelings, is no more than a disguise for the desire of the Will to manifest itself further by bringing a new individual into existence. However refined and personal the sentiment of love may seem to the lover, his—or her—interest in the beloved is fundamentally sexual or, more properly, procreative. What is experienced as 'love' is 'in reality the will to live of the new being, of which they shall become the parents'.[11] Such exalted sentiments as 'love' are deceptions practised upon us by the Will so that in realising its impersonal purposes we imagine we are acting for ourselves. The deception is necessary, Schopenhauer argues, because if we were consistently aware that life is largely suffering—as we would be if we were not deluded by feelings like love—we would neither wish to prolong life in ourselves nor create a new generation of men to share it.

Since he regards the Will as the ground of all being, Schopenhauer—again like Nietzsche and Lawrence—holds that intellect and consciousness are essentially instruments of instinct rather than independent faculties. At the beginning of the 'Psychological Observations' in the collection of essay in which Lawrence found 'The Metaphysics of Love', the object of the intellect is defined as being to act as 'the light and guide of the will on its path'.[12] This is, broadly speaking, a pragmatic view of intellect, one which sees it not so much as an instrument for discovering objective and permanent truths, but as something which interprets—and reinterprets—the world in accordance with the changing needs and interests which we develop as we grow. Intellect offers us temporary and provisional 'truths' not final ones. Schopenhauer sees truth in a way which is similar to the more developed accounts of intellectual function Lawrence would have found in Nietzsche and William James and his own view of truth as something personal and provisional, as that which is 'true in its own time, place, circumstance, and untrue outside of its own place, time, circumstance' places him squarely in this tradition. His debt to Pragmatic ways of thinking makes it clear that the impetus behind Lawrence's 'philosophy' is not adequately explained as the simple reaction against scientific rationalism it is sometimes taken to be because, as Walter Kaufmann points out, nineteenth-century science and, in particular, biology, was a major stimulus to Pragmatism:

> The teachings of evolutionism supplied the decisive impetus that prompted the development of pragmatic doctrines at about the same time—toward the end of the nineteenth century—in England, France, Germany, and of course the United States.
> The intellect, hitherto regarded as essentially eternal, now had to be accounted for in terms of evolution. Instead of having existed before the mountains were brought forth, it now appeared to have originated in time—not all at once, but through the struggle for existence and the survival of the fittest. It was an instrument, a tool, an asset in the struggle; and those possessing it had survived because of its great practical value.[13]

Although Schopenhauer thought that the intellect was normally the instrument of the instincts, he believed that some exceptional individuals were endowed with an intellectual capacity in excess of their instinctive needs and that in such cases intellect, detached from the immediate purposes of instinct, could turn against it. Such individuals are capable of reflecting on the activities of the instincts, of seeing them critically from the outside and freed in this way from the deceptions of the Will, they become aware of the true nature of things. Given Schopenhauer's emphasis on the negative aspects of existence, this experience is inevitably a disillusioning one, leading to the conclusion that life is not worth living:

> The development of the intellect to an abnormal degree of strength and superiority, thereby making it out of all proportion to the will ... is not only superfluous but actually an impediment to the needs and purposes of life.[14]

The result is an ascetic renunciation of all desire which Schopenhauer sees as the highest expression of human wisdom.

Both Nietzsche and Lawrence agree that consciousness and intellect can develop to the point where they undermine the 'needs and purposes of life' but both see this as a threat to the continuing vigour and even survival of man rather than as something to be admired. Both argue that reason and consciousness should remain in their subsidiary role as instruments of the unconscious, and that instinct rather than intellect should guide our lives. This conflict of opinion does not arise from the fact that Nietzsche and Lawrence see life in different terms from their predecessors; both emphasise, just as much as Schopenhauer does, the predominance of difficulty, pain and conflict in existence. The disagreement arises from different attitudes to exactly these pervasive features of the world and from a different and more active conception of the primary impulse of being. Lawrence follows Nietzsche in holding that the impulse does not aim simply at survival, but strives instead to grow, develop and increase at the expense of safety, of comfort and often even of survival itself. As Lawrence puts it in 'Study of Thomas Hardy', in man and other living things, the 'unappeased range of self-preservation' is balanced by a wasteful, extravagant impulse to expression, prudent accumulation by spending—

> Working in contradiction to the will of self-preservation, from the very first man wasted himself begetting children, colouring himself and dancing and howling and sticking feathers in his hair ...[15]

And, for Lawrence, it is this second phase that is 'all the story and all the triumph'. In the same way—and despite its name—Nietzsche's will to power is not a principle of continual greedy accumulation, but involves a rhythmic alternation of 'getting' and 'spending' and as G A Morgan says in his account of Nietzsche's thought, he himself 'seems to stress the last phase as the more important, as if getting were ultimately for the sake of giving'.[16] Human growth and fulfilment for both Lawrence and Nietzsche depend not on an ascetic withdrawal from the world but on an engagement with it in which struggle and suffering are the stimulus to fuller being. Both came to see Schopenhauer's attitude as a symptom of weakness, as a pathological response to life by someone too weak to face and affirm the discomfort inseparable from living fully.

Schopenhauer regarded sympathy as the highest of all moral qualities because he saw it as originating in the intuitive recognition that individuality is an illusion, since every being is a manifestation of a single entity—the Will. In the high value he attaches to compassion and related virtues, Schopenhauer is close to the Christian ethical tradition, despite the fact that he tended to disparage Christianity as a crudely superstitious creed. But even the possibility of sympathy is difficult to account for in the light of Schopenhauer's insistence that the world of our experience is a phenomenal one. How do we obtain that direct knowledge of the ultimate ground of being from which sympathy arises? Nor is it easy to understand how the Will can turn against itself when embodied in unusually intelligent human beings. In fact, the existence of altruistic and self-sacrificing behaviour is difficult to

reconcile with Schopenhauer's metaphysical premises and he has to intro-
duce a special, privileged kind of insight to explain it. Rationalists like
Huxley, who argued that human life is governed by an ethical process which
is opposed to the laws governing nature as a whole, face a similar problem
in explaining how traits which would originally have threatened survival
could become the dominant ones.

For Nietzsche, this kind of problem arises because thinkers like Schopenhauer and Huxley have not emancipated themselves successfully from the
dualistic habit of mind engendered by Christian tradition and consequently
think of man's 'good' qualities as wholly different from his 'bad' ones and
as having an entirely different origin. And they also accept traditional
definitions of what is good and bad, virtuous and vicious. Nietzsche's own
attitude is more rational, consistent and naturalistic, centering on the idea
of sublimation whereby 'bad' impulses can be transformed into 'good' ones.
It was this view of the relation between the 'lower' and the 'higher' elements
of the psyche which Lawrence adopted and it follows that for the novelist,
as for the philosopher, man's spiritual achievements depend not on weakening or suppressing his animal nature, but on strengthening and cultivating it.

Lawrence spent three years or so living in Croydon and Jessie's memoir
does not say exactly when in that period he discovered Nietzsche, but his
interest is likely to have been aroused shortly after his arrival there in the
autumn of 1908 because it was at just this time that Nietzsche's reputation
was beginning to grow again in Britain after a decade of neglect. *Beyond
Good and Evil*, which appeared in 1907,[17] was the first relatively successful
volume in a projected complete English edition of Nietzsche which had
started to appear as long ago as 1896. The modest success of the 1907 volume
was not enough to save this particular venture from collapse, but continental
interest in Nietzsche, which was particularly strong in France, had begun to
spread to Britain. Perhaps the most important vehicle for bringing before the
educated British reader the ideas of the man who in Arthur Symon's words
had 'spoken to his end of the century with a formidable voice' was the
magazine *The New Age*, particularly after A R Orage assumed full charge of
it late in 1907. It is clear from the literary memoirs of the time that under
Orage's inspired direction the magazine had an influence out of all proportion to its modest circulation and it played a central part in creating the
contemporary interest in Nietzsche which allowed Oscar Levy to embark on
the new complete English edition which began to appear in 1909.[18]

The *New Age* introduced a number of important writers to Nietzsche's
ideas and it may have been instrumental in arousing Lawrence's interest since
he subscribed to the magazine for a time. His attention was first drawn to
it by a member of the Eastwood discussion group to which both he and Jessie
belonged—

> It was a member of this little circle, a Socialist and a Suffragette, who first
> showed us A R Orage's *New Age* which Lawrence took regularly for a time ...
> We used to enjoy particularly the Literary Causerie by Jacob Tonson.
>
> (**PR** p 120)

Arnold Bennett began his 'Books and Persons' column, writing as 'Jacob Tonson' in March 1908 and in the early autobiographical play, *A Collier's Friday Night*, written originally in 1909, Mrs Lambert, who is clearly based on Mrs Lawrence, reads her student son's copy of the *New Age*. Taken together, these facts suggest that Lawrence was reading Orage's magazine at just the time when its editor was trying to arouse interest in Nietzsche in general and in Levy's new edition in particular. And of course Lawrence's interest in Schopenhauer would have led naturally on to an interest in the man who was his greatest admirer and direct intellectual successor.

Nietzsche is mentioned in several of Lawrence's earliest works, but such references are less helpful than they seem at first in assessing possible intellectual debts. The fact that a number of Lawrence's comments are critical or even hostile and are often directed not at peripheral or inessential areas of Nietzsche's thought but at his central conception, the will to power itself, might seem to dispose immediately of the idea that Lawrence was significantly influenced by Nietzsche. Many of the critics who have considered the matter, naturally more interested in the writer than in the philosopher, have been content to accept Lawrence's version of what Nietzsche thought and of how his own ideas differed—even if they conclude, as Graham Hough does at the end of the best short account of Lawrence's ideas that 'It is probable that his doctrine would not have been what it is if the Nietzschean influence had not been felt'.[19] The general critical conclusion has been that Lawrence was certainly interested in Nietzschean ideas and aware of their contemporary appeal, but was concerned to combat them rather than apply them. In his book on Lawrence's shorter fictions, for example, Kingsley Widmer, referring to the novelist's 'repeated criticism of "Will"' which is linked both with feminine destructiveness and industrial civilisation, adds that it

> ... may derive some of its force and pertinence as a critique of Nietzsche's 'will to power'. This seems to be the implicit context for Lawrence's statement: 'We have a confused idea that *will* and power are somehow identical. We think we can have a will to power.' Since Lawrence finds power primarily in unwilled sexual charisma, he condemns will to power as 'just bullying'.[20]

Commentators who have approached the question of influence from the opposite direction, from an interest in Nietzsche's reputation and in the spread of his ideas, and who therefore have a wider and more accurate knowledge of his philosophy, have found the question of the relationship between the two men more problematic. Patrick Bridgwater, for instance, discussing an exchange in *Aaron's Rod* in which Lilly explicitly links Nietzsche's *macht* with a kind of power which is conscious, intellectual and benevolent, concludes that Lawrence must have misunderstood Nietzsche and he goes on to emphasis that Lilly's view of power—which is presumably that of Lawrence himself—is very close to, indeed indistinguishable from, Nietzsche's:

> The urge to dominate, to which Nietzsche devoted not a little of his psychological acumen, as well as not a little of his tendency to over-generalise, is much

more a question of 'dark, living ... power' than of anything more cerebral; to identify it with the 'love-will' is nonsense. Lawrence is here far closer to Nietzsche than he realised.[21]

As I shall argue, it is likely that Lawrence did indeed realise how close he was to Nietzsche on this, the central conception of his philosophy but that, for a variety of reasons, he 'covered up his traces'[22]—to borrow Eric Bentley's uncharitable phrase.

It is in 'Study of Thomas Hardy', written in 1915, that Lawrence makes his first clearly critical reference to Nietzsche in discussing the relation of will to power to human love and sexuality. He associates it with a masculine impulse to dominate of the sort Widmer refers to, contrasting this 'Nietzschean' kind of love relationship with his own conception of the proper relation between men and women as one based on mutual respect for and wonder at the mystery of sexual otherness. He sees what he claims to be Nietzsche's idea of male passion as the reflex of an unconscious uncertainty in the face of that unknown kind of being which is the feminine. The male attempt to dominate in relationships between the sexes is essentially compensatory, arising from weakness rather than strength:

> There are two attitudes to love. A man in love with a woman says either: 'I, the man, the male, am the supreme, I am the one and the woman is administered unto me, and this is her highest function ...
>
> The other attitude of a man in love, beside this of 'she is administered unto my maleness', is, 'she is unknown, the undiscovered, into which I plunge to discovery losing myself.'
>
> And what we call real love always has this latter attitude. The first attitude, which belongs to passion, makes a man feel proud, splendid. It is a powerful stimulant to him, the female administered to him. He feels full of blood, he walks the earth like a Lord. And it is to this state Nietzsche aspires in his *Wille zur Macht*.[23]

Lawrence distinguishes (real) love from (mere) passion, a more narrowly sexual feeling and compares the effects of the latter to those of a 'powerful stimulant' suggesting that it is an unhealthy and in the end debilitating condition. It belongs to a kind of relationship in which, on the surface, the man is dominant and the woman no more than an instrument for his gratification, but Lawrence insists that appearances are misleading and that, on a deeper level, such relationships testify to a deep masculine fear in the face of the feminine, a 'deep inner dread' arising from the weakness and insecurity endemic among men in certain societies. Realising unconsciously that the woman's withdrawal would leave him 'empty, like ash', such men feel threatened by feminine independence and set out to destroy it, reducing their women to mere functions of themselves. Far from being a mark of overflowing vitality as Nietzsche supposes, such an instinctive strategy is a symptom of weakness: the problem is that the 'proud and splendid' feeling aroused in the male by having the woman 'administered to him' can be mistaken for the 'amazing joy' created by more mutual kinds of relationship.

In all this, Lawrence is clearly aware of Nietzsche's insistence that the most important way in which the will to power expresses itself in adult life is through sexuality, while rejecting the idea that *Wille zur Macht*—at least as he defines it—is a state to which we should aspire. He argues that Nietzsche has mistaken its significance, seeing as an expression of strength something which is essentially a product of weakness. Lawrence's attack is shrewdly directed since it is in his observations on relations between the sexes and particularly in his comments on how men should treat women, that Nietzsche himself does least justice to the complexity and suggestiveness of his central conception; there is a crudely anti-feminist element in his exhortations to men to treat women firmly, even brutally, which testifies clearly—if unintentionally—to his own sense of being threatened in his contacts with the opposite sex.

But Lawrence's rejection of Nietzsche's ideas in *Study* is not as complete as it seems, because his argument about the different kinds of relationships possible between men and women depends on Nietzsche's own subtle analysis of the transmutations of the will to power. For Nietzsche, the different varieties of power form a hierarchy in which different ways of employing strength correspond essentially to different degrees of strength, so that what seem on the surface to be qualitative differences are fundamentally quantative ones. Nietzsche's point is that while overt, physical dominance is only capable of exacting an external and temporary obedience, power that is exercised more subtly, with respect for the individuality of the other in the relationship, is—paradoxically—more efficacious. Power subtly used is a symptom of substantial strength, a naked display of force or obvious arrogation of authority bespeaks inner weakness. It is this paradox that Lawrence uncovers in his analysis of the ideal of male supremacy in those societies where it has governed the relations between the sexes. Among the Greeks and the Jews in the past and among the Italians now, men were seen as 'supreme' and the woman's 'highest function' was to serve them; this 'conscious attitude', however, is contrasted with 'their unconscious attitude [which] was the reverse: they were in truth afraid of the female principle, their vaunt was empty, they went in deep, inner dread of her.'[24]

Although the need felt by many men to be the dominant partner arises from an unconscious sense of weakness and vulnerability, the assertion and enjoyment of power which it prompts are conscious things and it is with such conscious impulses that the *Wille zur Macht* is identified in *Study*. Lawrence also identifies will to power with the conscious assertion of power in *Women in Love*. In the chapter entitled 'Mino', Ursula Brangwen, incensed by Rupert Birkin's approval of his male cat's aggressive behaviour towards a female stray and sensing the implications his attitude might have for their own developing relationship, accuses him of being like Gerald Crich who, earlier in the story, had forced his terrified Arab mare to stand still at a level-crossing while a noisy train went by. She accuses Birkin of being 'just like Gerald Crich with his horse—a lust for bullying—a real *Wille zur Macht*—so base, so petty'. Since, as I shall argue, the train incident symbolises, among other things, the destructive domination of instinct by consciousness, 'bullying' is very much associated with the conscious exercise of the will in *Women in Love*. Replying, Birkin says

> I agree that the Wille zur Macht is a base and petty thing. But with the Mino, it is the desire to bring this female cat into a pure stable equilibrium, a transcendant and abiding *rapport* with a single male. Whereas without him, she is a mere stray, a fluffy sporadic bit of chaos. It is a *volonté de pouvoir*, if your like, a will to ability, taking pouvoir as a verb.
>
> (**WL** p 167)

There is a good deal of self-mockery of course in Birkin's philosophic analysis of feline behaviour, but Lawrence does seem to be suggesting quite seriously, through Birkin's switch from German to French, that *Macht* invariably refers to a crude, domineering, uncreative kind of power—rather as English 'might' tends to be associated with things like military strength. But as Lawrence must have known, both from his reading of Nietzsche and from having a German wife, *Macht* has a wider range of reference than 'power'; it is quite clear both from the contexts in which Nietzsche employs *Wille zur Macht* and indeed from the whole tenor of his arguments about power that the phrase cannot be taken to refer only, or even primarily, to the cruder and more obvious kinds of strength. Furthermore, as Birkin himself implies, the *volonté de pouvoir* displayed by his cat is something which can easily be confused with the Nietzschean will to power, even though it has a quite different significance. While the latter is an unhealthy impulse, lacking in real nobility and force ('Base and petty'), and is linked with human behaviour and therefore with conscious awareness, the latter is a spontaneous and instinctive form-creating urge. But the similarity of Birkin's names for these contrasting impulses makes Lawrence's dependence on Nietzsche clear: *volonté de pouvoir* is a derivative concept which takes its significance from its contrast with the Nietzschean original. In fact, Birkin's comments suggest that Lawrence himself had some difficulty in establishing just how his concept was different from, and superior to, *Wille zur Macht*.

The emphasis in *Study* and in *Women in Love* is on will to power as a conscious urge which aims at establishing dominance of an obvious, physical kind and while it is true that in some of his earliest works, Nietzsche does use *Wille zur Macht* as the name for a desire for power of just that kind—a desire which he tends to condemn—seeing it as just one (conscious) motive among many, his characteristic use of the term in most of his works is quite different. Will to power is nothing less than the ultimate metaphysical principle of Nietzschean philosophy, the ground of all being and in human life, as in all its other embodiments, nearly all its activity is unconscious. And although, from time to time, Nietzsche expresses that unfortunate enthusiasm often felt by intellectuals for the more brutal kind of man of action, for the conqueror and the tyrant, it is the subtler and more refined manifestations of will to power in figures like the artist, saint and philosopher that he admires most.

The possibility that Lawrence misrepresented Nietzsche because he had only a limited acquaintance with his work—unlikely anyway in view of his prior acquaintance with Schopenhauer—is ruled out by the fact that in several of the works written before the Hardy essay or *Women in Love*, Lawrence correctly links Nietzsche's ideas in general and will to power in particular, with the centrality of the instinctive and unconscious. In two of the essays in *Twilight in Italy*, both written in 1913, Nietzsche is identified with the archaic, instinctive, Dionysian mode of being. In 'The Theatre', Lawrence says that because north Europeans have become too conscious, they are tempted 'like Nietzsche, to return back to the old pagan Infinite, to say that is supreme'.[25] And in 'Italians in Exile', he contrasts those north Europeans with the Italians, who are still trying to escape from the limitations of the purely instinctive life:

> And now, when Northern Europe is turning back on its own Christianity denying it all, the Italians are struggling with might and main against the sensuous spirit which still dominates them. When Northern Europe, whether it hates Nietzsche or not, is crying out for the Dionysic ecstasy, practising on itself the Dionysic ecstasy, Southern Europe is breaking free from Dionysos, from the triumphal affirmation of life over death, immortality through procreation.[26]

And the will to power itself appears as something both unconscious and creative in the short story 'England, My England', written in the early years of the war. In it, the authority and decisiveness of Geoffrey Marshall a successful business man are contrasted with the irresponsibility of his artistic son-in-law. Marshall's 'will to power' (the phrase Lawrence uses) is clearly unconscious, coming, we are told, from his 'blind self' and it gives him an authority which does not depend on any overt assertion of power—and which, at the same time, is far more effective than any more obvious kind of influence would be. Marshall has

> ... a certain acrid courage, and a certain will-to-power. In his own small circle he would emanate power, the single power of his own blind self. With all his spoiling of his children, he was still the father of the old English type. He was too wise to make laws and to domineer in the abstract. But he had kept, and all honour to him, a certain primitive dominion over the souls of his children, the old, almost magic prestige of paternity.

> **(EME p 19)**

Evidently Lawrence could, on occasion, employ Nietzsche's concept in the proper way. The other places in his work in which will to power is associated with consciousness and with bullying, or with an interfering kind of benevolence probably do not indicate that Lawrence fundamentally misunderstood Nietzsche—after all, he was thoroughly aware of the importance of the unconscious in the tradition to which Nietzsche belonged—but that he wanted to conceal the similarity of their ideas. It may be significant that Lawrence was working on *Study* and on the material which became *Women in Love* during the First World War, at a time when Nietzsche was being attacked in this country as one of Germany's war-inspirers, as the apostle of brute force and naked aggression. He would have been associated in the popular mind with exactly those qualities Birkin attributes to the *Wille zur Macht*. Lawrence's misrepresentation of will to power had the double advantage of dissociating his own ideas from those of a thinker in thoroughly bad odour and establishing his own originality.

Both Schopenhauer and James are mentioned in Lawrence's first novel, *The White Peacock*, while Nietzsche is not, but the difference in conception between the first version of 1906-7 and the final revision in 1909 suggests that it was during this time that the influence of Schopenhauer gave way to that of Nietzsche. Jessie's summary of the original version—which she thought 'storybookish and unreal'—suggests that it centred on the Schopenhauerian virtues of selflessness and compassion:

> The upright young farmer, hopelessly in love with the superior young lady (very conscious of her social superiority) who had been served shabbily by a still more socially superior young man, married her after a puritanical exposition of the circumstances by her mother, and a highly dubious conjugal life began in the melancholy farmhouse, with, one imagined, Letty always in the parlour and George in the kitchen.
>
> **(PR** p 116)

In the published version there is a significant change in the treatment of the central character, George Saxton; he becomes a man who, because of his inability to break free of traditional attitudes and modes of behaviour, is incapable of creating the relationship with Letty which he needs in order to develop fully. George's predicament anticipates that of Tom Brangwen in *The Rainbow* and both characters embody essentially Nietzschean ideas about the relation of character to environment and about 'organic memory'.

The growing importance of Annable—Lawrence's first fictional game-keeper and the spokesman in the novel for a primitivism sometimes mistakenly attributed to Lawrence himself—also shows the influence of Nietzsche. Jessie records that the keeper first appeared in Lawrence's initial rewriting of 1907-8, and grew from being a 'cynically brutal' character to one with considerable symbolic stature. The keeper is often seen as Schopenhauerian figure, largely because he ridicules romantic and idealised love suggesting, in rather the way that Schopenhauer does in 'The Metaphysics of Love', that it is no more than a disguise for sexual desire. But the keeper is also associated with violence and with unrestrained sexuality so he certainly cannot be seen as representing Schopenhauerian enlightenment, that state in which, freed from the deceits and importunities of the Will, the individual leads an altruistic and ascetic existence. Jessie is right, however, about the keeper's symbolic stature because, as I shall show, Annable has indeed a representative significance: he embodies the 'nihilism' which Nietzsche regarded as one characteristic response to the modern crisis of values.

In *The White Peacock*, George Saxton abandons his pursuit of Lettie and settles for his cousin, the sensuous and less challenging Meg—a choice which condemns him to steady decline after a brief burst of creative energy. The attitude of his wife and daughter to George after his deterioration has begun reflects the influence on the novel of one major area of Nietzsche's thinking: his hostile analysis of Christianity as a religion of resentment and revenge, used by the weak to torment the strong. Mother and daughter use religion to humiliate Saxton and assert their own moral superiority. When the girl takes her father to task for not going to church, it is clear that she is not just expressing her own naively contradictory attitudes but also revealing something of the spirit which lies behind much institutionalised religion:

> 'Everybody that goes to church looks nice'—she glanced at her mother and herself, preening herself proudly—'and God loves them', she added. She assumed a sanctified expression, and continued after a little thought: 'Because they look nice and are meek.'
>
> (**WP** p 400)

The child is too young to be aware of the contradictions in what she has said, but the way in which pride masquerades as humility here and 'virtue' is used as a cloak for malice, echoes Nietzsche's attack on Christianity as the product of spite and resentment.

On their last meeting before her own marriage, Lettie obliquely reproaches George for failing to be determined enough in his wooing of her. Walking through the woods with him, she draws his attention to various examples of risk-taking and self-sacrifice in the natural world, implying that George has lost her because he was unwilling to risk himself in the same way. She ironically compares this lack of enterprise—which she evidently sees as characteristic of human beings—with the response to challenge and difficulty shown by 'lower' forms of life. The tree they see which is being strangled by ivy grows the more vigorously; human beings threatened in the same way would, she suggests, behave quite differently:

> In the hedge was an elm tree, with myriads of dark dots pointed against the bright sky, myriads of clusters of flaky green fruit.
> 'Look at that elm', she said, 'you'd think it was in full leaf, wouldn't you? Do you known why it is so prolific?'
> 'No', he said, with a curious questioning drawl of the monosyllable.
> 'It's casting its bread upon the winds—no, it is dying, so it puts out all its strength and loads its boughs with the last fruit. It'll be dead next year ... Look at the ivy, the suave smooth ivy, with its fingers in the tree's throat. Trees known how to die, you see—we don't ... If we were trees with ivy—instead of being fine human beings with free active life—we should hug our thinning lives, shouldn't we?'
>
> (**WP** pp 274-5)

Lettie is suggesting that human beings rebel against nature by refusing to take risks in the effort to grow further; like George, they would rather 'hug their thinning lives' than risk breaking with their accustomed mode of life even when, as in the Nethermere of the novel, that life is crumbling under pressure from various destructive forces. Although Lettie suggests to George that her observations on sacrifice may remind him of Schopenhauer she is not arguing for an ascetic withdrawal from life's challenges, but for a Nietzschean affirmation of existence in which struggle and even death are embraced in the effort to grow further. Particularly in its reference to the prolific but dying tree, the episode strongly suggests the section on 'Self-Overcoming' in *Thus Spake Zarathustra* where Nietzsche defines the fundamental impulse of life:

> And life itself told me this secret: 'Behold', it said, 'I am that *which must overcome itself again and again.*
>     To be sure, you call it will to procreate or impulse towards a goal, towards the higher, more distant, more manifold: but all this is one and one secret.
>     I would rather perish than renounce this one thing; and truly, where there is perishing and the falling of leaves, behold, there life sacrifices itself—for the sake of power.'[27]

Nietzsche's influence is also clearly evident in *The White Peacock* in the effects attributed in the novel to the music of Wagner. Nietzsche had started off as an admirer of the composer, but growing increasingly disillusioned, became a fierce opponent of what he had come to feel was powerful, but essentially decadent and debilitating music. In one of the last meetings between George and Lettie, at a point where he is acutely aware of how much he has lost in losing her, she makes his condition worse by singing to him from *Tannhauser*. This, according to the narrative, was 'the music of resignation and despair' and it increases George's melancholy. In *The Case of Wagner*, one of the first of Nietzsche's works to become available in English, he concedes the power of Wagner's music, but condemns it as undermining the hearers hold on life, contrasting it unfavourably with the invigorating music of Bizet, particularly in *Carmen*. Just before their marriage, George and Meg go to see Bizet's opera and both experience the exhiliration Nietzsche associates with it:

> Carmen fascinated them both. The gaudy, careless Southern life amazed them. The bold free way in which Carmen played with life startled them with hints of freedom. They stared at the stage fascinated. Between the acts they held each other's hands, and looked full into each other's wide bright eyes, and, laughing with excitement talked about the opera.

**(WP p 323)**

In Lawrence's second novel, *The Trespasser*, references to Wagner's music are pervasive, and enthusiasm for the German composer is associated primarily with Helena, the destructive heroine—which suggests that Lawrence continued to accept Nietzsche's hostile view of the composer.

It is in *The Trespasser* that Nietzsche is first mentioned by name; Helena brings one of his works to the Isle of Wight for her musician lover Siegmund, with whom she is spending a holiday there. In the novel as a whole, Nietzschean ideas are even more important that they are in *The White Peacock* and while these are fully discussed in a later chapter, one passage in which Nietzsche's influence is particularly clear is worth comment. One of the minor characters in the novel, Hampson, is a composer and his account of his vocation and its significance depends on Nietzschean notions about the position of the innovating artist and his relation to the more conventional majority and, at the same time, he links artistic activity in general to the Nietzschean idea of 'self-overcoming'. Taking to Siegmund, Hampson says:

> 'I can open the blue heaven with looking, and push back the doors of day a little, and see—God knows what! One of these days I shall slip through. Oh, I am perfectly sane; only I strive beyond myself!'
> 'Don't you think it's wrong to get like it?' asked Siegmund.
> 'Well, I do, and so does everybody; but the crowd profits by us in the end. When they understand my music, it will be an education to them; and the whole aim of mankind is to render life intelligible.'

(*Tr* p 85)

Human advance in any sphere depends on the pioneering activities of a few gifted individuals, whose new insights initially meet with incomprehension and disapproval, not only from the conventional majority, the 'crowd', but even from that powerful element in their own natures which sides with the mass in condemning their explorations as 'wrong' or 'mad'. In his early writings in particular, Nietzsche associated the discovery and propagation of new insights primarily with creative artists. Gradually, such insights and values become established and familiar and the spiritual horizons of the majority are thus far extended. In time, of course, what were once fresh insights become the conventional wisdom and a barrier to further exploration, which has to be broken down by a new generation of artistic explorers.

However, the fundamental importance of Nietzsche for Lawrence's work does not emerge from particular detached borrowings, however interesting and obviously Nietzschean these may be, but from the fact that Nietzschean ideas underly and determine the large-scale patterns and structures of Lawrence's writing. In the chapters that follow, I shall demonstrate that an awareness of Nietzsche's thought is essential for a full understanding of Lawrence's vision and that it constitutes a subtle and powerful interpretative framework for reading the novels, stories, poems and plays. I have not tried to offer a Nietzschean reading of any work in its entirety, but have organised my account round certain major groups of ideas, moving between the fiction and the philosophy as seemed appropriate. The usefulness of any interpretative scheme must be judged by its success in elucidating what is most original, powerful and perplexing in a writer's work and I have tried therefore to explore and resolve some of the critical puzzles and disagreements which arise particularly in discussion of *Sons and Lovers*, *The Rainbow* and *Women in Love* since I believe that it is in these novels above all that Lawrence's distinctive greatness is demonstrated. However the need for clear and—relatively—brief exposition has led me to range widely through Lawrence's work in a number of genres in search of evidence and my examples have not always been chosen because they represent the best of his writing. If I have said comparatively little about the middle-period novels— *Aaron's Rod*, *Kangaroo* and *The Plumed Serpent*—this is not because I

believe that they are less amenable to a Nietzschean reading, but because I
think that in them Lawrence turned away from what he did best—exploring
the fluid and intense world of personal feeling—to an area, that of political
belief and action, of which he had no experience and for which he had, in
fact, little sympathy.

Since most readers are likely to be primarily interested in and knowledge-
able about Lawrence rather than Nietzsche, I have devoted a good deal of
space to the exposition of the relevant parts of Nietzsche's 'system'. In calling
it that, I am following those modern commentators like G A Morgan, Walter
Kaufmann and Arthur Danto, who have argued that Nietzsche is, if in a
rather qualified way, a systematic thinker and not, as he is sometimes thought
to have been, an unsystematic or anti-systematic one, whose books are no
more than collections of brilliant but unconnected aphorisms. My own
presentation of Nietzsche's thought owes a great deal to the synthesising
labours of those commentators and others, who have worked to extrapolate
from Nietzsche's writings the system he never brought himself to articulate.

Doubts may remain in the mind of the properly sceptical reader as to
whether any mature creative artist could have been influenced as profoundly
as I suggest Lawrence was and by someone who belonged to what we usually
think of as a completely different and even alien sphere of activity from
literature. But Nietzsche is unusual among philosophers in that—in Britain
and America at least—his influence was at its strongest among writers and
artists, rather than among his fellow philosophers. The Anglo-American
philosophical tradition, strongly empiricist in tendency, was inhospitable to
Nietzsche's kind of philosophising, to his speculative audacity and
apocalyptic tone, and in many academic libraries, including that of my own
university, his works are classified, not under philosophy but under literature, reflecting his banishment, earlier in the century, from the ranks of the
speculatively sober and respectable. But the classification also reflects a real
ambiguity in Nietzsche's position; unlike most philosophers, even important
ones, he is a considerable literary figure in his own right and his distinction
as a stylist is evident even in the often stilted and inaccurate translations
available to the young Lawrence. Schopenhauer and James are also considerable stylists, refreshingly free from the awkwardness, obscurity and graceless
technical jargon which we tend to associate with nineteenth century philosophical writing, particularly in Germany. All three write about major
philosophical issues, especially those which have to do with human nature
and man's behaviour, in a way likely to interest the non-professional reader,
and in a style which is individual, attractive and comprehensible. Schopenhauer and Nietzsche appealed to creative individuals too because of the
importance they accorded to the arts in their philosophical thinking; particularly in Nietzsche's case, this did not involve just the endorsement of
imagination as valuable, but was carried directly into his own intellectual
activity. His language is highly coloured, he employs image, metaphor,
symbol, fable, anecdote and parable, and in *Thus Spake Zarathustra* tries
to create a myth for the modern age. He proceeds by extravagant seeming
intuitive leaps, is extreme, often abusive, in his language and in general

rejects the coolness and circumspection, the parade of lucid abstractions, we associate with responsible philosophical discourse. These things, together with an interest in psychological particulars which often resembles that of the novelist, help to account for the enormous fascination Nietzsche had for artists and writers around and after the turn of the century.

Even more important perhaps than the artistic affinities of Nietzsche's work was the fact that he was the thinker who made the boldest and most far-reaching attempt to follow through the implications of the new scientific world-view for our understanding of human nature and human behaviour, for the place of humanity in the universe at large and in general to answer the kind of question which perplexed the young Lawrence and his generation 'as to how the old religious ideas stood in relation to the scientific discoveries that were sweeping away the familiar landmarks'. Unlike the rationalist thinkers who attracted Lawrence to begin with, Nietzsche did not simply adopt science as a new dogma; instead he moved beyond them, using the discoveries of science to develop a critical perspective on scientific activity itself. And Nietzsche's significance was not just the negative one of finally demolishing the surviving remnants of now archaic error and superstition and prejudice—he was also the author of an audacious attempt at the 'revaluation of all values', an attempt reminiscent of the headiest ambitions of the romantic artist, to redefine man's purposes and rechannel his energies. His ambition, like that of Lawrence himself was 'to inform and lead into new places the flow of our sympathetic consciousness and ... lead our sympathy away in recoil from things gone dead'.

Perhaps more eloquent testimony to the influence of Nietzsche on Lawrence than any of the agreements or disagreements which have been discussed is provided by the titles which Lawrence proposed to give the philosophical essays he was working on in 1915. In February of that year, he wrote to Bertrand Russell outlining some of his ideas, and went on to say 'I wrote a book about these things—I used to call it Le Gai Savaire'.[28] Early in March, he wrote again to Russel saying, 'Also I feel very profound about my book *The Signal*—Le Gai Saver—or whatever it is—which I am rebeginning'.[29] Then, in June of the same year, he resumed his philosophical writing after a lapse, and wrote to Ottoline Morrell, 'Today I have begun again my philosophy—*Morgenrot* is my new name for it'.[30] Le Gai Saber is the old Provencal term for the art of poetry which gave Nietzsche the title for *Die Fröliche Wissenschaft*, and Lawrence's 'Morgenrot' is plainly a mis-spelling of the German *Morgenröte*, the dawn, which is, of course, the title of another of Nietzsche's major works.

In using the word 'influence' I do not want to imply that there is a mechanical and external application of Nietzsche's ideas in Lawrence's work. What is involved is a creative absorption and development of them which issues in a richly detailed and specific fictional world. Because Lawrence's direct references to those to whom he was indebted are often evasive or misleading, I have taken his own advice in what follows and put my trust not in the artist, but in the tale.

CHAPTER 2

# Character and Environment

Lawrence's first novel, *The White Peacock*, is set in a small rural community called Nethermere. The main story concerns an abortive relationship between a young farmer, George Saxton and a socially superior girl, Lettie Beardsall, whose brother Cyril tells the story. Both George and Lettie finally marry partners from their own social level but neither finds fulfilment and George's character in particular, after a brief flowering deteriorates steadily, till at the end of the book he is an alcoholic, broken in health, and, in the narrator's words, 'lamentably decayed' from what he has once been. But the story is not only a record of individual disappointment and decline—the community to which the lovers belong is also disintegrating. What has been till recently a populous and prosperous valley is now decaying because of the discovery by the local squire that selling rabbits in nearby industrial Nottingham is easier and more profitable than farming. The squire protects his livelihood by encouraging the growth of the rabbit population, employing a game-keeper to protect them against predators, animal or human, and uses his position as landlord to prevent his tenants taking effective action to protect their crops. Freed from the checks imposed by natural competition and human control, the rabbits multiply prodigiously, delighting the squire who 'glowed with thankfulness as he saw the dishevelled hillside heave when the gnawing hosts moved on', but while the 'army' of rabbits ensures his con-tinuing prosperity it puts so much pressure on the available food that the despoilation spreads from woods and common to the cultivated land nearby. Forbidden to protect themselves against the invasion, the farmers struggle for a time to maintain their holdings, but finally abandon the unequal struggle and move from the land leaving rabbits and keeper in sole possession:

> Farms were gnawed away; corn and sweet grass departed from the face of the hills; cattle grew lean, unable to eat the defiled herbage. Then the farm became the home of a keeper, and the country was silent, with no sound of cattle, no clink of horses, no barking of lusty dogs.
>
> **(WP** p 104–5)

The squire's prosperity is purchased at the cost of the destruction of a long-established rural community which has been till recently extremely prosperous (there are references to things like the large stable formerly kept by the local horse-dealer, now bankrupt) and which has represented not a crude and rustic mode of existence, but one marked by considerable style and refinement.

On a walk, George and the narrator come upon one of the more recently abandoned farms which is in good enough condition for the friends to think at first that it is still occupied. It is only when Cyril notices that 'there was no light or glow in any window, though the house had only the width of one room' that they realise it is derelict; he goes on in his description of the building to emphasise its architectural distinction, its 'handsome chimneys' and 'long, impressive front', which indicate that it is the product of a high degree of skill and taste, the creation of a prosperous, and cultured rural society. That impression is confirmed by the efficiency and conscientiousness with which the practical business of the farm has been carried on. Drawn to the outbuildings by George's 'farmer's instinct', the pair find them 'in splendid condition . . . well timbered, neat and cosy'; contemporary with the house, they have been 'restored within a small number of years', almost certainly at the occupant's expense since the squire's reluctance to offer more than vague promises of help to his tenants has been illustrated only a page or so before. The rapidity and extent of the devastation created by the squire's actions is dramatically underlined by the fact that such an investment was considered worthwhile only a short time before by a farmer who clearly knew his business, and this is one of a number of illustrations of the way in which an attractive and productive way of life is being rapidly and inexorably destroyed.

Where the farms on the rabbit-infested land are still worked, there has been a change in the kind of tenant occupying them. The old White House farm, with its 'green mounting steps', from which 'Ladies have . . . ridden towards the Vale of Belvoir', has clearly been the house of a wealthy farmer; now the steps are mouldering and the farm is held by a labourer—a fate which is to befall the Saxton's own farm at Strelley Mill. The active independent natives of the area are being steadily driven from it and their places taken by immigrants of lower social status, who are willing to put up with the more marginal kind of existence which is all that is possible in competition with the rabbits. What the squire has brought about is a kind of reversal of the normal sequence of social development, so that an agricultural community is being turned back into a hunting one and a developed kind of social and economic order is now steadily reverting to a more primitive state. Ironically, it is the person whose traditional social role is to form the centre of order and cohesion in the community who is responsible for its destruction—in his small way the squire symbolises that abnegation of responsibility by the governing classes which, for Lawrence, as for Nietzsche, is the major cause of contemporary social disintegration and which has a consequence and corollary, the pressure of democratic and socialist ideas from below.

In this man-made desolation, the Saxton's farm is one of the few surviving outposts of the old rural order, but the ruinous state of the land around underlines the vulnerability of the Mill itself which 'on three sides ... was skirted by woods, the dens of rabbits, and the common held another warren'. As the story proceeds the 'gangrene' spreads to the Mill and the Saxtons' experience vividly illustrates just how quickly the contagion travels. Saxton's casual remark to his wife at the beginning of the novel that the rabbits are eating the turnips suggests nuisance rather than crisis, but in the autumn of the same year, only three or four months later, the problem has assumed such proportions that a direct approach to the squire is necessary. But the interview has no practical result and when, soon after it, they come upon the deserted farm on the hill, George predicts to Cyril that the Mill will soon be in the same state. As it is the Saxtons can no longer survive by farming alone and have had to diversify so that they have become, as George bitterly says 'a miserable mixture of farmer, milkman, greengrocer, and carting contractor'. The satisfying wholeness of a purely agricultural life has been lost and George's distaste for the fragmentation of effort which economic necessity has forced on them is clear; engaging in several quite different kinds of activity means that no one thing can be done with the thoroughness and efficiency which bring satisfaction. And George feels that his father's conservatism will prevent the recovery of a more integrated and fulfilling kind of existence in either of the two ways which might be possible—through a complete change in farming methods or through moving somewhere else. Without some initiative of this kind the Mill will continue to decline and their diversification of activity do no more than postpone the day when the Saxtons can no longer make a living there.

George's forebodings seem well-founded since neither he nor his father seem capable at this point of constructive action; yet, when it does come, their departure is not the result of passive submission to increasing pressure from 'rabbits and one thing and another', but is brought about by the spirited counter-attack Saxton mounts on the chief cause of their difficulties. In the spring following the summer on which the story opens, the scale of destruction on his land prompts him to desperate measures, and despite the squire's ban, he buys a gun and begins shooting the rabbits, action which will inevitably end his tenancy. The initiative is surprising for various reasons, the most obvious being that, with middle-age, Saxton's energy has declined to the extent that, earlier in the story, he has become increasingly inclined to relax the steady routine of the farm work. As a result, his determined onslaught on the rabbits in the cold and dark of the early spring morning is most unexpected, and suggests a dramatic renewal of vigour. But even more surprising than this upsurge of physical energy is the psychological change implied by Saxton's open defiance of the squire's wishes. Hitherto, his social attitudes have been strongly traditionalist and he has been respectful to his social superiors even when their right to such respect is doubtful. For such a man the head of the 'ancient' family, whose land his forebears has farmed for generations would normally command immense respect and his rebellion indicates just how much he has broken with his habitual attitudes.

So the 'settling down to an easy contented middle age' which we would naturally expect of someone who is, according to the narrator 'a pure romanticist, forever seeking the colour of the past in the present's monotony' is interrupted and by an action which will inevitably bring the expulsion of the family from the place to which Saxton is deeply attached and a break with their accustomed mode of life. His nostalgia when they are finally given notice is emphasised but, paradoxically, this serves to underline even more firmly, the force in him of the new and opposite impulse to cut the link with the valley and move, not just to a fresh life but also to a new country. The 'vague sadness' which he feels 'over the thought of their departure' indicates that the old loyalties still survive, but the mood is brief, giving way to a hopeful, but realistic, concern with the future:

> Over supper he became enthusiastic about Canada, and to watch him his ruddy face lighted up, his burly form straight and nerved with excitement, was to admire him; to hear him, his words of thoughtful common-sense all warm with a young man's hopes, was to love him. At forty-six he was more spontaneous and enthusiastic than George, and far more happy and hopeful.
>
> (**WP** p 252-3)

In this contrast between George Saxton and his father, the characteristics we usually associate with youth and age are reversed and the break with established patterns of living and the planning of new possibilities we would normally expect to come from the younger man comes, in this case, from the older. This unexpected reversal of roles has less to do with the way in which 'Women undermine men's hold on life'[1]—though a number of critics have seen George's experience in the novel as an illustration of this process—than with a more general failure of energy and initiative which has characterised him from the start. Even at the very beginning of the story, before he has so much as met the girl often alleged to have undermined his male integrity, George is far from representing the Dionysian forces, the 'turbulent and anarchic energies'[2] which many critics take to characterise natural, unspoiled maleness in Lawrence's work. In fact, in the opening chapters of the novel the traits most prominent in his nature are indolence and self-satisfaction and Cyril's comments make it clear that this is his normal state and not some temporary lapse from a more active and enterprising outlook. Looking out over the mill-pond in the opening scene of the novel, the narrator is '. . . almost startled into the water from my perch on the alder roots by a voice saying:

> 'Well, what is there to look at?' 'my friend was a young farmer, stoutly built, brown eyed, with a naturally fair skin burned dark and freckled in patches. He laughed, seeing me start, and looked down at me with lazy curiosity.
>
> 'I was thinking the place seemed old, brooding over its past.'
>
> He looked at me with a lazy indulgent smile, and lay down on his back on the bank, saying:
>
> 'It's all right for a doss—here.'
>
> 'Your life is nothing else but a doss. I shall laugh when somebody jerks you awake,' I replied.
>
> He smiled comfortably and put his hands over his eyes because of the light.
>
> (**WP** p 41)

Despite his jocular tone, it's clear that Cyril is aware of a real potentiality for fuller and more vivid being in the young farmer, which his present lazy complacency prevents him realizing spontaneously and which it would take some powerful external force to bring out.

George's inability to act in the face of something as serious and immediate as the crisis facing the farm bears out this initial impression; despite his dislike of the miserable mixture of jobs they now have to do and despite his awareness that the Mill cannot survive for long as a profitable undertaking, George confines himself to grumbling about his father's inaction, and takes no practical steps himself. Even more than the older man, he is reluctant to sacrifice present comfort—though he knows it cannot last—to future benefit, and expend the physical and psychological energy needed to embark on the creation of a new life. When his father finally does act, George entirely approves although, significantly, 'he had never had the initiative to begin the like himself, or even to urge his father to it.' He is disturbed at the prospect of leaving the farm to find another place but, again characteristically, 'postponed the thought of the evil day till the time should be upon him'.

What is evident here, as in his dilatory wooing of Lettie, is a kind of psychic inertia which makes it extremely difficult to break with established (and therefore comfortable) modes of behaviour and engage in the necessarily risky and uncomfortable commitment to the untried and unfamiliar. His failure to persist and win the girl is due to this constitutional slowness in translating desire into action rather than a 'pathological oversensitivity' to 'feminine rebuke and resistance'[3] or a general collapse in the face of the 'mysterious power' of Lettie and the cultured middle-class world she represents. His last chance to claim her is lost for the prosaic reason that he has 'as usual ... been dawdling in the portals of his desires, when the doors came to with a bang' and his belated attempt to recover his position is frustrated by his rival's motor accident and subsequent illness, because it is this more than any submission to family or class expectations which makes Lettie decide to keep her engagement and marry George's rival, Leslie.

The marriage which, on Lettie's side, is based on sympathy rather than passion is one of the first treatments in Lawrence's fiction of a theme he was to return to again and again; Lettie side-steps the difficult task of self-development through a challengingly mutual kind of relationship and chooses instead a relationship which, because it depends on compassion, is one-sided and manipulative. Lettie is the dominant partner in her marriage, though her dominance is subtly exercised and maintained; though socially and economically superior to her, Leslie is no match for her, humanly speaking. In contrast, in the relationship with George, it is clear that while he is disturbed and unsettled by what she represents and the challenge she offers to his mode of life, she is almost equally disturbed by what he stands for and it is exactly this element of challenge on both sides which ensures that each grows and changes significantly in contract with the other, despite the fact that their intimacy is brief. The contrast between the pair and the disagreements, tensions and even antagonisms their differences give rise to are far from being signs of an unhealthy kind of relationship; for Lawrence it is exactly this kind of relationship which has most dynamism and vitality and which is therefore likely to contribute most to the development of those involved.

The laziness which is emphasised from the opening chapters does not, however, extend to all George's activities—in the opening chapter, his father asks him about a job he has been doing in the coppice close, and is clearly surprised when his son tells him it is already finished: this is one of a number of examples which show that, in the routine work of the farm at least, George is quite unusually rapid and efficient. The apparent contradiction between the abundant vigour George displays in scenes like the one later in the novel in which Leslie tries his hand at mowing, and his lack of initiative in other directions, has puzzled many critics and they have concluded that his failure to win Lettie has to do with the fact that he is involved with a member of the opposite sex. In the same way, the tragic conclusion of the novel is seen as the outcome of that general crisis in the relations between the sexes which is a recurrent theme in Lawrence's fiction. Because of a dissociation between masculine and feminine values—so the argument goes—values which are associated with nature and culture respectively, women undermine masculine energy and enterprise, making fulfilment impossible for either sex. Kermode reflects the critical consensus in his comment that although derivative and novelistic in many ways, *The White Peacock* is the first expression of the basic Lawrentian 'myth' of 'man trapped between culture and nature'.[5] At the same time many of the critics who see the fate of the main characters in the novel as a consequence of a pervasive crisis in which feminine values have become inimical to masculine ones also feel that Lawrence does not convincingly explain how this disaster has happened. George suffers from a 'mysterious disability' while the nature of Lettie's allegedly damaging influence is also difficult to understand:

> The nature of this deadly power is never satisfactorily explained ... nor does he ever attempt to account for the extraordinary weakness of the men, which causes them to go under so easily in the sex war Lawrence envisions as the norm of erotic and marital relations.[6]

In this reading of the novel, George's failure with Lettie is an example of a general and inexplicable masculine weakness in the face of women and what they have come to represent, and their relationship resembles a less extreme version of the destructive relationship which has existed between the gamekeeper Annable and the aristocratic Lady Chrystabel. The thesis offers interpretative neatness and economy, but these are purchased at the cost of ignoring the fact that George's lack of enterprise is apparent even before he becomes involved with Lettie. In fact, as I have suggested, his failure to be persistent enough in his wooing reflects his more general difficulty in breaking with familiar and accustomed routine. Consider for instance, the description of George at work with a scythe:

> The sun being mild, George had thrown off his hat, and his black hair was twisted into confused half-curls. Firmly planted, he swung with a beautiful

rhythm from the waist. On the hip of his belted breeches hung the scythe stone; his shirt, faded almost white, was torn from just above the belt, and showed the muscles of his back playing like lights upon the white sand of a brook. There was something exceedingly attractive in the rhythmic body.

(**WP** p 93)

The mastery is not effortless of course, as George's moist hair reminds us, but what is emphasised here is economy, efficiency and grace rather than toil and effort. And the ease and authority of George's rhythm is further under-lined by Leslie's attempt at moving—although the latter has a 'fine, lithe physique' and is 'wonderfully ready at everything' he is very quickly tired out. It is clear from this and from other descriptions of the same kind that George is very far from representing Moynahan's 'turbulent and anarchic energies'; certainly he has abundant physical strength, but it is deployed with a precision, control and economy which ensure that none of his accustomed tasks ever extend him fully. In Lawrence's Nietzschean conception of development, growth always depends on the stimulus offered by challenge and difficulty and because he lacks any innate impulse to seek sterner tests, George's awakening has to depend on intervention from outside.

When his failure with Lettie is seen as just one example—if the most important one—of a general incapacity for creative action, the mystery surrounding it disappears. When changes in the circumstances around them have emancipated George and his father from their contentment with their present life, each links the difficulty they have found in breaking free from habitual ways of seeing, feeling and acting with one fundamental fact—that the family has been in the same place, living the same kind of life, for many generations. On the narrator's first visit to the Mill after Leslie's accident he sees George, who is about to go courting his cousin Meg, complacently examining his reflection in the old mirror above the mantel-piece:

> I wondered that he found such satisfaction in his image, seeing that there was a gap in his chin, and an uncertain moth-eaten appearance in one cheek.
>
> (**WP** p 268)

The joking exchange between the two young men which follows prompts Emily, George's sister, to recall what she once believed to be the reason why the mirror 'left gaps and spots and scratches in one's countenance' and 'gave one's reflexion a far-away dim aspect'

> I always used to think ... that the black spots had swallowed so many faces they were full up, and couldn't take any more—and the rest was misty because there were so many faces lapped one over the other—reflected.
>
> (**WP** p 268-9)

Emily's fancy was that the mirror obscured individual contours in proportion to the number of previous images it had 'absorbed' and at best offered an image which was not fully distinctive because blurred by those of previous users. Where it has taken in most reflections it gives back nothing at all.

George gives the idea serious application, using the blurred and incomplete reflection returned by the mirror as an image of individuality incompletely realised because of the prominence in the self of traits inherited from our forebears:

'You do see yourself a bit ghostish—' said he, 'on a background of your ancestors. I always think when you stop in an old place like this you sort of keep company with your ancestors too much; I sometimes feel like a bit of the old building walking about; the old feelings of the old folks stick to you like the lichens on the walls; you sort of get hoary.'

(**WP** p 269)

What George is suggesting is that over generations of human development in the same environment real processes occur which are rather like those fancifully suggested as explaining the deficiencies of the mirror and that through them feelings, acquired at some time in the past, are transmitted to succeeding generations. These ancestral responses, the 'old feelings of the old folks' are passed on with increasing emphasis, making any new and individual response more and more difficult, rather in the way that Emily had thought of the contours of the individual face in the mirror becoming obscured as the number of past reflections increased. Those who came late in a stable line of inheritance, as George does, find it nearly impossible to break free of their inherited perspective and respond freshly. And just as there were parts of the mirror which did not reflect at all and which Emily thought were full up, so this process of the inheritance and reinforcement of feelings can end in a state where a genuinely individual response is no longer possible.

Even more than most of the thinkers influenced by evolutionary ideas, Nietzsche emphasises the fundamentally dynamic and imperialistic character of life and the centrality of will-to-power in his thinking reflects his disagreement with what he thought was an over-emphasis in contemporary biological theory on the passivity of living things in the face of environmental pressures. In his view, thinkers like Schopenhauer and Herbert Spencer—and Darwin himself—had mistaken a special and marginal vital response for the characteristic impulse of life: by concentrating on the responsive, adaptive behaviour displayed by organisms in extreme conditions, they had mistakenly concluded that the fundamental life instinct is an 'instinct of self-preservation' or 'will-to-live' and that this goal was typically reached by adaptation. For Nietzsche, on the other hand, aggression and exploitation of what is around are the basic impulses of living things—typically, the healthy organism does not wait to be acted on but takes the initative to change the environment, working not just to maintain itself, but to grow and increase.

Young and strong, George Saxton represents, in Nietzsche's phrase, 'rising life' and might be expected to display the outgoing, expansionist character of the will-to-power to a high degree. How can this lack of initiative be explained if Lawrence's assumptions are, in fact, Nietzschean? A satisfac-

tory answer to this question depends on understanding the complex of
Nietzschean ideas concerned with the operation of the will to power, which
is not just a crude urge to absorb increasing quantities of whatever the
organism can seize from its environment. The primary movement of healthy
life is indeed an active, spontaneous reaching out to grasp and make over
what is in the vicinity, as a result of which the organism 'takes into itself
absurdly more than would be required to preserve it'[7] but the impulse
operates with a high degree of intelligence, identifying the things which have
a significance for further development, and building up a simplified picture
of the environment which will serve the organism as a kind of campaign map
for its subsequent forays. So whether the investigative tools the organism
employs are the simple 'pseudopodia which the single cell creature extends
or the complex and differentiated perceptual, affective and intellectual
apparatus of higher organisms—however it is constituted, the entire
apparatus of knowledge is an apparatus of abstraction and simplification—
directed not toward knowledge but rather toward taking possession of
things'.[8] What we think of as 'knowledge', whether of the world around or
of ourselves, is not a neutral reflection of things but an interested interpretation of them. It is, to use Nietzsche's terms, a 'perspective' which embodies
our present unconscious preferences and helps us in our efforts to reach
them. As an organism grows in power, its preferences change because 'The
strength of the aggressor has a kind of measure in the opposition which it
needs' and 'every growth reveals itself in the search for a more powerful
adversary'.[9] 'Knowledge' which is the perspective we have constructed so as
to gain possession of what we currently (though unconsciously) adjudge
significant for our development will naturally alter as that judgement is
(again unconsciously) revised and a new perspective, a fresh experiential
world will take the place of the old. For Nietzsche, as for Lawrence 'There
is no absolute good, there is nothing absolutely right' and the 'ugly
imperialism'[10] of the absolute is to be rejected.

Words like 'opposition' and 'adversary' are reminders that living things
do not seek their needs in an inert environment, but in a gladiatorial world
where similar efforts are being made by every other creature. In this
Darwinian realm, the aggressor struggles to overwhelm, to reshape, to reduce
to a function, while the victim seeks to maintain independence and integrity.
Conflict and even destruction are therefore inseparable from creation and the
will to grow inevitably implies a will to struggle as a means to that end. In
its efforts to grow, the organism naturally directs its energies at targets which
seem appropriate to its present degree of strength, attacking these things it
might be able to master and avoiding those likely to master it. Despite this
instinctive ability to assess the likely outcome, the outward movement of the
organism remains an adventurous, even dangerous act since the 'prodigality
of force' is 'the most essential character even of the most appropriate
actions'.[11] To gain more power, to grow—the two are synonymous for
Nietzsche—the organism has to risk itself by 'spending' a significant amount
of the force it has already accumulated and Zarathustra sums up the hazards
of the process:

> In all commanding there appeared to me to be an experiment and a risk: and the living creature always risks himself when he commands.[12]

The foray outward is followed by a struggle which will vary in length and intensity according to the relative strength of the antagonists. The aim of the aggressor is 'Appropriation and assimilation ... a desire to overwhelm, a forming, shaping and reshaping, until ... that which has been overwhelmed has entirely gone over into the power domain of the aggressor and increased the same.'[13] Clearly if the process is completed 'that which has been over-whelmed' will no longer have a separate existence, nevertheless the will to power is not simply destructive. What has been seized is reshaped and incor-porated in the developing organism. For Nietzsche, 'the essential thing in the life-process is precisely the tremendous shaping, form-creating force working from within which utilizes and exploits external circumstances'.[14]

But alongside this insistence that life is inherently active and expansionist, Nietzsche, often invokes another and apparently contradictory principle of 'need', especially when he is writing about human affairs. Some passages in his work suggests that the development of maximum power depends on the action of some strong stimulus, almost as if lethargy rather than will to power was the normal human state. Evidently the aggressiveness of the will to power can vary; in Morgan's words 'it is not insatiable in every respect, but becomes canalized and often settles into a routine which limits the urge for growth ...'[15] In other words, the engagement with larger 'targets' which we would expect to accompany growth sometimes does not occur. Particu-larly in human contexts, the expansion of power, which is essentially what growth is, may somehow fail to find expression in the redirection of interest and energy to proportionately more resistant objectives and life comes to be no more than a recurrent engagement with the sort of opposition which we have already proved capable of mastering.

The explanation for this lack of enterprise has to do with another Nietzschean concept—that of 'organic memory'. Nietzsche usually thought of will to power as explaining the whole range of vital phenomena, as the urge which lies behind all organic development, but he also thought that it probably had a much wider explanatory significance and might even be sufficient to account for all being, living or non-living. In the kind of universe he postu-lated, constituted by a multiplicity of wills to power in constant conflict, the chief differences between these two categories of being lies in the fact that a living thing 'gathers experiences, and is never identical with itself in its pro-cesses'.[16] Characteristics of living things like 'biological heredity, the trans-mission of social traditions, and human memory and habit formation which all retain or re-enact the past in the present'[17] are examples of this. Heredity is the most important of these mechanisms even in human beings and to account for it, Nietzsche adapts and extends the meaning of 'organic memory', which, in contemporary biology, meant the 'persistence of the effects of repeated stimuli and responses on any organ of a higher animal'.[18] The term had been coined to indicate 'that this persistence of the effects of previous activities in muscles and other origins is akin to the persistence of previous experience in the nervous system which we commonly call memory'. 'Organic memory' (which contemporary biologists often located in the ganglionic cells) accounts for the fact that, for example, 'A muscle which has contracted many times in a definite way ultimately becomes "trained", so that it responds more rapidly and accurately than an untrained muscle'. When the idea of 'organic memory' is employed by someone belonging to the orthodox Darwinian tradition, it carries no suggestion that such acquired abilities can be transmitted to future generations. Nietzsche, in contrast 'maintains the essentially Lamarkian view that heredity, being a transmission of past "experience", is the inheritance of characters in some past, however remote. He believes that feelings, valuations, and habits pass from father to son, and that reproduction is possible because every cell, especially every germ cell, contains all the past in condensed form'.[19] Memory in this sense is not a passive accumulation of material, but an active assimilation, a reshaping and summation of experience:

> One must learn anew about memory: it is the mass of all experiences of all organic life, alive, arranging themselves, shaping each other, wrestling with one another, simplifying, compressing and changing into many unities. There must be an inner *process* which is like the formation of concepts from many particular cases: the stressing and ever fresh underscoring of the basic scheme and omission of secondary features.—As long as something can be recalled as a separate fact, it is not yet melted down: the latest experience still swims on the surface.[20]

George's sense that staying for many generations in the same environment means that 'the old feelings of the old folks' are passed on to their descendants with ever-increasing emphasis depends on the Lanarkian conception of inheritance developed by Nietzsche, in which acquired characteristics like 'feelings, valuations and habits' can be passed on down the generations. And George's emphasis on the importance of inherited *feelings* in determining character is significant, because, for Nietzsche, feelings 'embody habitual ancestral judgements'[21] and are therefore psychologically more fundamental than, for example, perceptions or thoughts—although even feelings are not ultimate or original since 'behind [them] stand judgements and valuations which we inherit in the form of feelings (inclinations, disinclinations).'[22] Such ancestral judgements and valuations originate in need, growing up as conditions of survival in particular circumstances, but because of the operation of organic memory may, in a stable setting, be inherited long after they have ceased to be needed.

George's attempt using the mirror as a kind of metaphor, to explain the force and persistence in him of 'old feelings' is essentially a figurative account of the processes of organic memory just discussed: he links inner processes with a continuing sameness of external conditions just as Nietzsche had derived the 'creation of stable forms' from the 'recurrence of similar experiences'. The intimate link between character and circumstances which this complex of Nietzschean ideas involves is apparent when after being beaten in a fight by the gamekeeper Annable, George for the first time feels dissatisfied with the life he is leading. He complains to the narrator about the narrowness and triviality of his present existence, but feels it will be very difficult to break with it, not so much because of the admittedly strong social pressures in the conservative local community, but because of the unchanging character of the surroundings themselves. In the Valley, 'everything round you keeps the same, and so you can't change yourself—because everything you look at brings up the same old feeling, and stops you from feeling fresh things'. (**WP** p 113)

Settled in the same place for generations, the Saxtons have been exposed to that 'recurrence of similar experiences' which tends to analize the will to power and so limit the urge to grow. In such circumstances, increase in power tends to bring no realignment of interest towards 'larger' and therefore more appropriate targets, and the same things continue to be valued and sought. At the same time organic memory gives living things the power to gather and transmit experience so that the business of taking possession of what is valued becomes easier—the organism 'learns' from experience and becomes more expert, that is able to achieve its ends with the expenditure of less and less effort: hence the apparently paradoxical combination of vigour and indolence which George displays.

The amount we see, feel and understand, what Lawrence calls in *The Rainbow* our 'range of being' depends on an 'apparatus of knowledge' which has developed not as a means to discover objective 'truth' or 'reality' but as a means to 'taking possession' of things, which works in the service of our (unconscious) ruling valuations. Long dominance, as in the Saxtons, of one particular group of valuations will restrict the individuals 'range of being', developing and strenghthening only the limited kinds of awareness originally needed. Before George himself has recognised that his individuality has to struggle against powerful inherited responses, Lettie comments on the narrow range and conventional character of his perceptions calling him 'a piano which will only play a dozen common notes'. Her comment is provoked by his failure to see the merit of a painting she has shown him and she links the obtuseness of his aesthetic judgements with his inability to see the world itself with freshness and sensitivity. For her the artist (George Clausen) is

> a real realist, he makes common things beautiful, he sees the mystery and magnificence that envelops us when we work menially ... If I hoed in the fields beside you ... you'd be just that colour in the sunset ... and if you looked at the ground you'd find there was a sense of warm gold fire in it, and once you'd perceived the colour, it would strengthen till you'd see nothing else. You are blind; you are only half-born.
>
> (**WP** p 71)

Since breaking with established perceptions and established patterns of living becomes more difficult with each generation, George's father finds it easier to leave Nethermere than George does and, oddly, seems the more 'youthful' of the two. A generation further on, George has accumulated a greater burden of inherited 'inertia'—as Morgan calls it—and the modes of feeling, thinking and perceiving which have ensured his ancestors survival, have through long repetition accumulated almost overwhelming force in his nature. George's irresolute pursuit of Lettie is one example of the difficulty both he and his father find in breaking with their accustomed life—and this difficulty is largely a consequence of the length of time the Saxtons have settled in Nethermere. As the father says, when

> ... you stay in one place generation after generation ... you seem to get proud, an' look on things outside as foolishness. There's many a thing as any common man knows, as we haven't a glimpse of. We keep on thinking and feeling the same year after year, till we've only got one side.
>
> (**WP** pp 269)

Behind Saxton's remarks lies Nietzsche's idea that the action of organic memory and hereditary inertia can ultimately lead to a state of 'fixation', in which the traits essential for life in a particular stable environment have been reinforced so often and so strongly that their possessors become incapable of further change, and have indeed 'only got one side'. Conversely a change in mode of life tends to unsettle previously acquired traits and encourage the development of new ones. Agreeing with his son's remark that their kind of family history has made them feel 'a bit ghostish ... on a background of their ancestors', Saxton contrasts their state with that of people 'whose families have shifted about' who therefore 'don't know how it feels' and he goes on to use this idea that mobility prevents fixation to explain his decision to emigrate—'That's why I'm going to Canada'. It is this Nietzschean emphasis on the intimate relation between character and local conditions which led Lawrence to alter the actual circumstances of the Chambers family on whom the Saxtons are clearly based. While the Chambers family had moved to the Haggs Farm only two or three years before Lawrence met Jessie, their fictional counterparts have lived and farmed in Nethermere for some hundreds of years.

The same kind of association between a stable, long-established way of life an an inertia which impedes any attempt to extend experience is evident at the beginning of *The Rainbow*. The opening pages of the novel evoke and celebrate what Leavis describes as the 'immemorial life of the Marsh'[23]—its unchanging character underlined by the absence of any precise reference to time. But while Lawrence powerfully conveys the significance and value of what the Marsh represents in his opening description, he also suggests its limitations by using words like 'full', 'heavy' and 'surcharged' which imply inertia and satiety, to describe the state of the Brangwen men. Although he sees the almost wholly physical and instinctive traditional life as valuable, Lawrence does not set out to 'exalt this order of things as finally adequate' and his interest is rather in the 'struggle towards self-responsibility in the individual—self-responsibility and a wider scope, things which entail a freer play of intelligence and a direct part in the intellectual culture and final civilisation of the age ...'[24] Immobilized by generations spent in the same surroundings and in the same activities—Tom Brangwen later tells his future wife that the family have held the Marsh Farm 'above two hundred years'— the Brangwen men have become incapable of taking any spontaneous step towards fuller being, and some outside force is needed to provide the impetus for further development. 'Dazed with looking towards the source of generation, unable to turn round', the Brangwen men are not as alert, sensitive and active as they might be; their state resembles that of George Saxton at the beginning of *The White Peacock*, his life 'nothing else but a doss' from which somebody will sooner or later rouse him.

In the later novel, as in the earlier, one important element in rousing the male character to fuller awareness is feminine influence. George's development is closely bound up with Lettie's increasing interest in him and, in *The Rainbow*, Tom Brangwen's dissatisfaction with the traditional mode of life is bound up with the fact that as the last child, very much younger than his brothers, he 'had belonged rather to the company of his sisters' and is, in addition 'his mother's favourite'. Far more than Alfred or Frank, he has been exposed to the restless aspiring spirit characteristic of the Brangwen women, and it is clearly this which prevents him from unquestioningly adopting the traditional attitudes of the Brangwen men, and which leads to him being divided against himself. For instance, he accepts that his mother's ideal of educated gentility is valid for him while recognising, at the same time, that he is incapable of realizing it. His natural wholeness and happiness, his inheritance from his forbears, is undermined, and he comes to feel ashamed of his essentially physical and sensuous nature:

> He believed his mother was right in decreeing school for him, but he knew she was only right because she would not acknowledge his constitution. He knew, with a child's clear, instinctive foreknowledge of what is going to happen to him, that he would cut a sorry figure at school. But he took the infliction as inevitable, as if he were guilty of his own nature, as if his being were wrong, and his mother's conception right.
>
> (**R** p 15)

It is tempting to interpret Tom's experience here in terms of the sort of destructive clash of masculine and feminine values often said to be central to Lawrence's work—Kermode, for instance, argues that

> When Lawrence opened *The Rainbow* with an account of the way in which outward-looking, aspiring women changed the life of their contented men-folk, so inaugurating the changes which would come to crisis in the life of Ursula Brangwen, he was thinking of his mother and of the girl Jessie Chambers, whose culture and sexual unresponsiveness he treated as evidence of a female sell-out to the bad kind of consciousness.[25]

But female ambition is not the only or even the decisive factor in upsetting the settled life of the Marsh Farm or Strelley Mill. Even in the opening section of *The Rainbow*, which is unlocalized in time, Lawrence contrasts masculine and feminine attitudes, suggesting that he sees the difference as rooted in the nature of each sex rather than as something which has arisen at a particular time through a 'sell-out' to a 'cult of castration' with 'definable historical origins'.[26] In any event, the interest the Brangwen women feel in the 'far off world of cities and governments' has no practical influence on the traditional pattern of life until industrialisation comes to the valley and the Brangwens are confronted by the rapid and radical transformation of their own immediate surroundings. Feminine restlessness, whatever its source and significance, may be a necessary condition for change but is not, apparently, a sufficient one. One might add that, whatever its precise mechanism, a process that produces an individual as vital and attractive as Ursula Brangwen can hardly be seen in the negative way Kermode suggests.

Even before the industrial invasion, the Brangwen women had concluded that 'education' together with 'experience' was the key to the fuller life they recognised in their social superiors. However, like their menfolk, they are sunk at this point in 'the drowse of blood-intimacy' and so are satisfied themselves with merely imaginative participation in the wider life beyond the rural community and even fail to act on their ambition that their children should gain direct access through education to the 'finer, more vivid circle of life'. It is only when the industrial development of the eighteen-forties has unsettled the traditional ways that one of the Brangwen women is able to shake off her 'drowse', and even then such a radical initiative demands an unusual effort of will because we are told that Tom's mother 'roused herself to determination and sent him ... to a grammar school in Derby'. But in the event, Tom's dissatisfaction with the old life has less to do with what he learns at school than with his willingness to accept his mother's ambitions for him in the first place. The fact that he does so indicates that the intrinsic self-confidence and self-esteem, which has marked previous generations of Brangwen men—and kept them immune from feminine influence—has somehow broken down. If his mother has a quite unusual degree of influence over him, it is not just because he is her favourite or has spent a lot of time in female company, but is also the result of an inner change which has made him more amenable to that influence.

Tom is different from his forebears because he has grown up during the industrialisation of the area round the farm. In *The Rainbow*, in other words, that 'change in mode of life' which works to 'unsettle the previously acquired forms' comes about not as a result of a move to a fresh environment—as in the Saxton's case—but as a result of a radical change in the surroundings themselves. Like the Saxtons, the Brangwens have been in one place for so long that 'hereditary inertia' is a powerful force in them and it is this, in the men in particular, which accounts for the seemingly paradoxical fact that, in H M Daleski's words, 'the disposition of the Brangwen men is essentially female'.[27] Instead of exhibiting the outgoing, enterprising traits which Lawrence defines as 'male' in 'Study of Thomas Hardy', they are linked with the 'female', with the unchanging life of the body, senses and instincts. The process of stabilisation is interrupted by the radical alteration in their surroundings which begins in the eighteen-forties and so it is in Tom's parents' generation—the first to experience the changes—that the first clear signs emerge of the new awareness and new interests which are more fully developed in their children; in Alfred and in Tom himself in particular.

Although the change in the area round the Marsh Farm is considerable,

it is far from being as complete as the sort of alteration their their circumstances experienced by the people Saxton refers to, 'whose families have
shifted about'. The farm is reduced in area and cut off from its hinterland
but is itself essentially unchanged; still 'remote and original on the old quiet
side of the canal embankment', it remains 'just on the safe side of civilisation,
outside the gate'. The result is that, in the Brangwen's experience, the
familiar and the novel, the influences making for stability and those encouraging change, are intermingled—as they go about the traditional rural
tasks, they meet with the sights, sounds and smells of the new industrial
order:

> At first the Brangwens were astonished by all this commotion around them.
> The building of a canal across their land made them strangers in their own
> place, this raw bank of earth shutting them off disconcerted them. As they
> worked in the fields, from beyond the now familiar embankment came the
> rhythmic run of the winding engines, startling at first, but afterwards a narcotic
> to the brain. Then the shrill whistle of the trains re-echoed through the heart,
> with fearsome pleasure, announcing the far-off come near and imminent.
> As they drove home from the town, the farmers of the land met the blackened
> colliers trooping from the pit-mouth. As they gathered the harvest, the west
> wind brought a faint, sulphurous smell of pit-refuse burning. As they pulled
> the turnips in November, the sharp clink-clink-clink-clink-clink of empty
> trucks shunting on the line, vibrated in their hearts with the fact of other activity
> going on beyond them.
>
> **(R** pp 12–13)

It is this duality in their experience which creates, in the new generation of
Brangwens and particularly in the youngest, Tom, a conflict between old
feelings and habits and a wider awareness and fresh interests. The family's
most immediate circumstances do not change in any essential way—indeed
far from causing an 'up-rooting',[28] industrialism brings increasing prosperity to the farm—so the inertia which is created by stable conditions
continues to increase. At the same time, the Brangwens are constantly faced
with the evidence of the great changes which have taken place around them,
and this contrasting element in their experience has an opposite, destabilising
effect encouraging the development of new 'feelings', valuations and habits'.
The result is an increasing tension which can be seen in their divided, ambivalent response, their 'fearsome pleasure', for instance, at the whistles of the
trains which announce 'the far-off come near and imminent'. They are
frightened and excited at the same time by this intimation that the Marsh is
no longer remote from the 'far-off world of cities and governments and the
active scope of men' which, in the past, the Brangwen woman had had to
strain her eyes to see.

While the old pre-industrial order is still the predominant influence in the
lives of Tom's parents, the rapid changes around them do awaken an interest
in, and an excitement at, the 'other activity going on beyond them', though
they have no desire to participate actively in it and, outwardly at least, the
traditional mode of life continues unchanged. Tom and his brothers, on the

other hand, grow up in a divided world and the potential for change in them is correspondingly greater. At the same time, their relation to the old life and their impulse to 'learn' in a general sense by extending their experience, varies a good deal. In Alfred and the unnamed oldest brother, the urge to break with the traditional life is spontaneous and the latter in particular makes a complete and final break, exchanging the stability and continuity of the life at the Marsh for its opposite, the nomadic existence of a sailor. And we are told, significantly, that he 'did not come back'. Alfred, the second son, also manages to leave the Marsh, but only after a considerable struggle and he gets no further than nearby Nottingham, where he becomes a draughtsman in a lace-factory. While the eldest makes an early and apparently easy departure, Alfred's nature is dominated much more by the old feelings and habits and he escapes only after an intense and powerful inner battle.

At school his strong desire to learn is in conflict with a native incapacity, because it is his senses rather than his intellect which are developed, and he makes real progress only in the one subject, drawing, which depends on the senses. Although Alfred recognises his artistic ability as his 'hope', his one chance of moving beyond the world of the farm, he does not find it easy to break with that world and settle in the kind of job for which his talent qualifies him. It is only after 'much grumbling and savage rebellion against everything, after much trying and shifting about 'that he settles in the job in Nottingham. And unlike the eldest son who never returns, Alfred is regularly drawn back to the Marsh despite the fact that he feels 'some contempt' for the life and for those who have remained there.

Despite his difficulties at school, Alfred is at least keen to learn but Tom shows no spontaneous enthusiasm for education and resists his mother's plan to send him to grammar school at Derby. Like the degenerate Frank who 'refused from the first to have anything to do with learning', Tom has no innate urge to extend his experience and only his mother's determination ensures that he is sent to school. And once there, in contrast to Alfred's 'yearning' for knowledge, Tom feels a positive and powerful revulsion against 'deliberate learning', which has its origins in a 'physical inability to study'. The recalcitrant facts of his own nature are an insuperable barrier to Tom's intellectual progress and he is incapable of the perseverance and self-discipline, the 'dogged' effort which, if it brings Alfred little profit except in his drawing, at least allows him to master the rudiments of his other subjects as well. Later, as a young man, Tom becomes deeply disillusioned with life on the farm and desperate to leave it, but he finds it impossible to go even the short distance away that Alfred has managed and stays at the Marsh till his death.

Each of the three brothers tries to widen his experience and change his life but experiences increasing difficulty in doing so: they form a continuum, each displaying a greater degree of inertia which appears in increasingly limited freedom of movement both physically and psychologically. The Brangwen sons illustrate the way in which the process of stabilisation can proceed within a single generation, whereas in *The White Peacock* its effects are most evident between generations, in the way in which, in the Saxtons, the traits associated with youth and age are reversed. In *The Rainbow* it is the fact that the Brangwen parents' most immediate experience continues to be the same, despite the changes round them, that serves to consolidate the dominant responses further and ensures that they are passed on with increasing emphasis to each successive child.

Like Alfred, Tom is 'sensitively developed ... refined in instinct' though his is a sensitivity of feeling rather than of seeing and his interest is aroused by poetry rather than by drawing. Spoken verse in particular conveys 'enlightenment to him through feeling' but his attempt to follow up this rewarding kind of experience on his own is frustrated by a revulsion from the printed word caused largely by his inability to 'voluntarily control his attention':

> He sat betrayed with emotion when the teacher of literature read, in a moving fashion, Tennyson's 'Ulysses' or Shelley's 'Ode to the West Wind'. His lips parted, his eyes filled with a strained, almost suffering light ... Tom Brangwen was moved by this experience beyond all calculation, he almost dreaded it, it was so deep. But when, almost secretly and shamefully, he came to take the book himself, and began the words 'Oh wild west wind, thou breath of autumn's being', the very fact of the print caused a prickly sensation of repulsion to go over his skin, the blood came to his face, his heart filled with a bursting passion of rage and incompetence. He threw the book down and walked over it and went out to the cricket field. And he hated books as if they were his enemies.
>
> (**R** p 16)

He finds that a kind of experience which is more intense and exhilirating than anything he has felt before has to depend on action by someone else, because despite his intense desire to recapture it for himself, he is unable to do so. His effort collapses in the face of his instinctive resistance to the printed word and the anger and disappointment he feels when he fails are the measure of how much the experience has meant to him. And the profound conservatism of his nature is further underlined by his own feelings about his response to poetry: during the readings in class, he sits 'betrayed with emotion' and his attempt to explore the experience for himself is made 'almost secretly and shamefully'. His ambivalence, reminiscent of the 'fearsome pleasure' with which his parents' generation responded to new kinds of experience, indicates that Tom feels uneasy, even guilty, about the fact that his feelings are 'exceptional'.

Later, as a young man, Tom meets a sexually emancipated girl and her foreign lover at Matlock and this encounter extends and develops the intimations of 'fuller being' first felt at school. The meeting makes him aware of sexual and social satisfactions unavailable in his present life, but once again the revelation of new possibilities is the result of the actions of others. The girl takes the initiative in love-making, and the foreigner makes the social approach, while Tom remains largely passive and responsive. His experiences at Matlock become the basis for a dream of a finer, more fulfilling life which, for a time, is more vivid than the mundane reality of Cossethay and Ilkeston.

But the intoxication the contact has brought fades, despite Tom's attempts to maintain it by drinking more than usual, and 'the cold material of his ordinary life (begins) to show through'. Forced to confront the commonplace again, Tom now finds it intolerable, but is also unable to take any active and practical steps to escape from it. He realises that neither his sexual nor his social aspirations can be realised in the community he knows, but he also finds that despite their urgency, he cannot leave it:

> He wanted to get out of the quandary he found himself in. But how? He had seen a little creature caught in bird-lime, and the sight was a night-mare to him. He began to feel mad with the rage of impotency.
>
> (**R** p 26)

The feeling of anger and frustration and impotence gives way to a withdrawn, musing state which alcohol helps him to sustain until

> ... a fever of restless anger came upon him. He wanted to go away—right away. He dreamed of foreign parts. But somehow he had no contact with them. And it was a very strong root which held him to the Marsh, to his own house and land.
>
> (**R** p 26)

Marvin Mudrick argues that Tom's difficulties arise because the industrialisation of the region has brought such a rapid and unexpected break with the past that the 'impulse outward' released by it has had no chance to assume definite shape. Tom finds his present life unfulfilling, but has no definite idea where or how fulfilment is to be found—mines, canal and railway have 'cut across the past and offered a promise of the future' so that 'the individual is freed from traditional, unquestioned preoccupations to think and do— what?'[29] But the 'impulse outward' *had* assumed definite shape in the minds of the Brangwen women even before industrialisation, when they wished to help their children towards the 'higher form of being' embodied in their social superiors. And even then, the women had definite ideas about how their goal could be realised, concluding that it was 'education and experience' rather than money or class which were the way to the 'finer, more vivid circle of life'. If, at first, the women fail to act on their ambitions it is not because the ambitions themselves are vague or because they cannot see how they might be realised but because, like the men, they are affected by 'the drowse of blood-intimacy', by the immobility created by generations spent in the same surroundings, leading the same kind of life. And like the Brangwen women, Tom knows exactly what he wants, because his idea of a fuller, finer life, like theirs, is rooted in actual contact with people who embody such possibilities. It is the episode at Matlock which provides the material for the dream which comes to dominate his thoughts:

> The result of these encounters was, that he dreamed day and night, absorbedly of a voluptuous woman and of the meeting with a small, withered foreigner of ancient breeding. No sooner was his mind free, no sooner had he left his own

companions, than he began to imagine an intimacy with fine-textured, subtle-mannered people such as the foreigner at Matlock, and amidst this subtle intimacy was always the satisfaction of a voluptuous woman.

(**R** p 25)

While this kind of imaginative involvement in a fuller life had been enough for the Brangwen women of previous generations, each of whom 'lived her own fulfilment' in the life of the squire's lady, in Tom the desire for change has become stronger, more direct and urgent, so that the vicarious satisfactions of the imagination are no longer enough. He must actually participate in the kind of existence he dreams about if he is to attain his fulfilment. So his first reaction when the dream fades and the commonplace resumes its hold is to consider marrying, feeling, that if he could at least find the sexual fulfilment, the 'satisfaction of a voluptuous woman' which seems the most attainable element of his 'dream', he will be able to settle down again, free of much of the frustration which now troubles him. But, as his previous experiences with the local girls, both 'loose' and respectable, has suggested, the kind of satisfaction he seeks is not to be found with them and he comes to feel that the only possibility of finding fulfilment depends on moving away from the Marsh, which he is unable to do.

So Tom's inactivity stems, not from the indeterminate nature of his aspirations, nor from an inability to see how he might realise them, but from the same kind of inertia that marked his forebears. There are powerful forces for change in his psyche, generated by altered circumstances, but they are in conflict with even stronger forces—feelings and habits reinforced over many generations—which have accumulated an almost overwhelming weight and offer virtually insuperable resistance to any new initiative.

George Saxton in *The White Peacock* experiences the same rapid disillusionment with what had seemed a satisfactory life. Meeting him shortly after his fight with Annable, Cyril is surprised by the new attitude expressed in George's bitter question 'What's worth having in my life?' because in their last conversation, the young farmer had said that his domestic comfort outweighed the other unsatisfactory aspects of life in the valley. Like Tom's disillusionment, George's dissatisfaction with his present life is not just created by damage done to his physical self-confidence and instinctive self esteem—it is also linked with a positive vision of a more attractive and fuller kind of existence, with the idea of the 'free kind of life' which he asks Lettie about. But despite the greater ease with which his aspirations could be realised, (they are, after all, centred on a particular and available girl) George, like Tom, seems to be incapable of positive action and like him takes refuge in dream and fantasy. When Cyril tries to encourage his friend, hinting that Lettie would favour his suit, George misinterprets his reference to doing 'something decisive' about things, replying 'I don't know what can happen—unless the squire turns us out'. It is as if George can only think of decisive action being taken by someone else, of change as something which comes about not by acting, but by being acted on. And even when Cyril makes his meaning clear, George can only express his feeling of utter helplessness—'Don't make me feel a worse fool ...' he replies, despairingly.

George's difficulties stem partly from the fact that marriage to the socially superior Lettie is an essential part of his 'dream' and in wooing her he would be rebelling against the feelings about class which prevail in the community. But his failure to act does not come wholly or even primarily from deference to local opinion—despite his complaint that in the valley 'You've no freedom for thinking of what the other folks think of you'—but rather from the continuing force in his own nature of the traditional responses, the 'old feelings' which are maintained and strengthened by the familiar surroundings. It is because he realises that these influences are likely to frustrate his newly awakened desire for change that George thinks for the first time of leaving Nethermere and emigrating, with the rest of the family, to Canada.

Trying to explain his predicament to Cyril, George refers to something Lettie has said about the lack of freedom experienced by members of small, long-established communities:

> Lettie said to me: 'Here, you can't live as you like—in any way or circumstance. You're like a bit out of those coloured marble mosaics in the hall, you have to fit in your own set, fit into your own pattern, because you're put there from the first. But you don't want to be like a fixed piece of mosaic—you want to fuse into life, and melt and mix with the rest of folk.'
>
> **(WP** p 113)

Her reflections are prompted by a question from George about her attitude to the 'free kind of life' which—picking apples together—they are temporarily sharing. Involved for the moment in a kind of experience and relationship different from those customary in the social group to which she belongs, Lettie admits she feels a desire to explore life more freely than convention allows. She wants to 'fuse into life' and 'melt and mix with the rest of folk' outside her own 'set', but she feels that such freedom is impossible in places like Nethermere. Her fatalistic conclusion reflects her own dilemma; she is dissatisfied with the suitor, Leslie, who belongs to her own social group and increasingly attracted to the 'unsuitable' George, but nevertheless finds it impossible, by herself, to break with conventional expectations and end her engagement. And she sees her situation as general in, and created by, the sort of community she and George belong to, while implying in her introductory 'here' the existence of other, freer, kinds of environment. Both characters, then, find themselves in the same kind of predicament, where a powerful impulse to move in new directions is frustrated by an even more powerful inertia created by the kind of community in which they live. And because George's deepest desires, like Tom's, cannot be released in action, he too takes refuge in vivid day-dreams of fulfilment, in that habit of building 'castles in Spain' which Cyril censures in his friend. Exasperated, he asks George why he doesn't 'scheme for getting what you want, instead of dreaming fulfilments' but his exhortations have no effect. Like Tom

Brangwen after the Matlock encounter, George is 'absorbed in the interest and actuality' of his dream and so content to go on dreaming.

George is like Tom too in that the sense of new possibilities in life comes to him from outside. Just as an awareness of potentialities beyond his present state of existence is brought to Brangwen by others—by his English teacher's reading of poetry, by the girl and the foreigner at Matlock, so George's vision of fulfilment with Lettie in a 'free kind of life' originates in the idea of her working alongside him in the fields which she had introduced in their discussion of Clausen's 'Hoeing'. At the time, that idea had seemed 'very new to him, almost a shock to his imagination'. Like Tom, he cannot think of alternatives to the conventional pattern of life by himself and this is because both come from the kind of long-established, stable environment in which one particular set of valuations has been constantly reinforced. As a result, both have a restricted and inflexible 'apparatus of knowledge' and a limited range of deeply rooted traits developed in the service of these valuations; confined within a particular and traditional 'interpretation' of things, neither is capable of even conceiving of alternatives.

The effect on Tom of the meeting at Matlock is compared to that of a man forced out of his house by a fire:

> His mind was one big excitement. The girl and the foreigner; he knew neither of their names. Yet they had set fire to the homestead of his nature, and he would be burned out of cover.
>
> (**R** p 25)

The phrase 'the homestead of his nature' aptly conveys the characteristics of the experiential world Tom has lived in up to now. It suggests first that the 'reality' in which we live (like the house in which we live) is essentially a human construction, and in its echo of the earlier description of the Marsh Farm itself ('The homestead was just on the safe side of civilisation ...') it links the 'reality' human beings create for themselves with the place in which their 'perspective' develops. Further, the kind of dwelling-place which the metaphor suggests indicates the sort of 'interpretation' the Brangwen's have of the world, 'homestead' suggesting familiarity and comfort, but also narrowness and rusticity. In *The White Peacock*, George employs the same kind of image to describe his own sense of being imprisoned within an inherited pattern of living, saying he sometimes feels 'like a bit of the old building walking about'. In his case, however, emancipation from the traditional outlook is slow and difficult; his house is not 'burnt down' as Tom's is, but slowly decays. As he himself says to Cyril just after Lettie's marriage:

> It is in my nature to linger an unconscionable time, yet I dread above all things this slow crumbling away from my foundations by which I free myself at last.
>
> (**WP** p 309)

The occasion of the remark is significant, because the marriage which has just taken place is the main testimony in the novel to George's inability to free himself from conventional responses. And having lost Lettie, he now lacks the stimulus he needs to create a new 'perspective' in place of the old. To use his own idiom, he cannot now build a 'house of life' which would be his own rather than merely something inherited from his ancestors, and which would have the greater scale and spaciousness suggested by his use of 'castles'.

> 'You see I built on Lettie',—he looked up at me shamefacedly, then continued tearing the shavings—'you must found your castles on something, and I founded mine on Lettie. You see I'm like plenty of folks, I have nothing definite to shape my life to. I put brick upon brick, as they come, and if the whole topples down in the end, it does. But you see, you and Lettie have made me conscious, and now I'm at a dead loss. I have looked to marriage to set me busy on my house of life, something whole and complete, of which it will supply the design.'
>
> **(WP p 310)**

Tom escapes from his inherited 'perspective' more quickly and completely than George, so despite his inability to move away from the Marsh and seek satisfaction elsewhere, he *is* able to act decisively when an opportunity for fulfilment presents itself within the area to which he is confined. In this case the intervention from outside which changes Tom's life takes the form of the chance arrival in the district of Lydia Lensky, the widow of a Polish doctor and a woman of aristocratic background. Lydia seems to embody in herself all the elements which make up Tom's dream of fulfilment, and although he is frightened as well as fascinated by her and what she represents, so that 'He was a long time resolving definitely to ask her to marry him', he puts his hard-won resolution into effect. George Saxton on the other hand, although separated from Lettie only by class is, at first, incapable of the kind of initiative needed to win her and, ironically, it is only when she is beyond his reach that he announces his determination to 'wrench' himself away from such residues of the traditional outlook as remain in him. This contrast between two otherwise very similar characters—Graham Hough describes Tom Brangwen as 'a more successful George Saxton'[30]—has its roots in their early experience. At the beginning of *The White Peacock*, Mrs Beardsall refers scornfully to George's immaturity and links it with his mother's over-indulgent treatment of him:

> As for him—he's an unlicked cub. What can you expect when his mother has spoiled him as she has.
>
> **(WP p 21)**

Tom is also his mother's favourite, but has been subject to feminine influence of a more bracing kind, which has undermined rather than strengthened any tendency to self-satisfaction, and he becomes convinced of his own limited-ness and inadequacy at an early age. Tom also discovers that the schooling his mother insists on centres on the kind of intellectual skills which he simply cannot begin to attain, while his sensitivity in other than 'mental things' is irrelevant, or even inimical, to academic success. The result is that Tom's school career is largely one of failure and humiliation, relieved by a few rewarding occasions—like the poetry readings—when enlightenment comes to him through feeling. It is hardly surprising, then, that rather than bringing a break with the old life as his mother had intended, Tom's sojourn at grammar-school creates in him a strong desire to return to the simple life of the land.

When he leaves school, Tom goes back to the farm 'where he was in his own again', but the aspirations he has absorbed through his close contact with his mother and sisters remain alive—and so, while he is relieved to escape from his 'ignominious position' in the place of learning, 'Yet his soul was wretched almost to hopelessness' at the apparent impossibility of moving beyond his present state. The result is that Tom's return to the land is only superficially a return to that oneness with nature and its processes enjoyed by his forebears. The conservatism which predominates in his nature makes him largely content to resume the old life, but his less than complete adjustment to it shows itself in the violent, unprovoked rages which sometimes afflict him. Nevertheless, until the episode at Matlock he is reconciled to carrying on the traditional pattern of life, having convinced himself—under the influence of the excessive modesty produced by his experience at school—that he is incapable of anything higher. As he says to his exasperated mother, 'I have got a turnip on my shoulders, let me stick to th' fallow'.

If his schooldays have made him want to regress to the simple life on the land, his meeting with the girl and the foreigner at Matlock has the opposite effect. After it he is disillusioned with the Marsh and all it represents and eager to move towards the fuller life which he has glimpsed. The revolution in his attitudes takes place because what happens at Matlock demonstrates to him that, despite his failure at school, he is not finally excluded from experiences beyond the traditional range; it shows him that entry to 'the more vivid circle of life' does not have to depend on the mental progress of which he has found himself incapable. At Matlock he is involved in a sexual encounter far more exciting and fulfilling than any he has had with the local girls and he also participates in a kind of social intercourse which is more developed, more subtle and delicate, than any he has known before. What is said in the conversation with the foreigner matters less to Tom than the 'subtle intimacy' which, for the time, they share:

> He was transported at meeting this odd, middle-aged dry-skinned man, personally. The talk was pleasant, but that did not matter so much. It was the gracious manner, the fine contact that was all.
>
> **(R** p 25)

So Tom gains entry for the moment to an existence where feelings have a depth, range and refinement beyond those of the familiar world of the Marsh Farm, Cossethay and Ilkeston; a realm of more vivid experience to which his unusual emotional sensitivity allows him access. The episode at Matlock is a turning point because it shows that in resigning himself to 'th' fallow' he has shown 'too low an opinion of himself'. It revives the hope his 'soul' seemed to have lost when he left school and in contrast to the glamorous possibilities it reveals, his present narrow round now comes to seem worthless and unreal.

The 'old feelings' which predominate in George and Tom represent inherited and embodied judgements, estimates of 'use' or 'harm', arrived at by their ancestors in some remote past in relation to their growth and development. Feelings originate in valuations which were once 'conditions of existence' in a particular setting and in stable conditions are assimilated and strengthened through the action of organic memory, and continue to function as spontaneously acting urges, although their utility has been lost. Neitzsche sums up the evolution of urges in this way:

> All human urges, like all animal ones, have been developed and placed in the foreground as conditions of existence under certain circumstances. Urges are the after-effects of long-fostered valuations which now function instinctively, as a *system* of judgements of pleasure and pain. First compulsion, then habituation, then want, then natural propensity (urge).[31]

The experience of the Brangwens illustrates how behaviour which begins under compulsion can become instinctive and spontaneous. By the period in which the novel opens they have 'forgotten what it was to be in straitened circumstances' but habits of industry and prudence originating in some earlier period have been retained, their persistence suggesting that over the generations the family have been involved in a long struggle with circumstances more difficult than those they now face:

> So the Brangwens came and went without fear of necessity, working hard because of the life that was in them, not for the want of the money. Neither were they thriftless. They were aware of the last half-penny, and instinct made them not waste the peeling of their apple, for it would help to feed the cattle.
> (**R** p 7)

The thrift compelled by harder conditions has now become an 'instinct' which continues to function despite the fact that the need for it has ceased.

If a stable setting encourages the continuing dominance of old valuations it also, for the same reason, brings an increasing economy of effort in the appropriation of what is valued. The operation of organic memory allows living things to learn from experience and so acquire increasing expertise in attaining their ends. Typically the progression is from actions which are comparatively clumsy and wasteful of effort to the efficiency and economy of instinctively exercised skills, so that even if the 'prodigality of force' remains 'the most essential character even of the most appropriate actions', the organism in the end gets far more than it has to give out, steadily accumulating 'power' and transmitting it to the next generation.

The traditional activity of both Brangwens and Saxtons is agriculture—a creation of the will to power at its most elementary level, acting to ensure the physical survival and growth of the human community. In it are displayed the formative characteristics of the will to power mentioned earlier: the natural world is initially prolific and chaotic, 'abundance and extravagance even to absurdity' predominate in it according to Nietzsche. As a result, he insists, the entire animal and plant world develops 'all at the same time, in utter disorder, over and against each other'.[32] In agriculture, this natural chaos is subjected to human control and made to serve human purposes— nature is reorganised in the service of human needs, wasteful abundance becoming useful fertility. The creation of a system of agriculture involves such a radical transformation of nature that it will inevitably be a long and difficult process; the power of the forces man has to contend with, if he is to impose and maintain control, is suggested by the speed with which the old rural order of Nethermere succumbs to the plague of rabbits. In that novel, it is the Saxtons and their farming neighbours who represent the 'human controlling principle in nature' without which it would run wild 'perverting human passion and endeavour'[33] and not, as the critic who uses these phrases perversely suggests, the gamekeeper Annable. His job is to encourage the rabbits, thus protecting the squire's profits, but also destroying the control over nature built up over generations of steady effort. In *The White Peacock* the threat to cultivated nature posed by uncontrolled natural abundance is artificially intensified, but serves as a reminder of the constant tension between human purposes and the natural order of things.

But in both novels, the basic task of establishing control over nature has long since been completed and the initial hostility of the environment has generated, in those who live and work in it, the strength to deal with its challenges. As a result their engagement with it, although not effortless, now no longer demands the entire energies of Brangwens or Saxtons. In *The White Peacock*, frequent references to the hunting and trapping of animals—the squire's rabbits are not the only victims—emphasise that an element of conflict and difficulty is always present in the human engagement with the natural world; in *The Rainbow*, on the other hand, what is stressed is the degree to which nature has become adapted to human purposes so that it actually seems to collaborate with, rather than resist, the Brangwen men. Aspects of it are even described in human terms suggesting that it has become thoroughly 'humanised'; as in the opening pages of the novel, where the distinction between the human and the natural and between inner and outer worlds is blurred. The will-to-power as a form-creating force comes from within and reaches out to make over external circumstances according to its own patterns so that inner and outer come to resemble one another:

> They knew the intercourse between heaven and earth, sunshine drawn into the breast and bowels, the rain sucked up in the day-time, nakedness that comes under the wind in autumn, showing the birds' nests no longer worth hiding. Their life and their inter-relations were such; feeling the pulse and body of the soil, that opened to their furrow for the grain, and became smooth and supple after their ploughing, and clung to their feet with a weight that pulled like desire, lying hard and unresponsive when the crops were to be shorn away. The young corn waved and was silken, and the lustre slid along the limbs of the men who saw it. They took the udder of the cows, the cows yielded milk and pulse[d] against the hands of the men, the pulse of the blood of the teats of the cows beat

into the pulse of the hands of the men. They mounted their horses, and held life between the grip of their knees, they harnessed their horses at the wagon, and, with hand on the bridle-rings, drew the heaving of the horses after their will.

(R p 55)

This degree of mastery means that what is taken in is vastly in excess of what is expended so that the Brangwen's way of life is, so to speak, an 'accumulative' one; their limbs and bodies are 'impregnated with the day, cattle and earth and vegetation and the sky' and their blood flows 'heavy from the accumulation of the living day':

So much warmth and generating and pain and death did they know in their blood, earth and sky and beast and green plants, so much exchange and interchange they had with these, that they lived full and surcharged, their senses full fed ...

(R p 56)

In the long struggle with hostile conditions, need and organic memory work together over many generations to build up power; Morgan calls this the principle of 'storage', saying that 'if things go well a species builds up tremendous power by this process' but he goes on to say that it cannot continue indefinitely, quoting Nietzsche's own warning that

The danger of those strong communities founded on like individuals of firm character is the stupefaction, gradually increased by heredity, which ... follows all stability like its shadow.[34]

'Storage' and 'stupefaction'—the terms seem appropriate to their case—continue side by side in the Brangwen men. 'Full' and 'surcharged' they are also 'dazed with looking towards the source of generation, unable to turn round'. And the same conjunction of vigour with slowness and heaviness is evident in George Saxton, and for the same reason.

If the long engagement with continuing unfavourable conditions produces individuals of strong though limited character, it also severely restricts individuality itself, creating a shared, communal identity because the same limited range of necessary urges is 'learned' and continually reinforced. In their conversation about pictures during George's first visit to her home, Lettie points out that his responses lack individuality as well as range—the notes he can sound, in her own piano image, are 'common' as well as 'few'. At this point, George's attitudes and reactions are those characteristic of the community. Later after the fight with Annable which begins his disillusionment, George is able to see and regret the rigidly conformist outlook of Nethermere although, like Lettie, he is pessimistic about his chances of escape from its confining categories.

The same uniformity of character both within and between generations is apparent at the beginning of *The Rainbow*. The Brangwens are not distinguished at all as individuals until the events of the eighteen forties begin the process of differentiation which the novel traces. The only contrast which is made in connection with earlier Brangwen generations has a sexual rather than an individual basis—Lawrence's repeated use in the opening pages of the generalising phrases 'the men' and 'the women' and his careful presentation of the different attitudes of the two sexes suggest a homogeneity of character *within* each of the sexes.

At the same time, this general difference seems inconsistent with my emphasis on how organic memory works to produce sameness in those living in identical conditions. The explanation lies in another important Nietzschean idea, that relative physical weakness is the great stimulus to the development of intelligence, which has its origins in a passive but sharp attentiveness and an ability to postpone and plan for gratification—things which are forced on those who are less able to get what they want by the direct exercise of physical strength. So Nietzsche consistently associates intelligence with the weak and with women as a sex. Those who are physically strong and therefore capable of dealing with the challenges of life in physical terms have less need of intelligence and so are less likely to develop is spontaneously, or to such a degree: like George or Tom, they need some outside force to encourage its growth.

It is these ideas which lie behind the close relationships between individuals of contrasting physical types which are a recurrent feature of Lawrence's fiction. Sometimes these relationships involve both sexes, but often they are between men, like that between Aaron and Lilly in *Aaron's Rod*, Somers and Kangaroo in *Kangaroo*, Ramon and Cipriano in *The Plumed Serpent* or, most notably, Birkin and Gerald Crich in *Women in Love*. Such relationships pair someone who is physically slight, but with an alert and mobile personality and highly developed intelligence, with an individual who is more physically solid and substantial, but also rather stolid, lacking the inner dynamism which would ensure maximum growth. Each partner has a complementary role; the strength and solidity of the physically strong individual helps to guard the other against the dangers inherent in a highly mobile nature (neurosis and breakdown) whereas the more dynamic partner acts as a stimulus to a personality which, if left to itself, would be complacent and static. In *Women in Love*, Gerald's refusal to continue developing his relationship with Birkin in the way suggested in the 'Gladiatorial' chapter impedes his further growth and helps to bring about his tragic end. Although physically 'weaker' individuals, having more need of intelligence, develop it more quickly and spontaneously than those who are stronger—it is no accident that in *The Rainbow*, Lawrence makes a woman his representative of the most developed contemporary consciousness—if the 'strong' can find a powerful and steady enough stimulus they are, in the end, capable of greater achievements, which is why, through history, men have outperformed women in creative use of the intelligence.

In *The Rainbow*, the Brangwen men constitute, in Nietzsche's words, 'A type with few but very marked traits'; their inferiority in 'range of being' to the vicar and to the other members of the gentry 'whose lives ranged over a great extent' is one of the things that preoccupies their womenfolk. Such traits as they do have are very strongly developed, as the description of Tom's father indicates:

> ... Brangwen himself had a humorous puckering at the eyes, a sort of fat laugh, very quiet and pale, and he was spoilt like a lord of creation. He calmly did as he liked, laughed at [his wife's] railing, excusing himself in a teasing tone that she loved, followed his natural inclinations, and sometimes, pricked too near the quick, frightened and broke her by a deep, tense fury which seemed to fix on him and hold him for days.
>
> (R p 13)

Tom himself has the same passionate nature. Normally 'fresh and alert, with zest for every moment of life' he is also capable of his father's 'deep, tense fury' so that at school respect for him is general, despite his academic shortcomings:

> Only one narrow, domineering fellow, the Latin master, bullied him and made the blue eyes mad with shame and rage. There was a horrid scene, when the boy laid open the master's head with a slate ...
>
> (R p 17)

But Tom is deeply ashamed of the attack so that 'he could not bear to think of the deed, not even long after, when he was a grown man'. Unlike his father, Tom feels guilty for having 'followed his natural inclinations' and this division in his being, clearly related to the feminine influence on him, is one of the main reasons why he develops beyond the limited state in which his predecessors have lived.

Nietzsche thinks of individual and social stabilization as parallel phenomena. The individual, like society is essentially a 'community' of wills to power, hierarchically organised, and 'fixation' occurs in each case when the power relationships in the organism have become unalterable. The accumulation of overwhelming inertia in certain stable forms produces a situation in the individual psyche like that in 'static human societies governed wholly by tradition'.[35] Both individual and society become a dead mosaic, in which each element is unchangeably fixed, instead of a living organism in which instability, change and interaction are present. In stable conditions an individual or community moves towards a state in which development is no longer possible. The condition of continuing individual growth or social development is an element of 'disorder', but because too much of it would lead to disintegration, 'the optimum situation is a firm basis of stability which is then repeatedly "innoculated" with not too great doses of "degeneracy" or "weakness" or "sickness" or "novelty".'[36]

But the very stability that threatens to stifle their development also means that those like the Saxtons and Brangwens are capable, given the right stimulus, of very considerable achievements. The consistency and initial hostility of their circumstances have encouraged the development of enormous power which has been 'stored' in abundance: in George's activities as a politician and businessman after his marriage we are given a glimpse of what he is capable of, even though he cannot sustain any of his efforts because he lacks the continuing creative stimulus Lettie would have provided. In the later generations of Brangwens and particularly in the lives of Gudrun and Ursula in *Women in Love*, we are given a more substantial sense of what is involved in 'utterance', which is Lawrence's usual name for the outgoing, 'spending' phase of will to power as it manifests itself in human lives.

CHAPTER 3

# The Processes of Life

For Nietzsche, the living organism is not a single entity but a community of wills to power, and he explains its structure and processes by analogy with the formation and evolution of the kind of aristocratic society which he thought had been the source of all the greatest human achievements. Every living thing is an association of wills, hierarchically organised and—in the healthy state—dominated by a ruling group which has shaped it; in it the 'rulers' treat the weaker, subordinate members of the community as 'functions', while the 'weaker', in their turn, enjoy the advantages to be gained from association with the stronger:

> Association is a consequence of the will to power because it is a means to power: the weaker obey the stronger for the sake of safety and of power over the yet weaker, and the stronger organise the weaker in order to use them as functions.[1]

The aggressive aspects of will to power are therefore 'mitigated and mutual sympathy is developed *within* a living association for the sake of joint action against outsiders'.[2] The principles of 'need' and 'organic memory' work together to make the rulers limit their ambitions in the interests of the community—'Each has something to perform, and in order to attain this *regularly*, the stronger *forgoes* further encroachments and accommodates itself to an *order* ...',[3] while, for the subordinates 'those "social" functions which begin under compulsion come by cumulative repetition to be second nature; obedience to "law" becomes instinctive, even pleasant ...'[4] But living things, like human societies, rarely become fixed and stable—most remain both 'a war and a peace'.

Since will to power is essentially something active and not a function which may or may not be exercised, the various elements in the organism continue to grow and develop and the internal power relationships remain fluid and '"Life" would be defined as an enduring form of processes of the establishment of force, in which the different contenders grow unequally'.[5] The result is that the 'social order' in the organism is liable to change; like all kinds of society it is 'a prolonged experiment in command and obedience ... living association displays a measure of persistent order which is continually being disturbed by fresh disorder. The centre of gravity shifts; masters and servants change roles'.[6]

Since Nietzsche rejects the idea that the human species has a special status in the order of things, his analysis of the general character of life applies to man as well as to 'lower' forms and the 'higher' qualities which have traditionally been thought to distinguish men from the rest of nature and to have their source in some higher realm are, like all organic functions whatever, specialisations of will to power. As a result, when Nietzsche applies his hypothesis to human life, he breaks with the philosophical tradition which takes introspection to be a source of certain knowledge (in *The Will to Power* he makes much of the philosophical audacity of Descartes famous *cogito*) and one which is free of the bias, distortions and imperfections which the senses impart to our apprehension of the external world. For Nietzche, our awareness of ourselves, like our awareness of 'objective reality', is an interested interpretation of what is happening, not a reflection of it—and in the case of our own natures, where our interests are likely to be most strongly engaged, there will be correspondingly less chance of discovering 'truth'. Inner sense, like outer sense, is perspectival and the ' "apparent *inner* world" is governed by just the same forms and procedures as the "outer" world'.[7] Any attempt to reach the truth about ourselves through introspection will be frustrated by the 'phenomenalism of the "inner world" ' which is created and maintained by the fundamental forces in our nature:

> The danger of the direct questioning of the subject *about* the subject and of all self-reflection of the spirit lies in this, that it could be useful and important for one's activity to interpret oneself *falsely*.[8]

In fact, introspection is an even less reliable guide than observation and 'nothing is so much deception as this inner world which we observe with the famous "inner sense".'[9] So Nietzsche decides that his main method for the investigation of human nature must be to 'question the body', to use physical rather than psychological phenomena as his main source of evidence. With

> The body and physiology the starting point ... We gain the correct idea of the nature of our subject-unity, namely as regents at the head of a communality ..., also of the dependence of these regents upon the ruled and of an order of rank and division of labour as the conditions that make possible the whole and its parts. In the same way, how living unities arise and die and how the 'subject' is not eternal; in the same way, that the struggle expresses itself in obeying and commanding, and that a fluctuating assessment of the limits of power is part of life. The relative ignorance in which the regent is kept concerning individual activities and even disturbances within the communality is among the conditions under which rule can be exercised. In short, we also gain a valuation of *not-knowing*, of seeing things on a broad scale, of simplification and falsification, of perspectivity. The most important thing, however, is: that we understand that the ruler and his subjects are of the same kind, all feeling, willing, thinking—and that, wherever we see or divine movement in a body, we learn to conclude that there is a subjective, invisible life appertaining to it. Movement

is symbolism for the eye: it indicates that something has been felt, willed, thought.

The observation of physical pehenomena gives a more adequate sense of the complexity of the living organism than introspection can; while 'The evidence of the body reveals a tremendous multiplicity', because we 'lack any sensitive organs for [the] inner world . . . we sense a thousandfold complexity as unity'.[10] Late in *The Rainbow*, when Ursula Brangwen is at College in Nottingham, she encounters the scientific materialism which had had such a disturbing impact on the young Lawrence. In conversation with her, a woman physics teacher argues that living things do not belong to a special order of being, but simply represent a greater complexity of physical and chemical processes than non-living things. A little later, looking at a protozoa through a microscope, Ursula has a moment of revelation in which she comes to understand the nature and purpose of life and the insight allows her to reject her teacher's reductive materialism. Significantly, the insight is gained not through investigating life in its most developed form in human beings, where the differences between the living and non-living might be assumed to be at their most marked, nor is the method used that of introspection, though we might think that this was the closest kind of observation possible. Instead Ursula finds her clue—as Nietsche does—in 'external phenomenology,' in looking at physical form and activity:

> The conversation had ended on a note of uncertainty, indefinite, wistful. But the purpose, what was the purpose? Electricity had no soul, light and heat had no soul. Was she herself an impersonal force, or conjunction of forces, like one of those? She looked still at the unicellcular shadow that lay within the field of light, under her microscope. It was alive. She saw it move—she saw the bright mist of it ciliary activity, she saw the gleam of its nucleus, as it slid across the plane of light. What then was its will? If it was a conjunction of forces, physical and chemical, what held these forces unified, and for what purpose were they unified?
> For what purpose were the incalculable physical and chemical activities nodalized in the shadowy, moving speck under her microscope? What was the will that nodalized them and created the one thing she saw? What was its intention? To be itself? Was its purpose just mechanical and limited to itself?
> It intended to be itself. But what self? Suddenly in her mind the world gleamed strangely, with an intense light, like the nucleus of the creature under the microscope. Suddenly she had passed away into an intensely-gleaming light of knowledge. She could not understand what it all was.She only knew that it was not limited mechanical energy, nor mere purpose of self-preservation and self-assertion. It was a consummation, a being infinite. Self was a oneness with the infinite. To be oneself was a supreme, gleaming triumph of infinity.
>
> (**R** pp 440–1)

Even at this most elementary level, where there is no community but only a single cell, physical observation offers evidence of 'feeling, willing, thinking', characteristics we usually associate only with more complex and highly developed life-forms. And the 'incalculable' physical and chemical processes in the cell do not act autonomously, but are held together, organised, by 'a will that nodalized them and created the one thing she saw. This organising will aims at the attainment of selfhood which, even at this simplest level, is not simply something given, to be maintained by self-preservation or self-assertion, but something to be striven for, an achievement—attained at the cost of struggle and effort, it is 'a triumph'.

The idea that the observation of the body and of physical activity will reveal the individual as a complex community finds its clearest and fullest expression in Lawrence's second novel, *The Trespasser*. The story centres on the relationship between Siegmund, a middle-aged violinist and his younger pupil and lover, Helena. Although based on an autobiographical manuscript by Helen Corke, a friend of Lawrence's Croydon years, the association between Siegmund and Helena strikingly anticipates that between Paul and Miriam in *Sons and Lovers*, which has its roots in the novelist's long and troubled relationship with Jessie Chambers. The resemblances are particularly close in the presentation of the two main female characters, both of whom deny and depreciate the physical (and especially the sexual) while valuing artistic and other activities which have their roots in and draw strength from the very instinctual energies they reject. As a result, both Helena and Miriam stimulate their lovers' creativity on one level while, at the same time, they attempt to stifle the very forces which lie behind their creative energy, so that their influence carries the threat of exhaustion and disintegration for the men involved.

Early in *The Trespasser*, Siegmund looks at his body after swimming and sees it as at once a multiplicity and a single self:

> He glanced at himself, at his handsome, white maturity. As he looked he felt the insidious creeping of blood down his thigh, which was marked with a long red slash. Siegmund watched the blood travel over the bright skin. It wound itself redly round the rise of his knee.
> 'That is I, the creeping red, and this whiteness I pride myself on is I, and my black hair, and my blue eyes are I. It is a weird thing to be a person. What makes myself among all these?'
>
> (**TR** p 41)

This recognition and affirmation of his own physicality and particularly of the inextricable link between his body and his intrinsic self-hood which are responses to Helena's denial of the physical, does not originate in Siegmund's conscious mind, but emerges from some more fundamental level of being. 'It was,' we are told, 'his physical self thinking'. Nietzsche tends to identify ordinary consciousness with self-consciousness, and sees it as an internal mirroring process which reflects complex inner events in a dim and incomplete way: things like 'thinking' and other activities often mistakenly identified with this reflexive consciousness can—and generally do—take place without it, so that in Nietzschean psychgology it is perfectly possible for the 'physical self' to 'think'. And Siegmund's understanding of himself is clearly based on physical observation, on 'external phenomenology' rather than on introspective self-examination. Such an approach reveals more because 'reflexive' consciousness is 'a simplifying—therefore falsifying medium'[11] which gives no real indication of the wealth of activity going on below conscious level.

In rather the same way, when Siegmund first makes love to Helena, his physical self is endowed with traits we would usually associate with intellect and consciousness. In his state of erotic excitement, he is 'a tense, vivid body of flesh without a mind', but the fact that his 'mental consciousness' is in abeyance does not mean that the physical, instinctive side of his being (the side both Lawrence and Nietzsche often refer to simply as 'the blood') lacks qualities like intelligence and purposiveness, often mistakenly thought to belong only to the higher intellectual levels of the psyche. If he is 'without a mind' his 'blood' is nevertheless 'alive and conscious'. These ideas of the multiplicity of the self and the 'intelligence' of the body come together in the description of how Helena sees her lover's hands:

> The room was black and red with firelight. Helena shone ruddily as she knelt, a bright, bowed figure, full in the glow. Now and then red strips of firelight leaped across the walls. Siegmund, his face ruddy, advanced out of the shadows. He sat in the chair beside her, leaning fowards, his hands hanging like two scarlet flowers listless in the fire glow, near to her, as she knelt on the hearth with head bowed down. One of the flowers awoke and spread towards her. It asked for her mutely. She was fascinated, scarcely able to move.
>
> (Tr p 35)

The girl's fascination parallels the wonder and admiration at his own body which Siegmund feels when he looks at it on the following morning and suggests that, like Miriam in *Sons and Lovers*, she has a latent capacity to respond to the complexity and integration of physical life, to recognise that it is not simply brutal and stupid, even if that capacity has been obscured by the idealistic values she has inherited. The flower image used to describe her lover's hands suggests at the same time the independence, beauty and subtlety of the different parts of the physical self and so helps to account for her momentary fascination.

Later in the novel, in a meeting between the hero and Hampson, a fellow-musician who is one of the Lawrencian spokesmen in the story, this kind of wonder at the physical is articulated and the reasons for it suggested. Hampson

> smiled, then looked down at the wall, where his own hands lay white and fragile, showing the blue veins.
>
> 'I can scarcely believe they are me,' he said. 'If they rose up and refused me, I should not be surprised. But aren't they beautiful?'
>
> He looked, with a faint smile, at Siegmund.
>
> Siegmund glanced from the stranger's to his own hands, which lay curved on the sea-wall as if asleep. They were small for a man of his stature, but, lying warm in the sun, they looked particularly secure in life. Instinctively, with a wave of self-love, he closed his fists over his thumbs.
>
> (Tr p 85)

The attribution of a separate individuality to the hands of both men recalls the lovemaking episode just discussed and the fact that while bathing on the morning after his arrival, Siegmund had seen his thighs as 'creatures pround in themselves'. This sense of the independence of different parts of the body is linked with an awareness of physical beauty which is evident in the flower image, in Siegmund's affirmation as he inspects his 'handsome maturity' that 'I am at my best ...' and in the admiration and love aroused in each man by the sight of his own hands. The elements of the physical self are seen as autonomous, as having their own interests and purposes which are not necessarily accessible to consciousness; in form and action, they have a precision, subtlety and coordination which owes nothing to conscious effort and which is registered as beauty. Because the body and its activities are independent of consciousness, they are ungraspable by the ego. The physical self is larger than and remains incomprehensible to and unpredictable for the 'I', the conscious self—hence Siegmund's conclusion that 'It is a weird thing to be a person' and Hampson's apparently humorous but fundamentally serious comment on his hands, 'I can scarcely believe they are me.... If they rose up and refused me, I should not be surprised'. In his 1913 review of Georgian Poetry: 1911-1912, Lawrence expressed the same idea in his own voice:

> I look at my hands as I write and know they are mine, with red blood running its way, sleuthing out Truth and pursuing it to eternity, and I am full of awe for this flesh and blood that holds this pen. Everything that ever was thought and ever will be thought lies in this body of mine. This flesh and blood, sitting here writing, the great impersonal flesh and blood, greater than me, which I am proud to belong to, contains all the future.[12]

In its healthy state the community which constitutes the organism is controlled and directed by a dominant group of wills and the ruling aristocracy at any particular time constitutes the 'self'—which is not to be confused with the 'ego', the limited conscious self. Because will is essentially something active in a specific direction rather than an abstract 'faculty', the ruling group will direct the organism as a whole towards the satisfaction of their interests and each action will therefore involve the 'commanding' of a not wholly enthusiastic host of subordinates with different interests. Nietzsche argues that if we usually think of will as making something happen by simple *fiat* this is because the full complexity of the way in which the rulers' intentions are translated into action is normally hidden from us and 'the commanding gets identified with all the work of the subordinates which execute it'.[13] Such insouciance is not spontaneous, but develops when a particular group of rulers has been dominant for long enough to ensure that both commanding and obeying have become habitual and the conflict and effort involved in them minimised. It is only when control begins to lapse, in the condition Nietzsche calls 'decadence' that the fact that the individual is a plurality of wills, organised through the efforts of a dominant group, becomes directly apparent. In decadence, the organising will is weak or ineffective, and each member of the bodily community acts independently, threatening the integrity of the whole. Decadence is characterised by

> ... anarchy of atoms, disintegration of will ... the vibration and exuberance of life forced back into the smallest structures, the rest *poor* in life. Everywhere paralysis, fatigue, torpor *or* emnity and chaos: both more and more evident the more one ascends to higher forms of organisation. The whole no longer lives at all.[14]

The essential nature of decadence is well illustrated in *The Trespasser* in the condition Siegmund finds himself in after sharing in one of Helens's states of heightened, exalted emotion. Exhausted, he becomes conscious for a time of the multiplicity of independent wills of which he is constituted—he is 'vaguely aware of a teeming stir of activity, such as one may hear from a closed hive, within him'. Earlier the plurality of the self had been suggested by the independence ascribed to major parts of the physical body, but 'hive' suggests that the components here are smaller and more numerous; the larger unities have evidently fragmented. The ideal of a swarm of independently active wills which the imagery calls up is closely related to the curious and wholly internal shuddering which he experiences. The separate elements of the bodily community have assumed, for the moment, a malign independence of action:

> He shuddered lightly now and again, as they stepped lurching down the hill. He set his jaws hard to suppress the shuddering. It was not in his limbs, or even on the surface of his body, for Helena did not notice it. Yet he shuddered almost in anguish internally.
>
> (Tr p 75)

Just after the shared 'ecstasy' his state had been even more serious, and the deliberate effort needed to co-ordinate his actions correspondingly greater—the 'great effort to control his body' which he needs to make then leaves him at first with the feeling that

> He wanted to lie down again, to relieve himself of the sickening effort of supporting and controlling his body. If he could lie down again perfectly still he need not struggle to animate the cumbersome matter of his body ...
>
> (Tr p 75)

This extreme feeling gradually abates, but still, when the pair come to a stile on the way back to their lodgings, Siegmund finds it very difficult to negotiate and 'As he stepped over it it needed a concentrated effort of will to place his foot securely on the step. The effort was so great that he became conscious of it'. Ordinary unreflective physical action is not effortless since the act of will inevitably involves putting one force against another in an experiment of command, but it is only if the effort is unusually great, that it is registered in the reflexive consciousness. Siegmund's difficulty here testifies to the fragmented state of his being and the extraordinary effort needed to translate intention into action in this condition makes him directly aware of things which usually go on beneath conscious level.

Puzzled by his condition, Siegmund attempts to understand it by comparing it with a near-fatal illness he suffered as a child which felt rather similar—

> He remembered distinctly, when he was a child and had diphtheria, he had stretched himself in the horrible sickness, which he felt was—and here he chose the French word—'l'agonie'. But his mother had seen and cried aloud which suddenly caused him to struggle with all his soul to spare her suffering.
>
> (**Tr** p 76)

The association between Siegmund's childhood diphtheria and the sort of disintegration he suffers after sharing Helena's 'ecstasy'—together with the way in which the progress of the disease is arrested by an act of will after the mother's cry—closely anticipate the more direct treatment in *Sons and Lovers* of the young Paul Morel's serious attack of pneumonia:

> Paul was very ill. His mother lay in bed at nights with him; they could not afford a nurse. He grew worse, and the crisis approached. One night he tossed into consciousness in the ghastly, sickly feeling of dissolution, when all the cells in the body seem in intense irritability to be breaking down, and consciousness makes a last flare of struggle, like madness.
> "I s'll die, mother!" he cried, heaving for breath on the pillow.
> She lifted him up, crying in a small voice:
> "Oh, my son—my son!"
> That brought him to. He realized her. His whole will rose up and arrested him.
>
> (**SL** p 175)

Paul's illness is even more dangerous than it might have been because of the effect on him of his mother's recent behaviour. Overwhelmed by the death of his elder brother William, she 'could not be persuaded to take her old bright interest in life' and although Paul tries to reawaken her she remains indifferent so that 'It drove him almost insane to have her thus'. The experience weakens Paul's will to live—essentially the will to control and integrate the organic community—and thereby reduces his resistance to the disease. His mother's anguished cry shows that her interest in him has revived and with it the organising will reasserts itself; the action of the 'whole will' arrests the process of fragmentation just short of the final disintegration which is death and his slow struggle towards re-integration begins. For Nietzsche, the essence of the kind of pathological decline illustrated here, as of the natural decline which is an inevitable part of the life-cycle, is the lapse of the will to assimilate and organise, which results in the progressive breakdown of the organism into ever smaller units—death is the end result of the process. So, when he mentally compares his present state with his memory of his childhood illness, Siegmund concludes that it too feels 'rather deathly' and in Paul's case the idea of death is directly linked with the idea of fragmentation happening at the most fundamental, cellular, level.

Nietzsche's term for the specialised forms of will to power which together constitute the ruling group or 'self' of the organism is 'urge' or 'impulse'. Our urges lie behind our values and on these in turn, 'Our intellect, our will, likewise our sensations are dependent'.[15] Perception, feeling and thinking are the instruments of our urges and so the kind and degree of their development depends on the character of these fundamental elements in our being. George Saxton's limited perceptual range, for example, is a consequence of the 'old feelings' which persist in him. Such 'feelings' have their beginnings as 'evaluations' which are functional in particular surroundings and in a stable setting evolve into an instinctively operating 'system of judgements of pleasure and pain' drawing us towards certain kinds of experience and repelling us from others. Feelings in this sense are, for Nietzsche, the decisive forces in human nature, whether as the causes of action or as barriers to it. The dominance of the 'old feelings' in George holds him to the customary interests and activities and any alteration in his mode of life will depend on his being able to feel 'fresh things'. Passion is then the moving principle in Nietzschean psychology—although the fundamental 'urges' are not identical with the passions we are aware of, because there have been subjected to the simplifying and synthesizing activity of consciousness. But unlike some other thinkers who have denied the efficacy of reason, Nietzsche does not argue that we seek to fulfil our desires to be freed from their importunity; on the contrary, urges find their satisfaction in 'unimpeded activity, not in some result of the activity'.[16] Life and desire are therefore inseparable and behind each want lies the ever-active will to power simultaneously (and unconsciously) evaluating and moving to action.

When, after returning from his holiday with Helena, Siegmund tries to escape from the discomfort of his domestic situation (he is a married man with children), he finds that 'Everything he suggested to himself made him sicken with weariness or distaste: the seaside, a foreign land, a fresh life that he had often dreamed of, farming in Canada'. He concludes that if nothing attracts him he 'had better be dead' because to have 'no want, no desire—that is death, to begin with'. But because he is not literally dead, Siegmund is in fact not without desire—there is one thing which does still attract him and that is death itself: 'The idea of death alone seemed entertaining'. In Nietzsche's view, decadence, like that which Siegmund suffers after and as a result of his holiday with Helena, does not involve the complete lapse of will to power. The decadent individual may not be able to act positively and creatively, but will to power survives in him and is exerted towards destruction. Since 'feelings', the flow and recoil of sympathy, are the fundamental forces in human development, the psychic impasse in which characters like Tom Brangwen and George Saxton find themselves is not one in which 'passion' is at war with 'reason'; old deeply rooted inclinations and not rational considerations prevent them from changing their lives in the way that they would like to. Since they are, by definition, kinds of activity, urges which are frustrated of direct expression in this way invariably find some indirect outlet—Neitzche offers dreaming and wishing as two examples of such vicarious modes of satisfaction, linking them by suggesting that wishing is 'a sort of dreaming, an expression of impotence or fatigue, escape from reality'.[17] Both Tom and George, finding themselves unable to act to realise their aspirations, find escape from their unsatisfactory circumstances in 'dreaming fulfilments'; each immerses himself in vivid, wish-fulfilling daydreams, shutting out for the time the despised ordinary world.

In their primal state, the urges which are the foundations of human nature are of awesome force; Nietzsche says that if we could 'look out and down from the chamber of consciousness' we would be able to see that 'man rests with the unconcern of his ignorance, on the pitiless, the ravenous, the insatiable, the murderous, and as if suspended in dreams on the back of a tiger'.[18] One of the characters in Lawrence's fiction who embodies this Dionysian substratum of human nature is Annable, the massively built gamekeeper in *The White Peacock*. But Annable does more than simply embody a philosophy of life founded on the claim that such energies are the only realities and should be allowed free expression. The keeper makes his appearance early in the book when he challenges George Saxton over some snares which have been laid on the squire's land. The episode is important because it leads to the fight between the two men, and it is George's humiliating defeat at the hands of the keeper which does the first real damage to his complacency.

Annable himself emerges as an important figure in the second half of the novel appearing like 'some malicious Pan' when Cyril, Emily, Lettie and Leslie are exploring the squire's woods. The exchange with the two couples gives the keeper an opportunity to express his idiosyncratic views on the state of contemporary society, which he sees as permeated by a perverse idealism, the product of pernicious feminine influence. His general diagnosis is derived from his own experience of marriage to the aristocratic Lady Chrystabel, who has hurt and rejected him and whose behaviour he sees as typifying that of cultured women. As a result he has come to see the whole social and cultural order, of which women are the inspirers and guardians, as designed to reduce and humiliate the sensual male; to preserve his masculinity intact a man must retreat from 'my lady's parlour' back into the woods. So his present life is as great a departure from civilized 'perversity' as he can manage. He avoids the society of 'human rot' preferring 'th' animals or th' birds' and tries to lead and have his large family lead, as unmitigatedly natural a life as possible. Since his philosophy involves simply following the natural instincts, he is as unrestrainedly prolific in his production of offspring as the rabbits or mice he admires, and the association between his own behavior and that of animals is underlined by his description of his children as a 'litter'. He compares his children approvingly to small but fiercely predatory creatures—foxes, weasels, ferrets—suggesting the egoism and violence which are part of man's essential nature. He is determined that they shall grow up untainted by the affectation and hypocrisy, the 'smirking deviltry' which he associates with conventional education and social training.

Experience of marriage to a 'refined' wife has convinced Annable that any attempt by human beings to lead more than a purely animal existence ends in perversity and degeneration—'When a man's more than nature he's a devil', he says. The idealistic attempt to repress impulses stigmatised as 'base' or 'animal' does not free man from them, instead they remain active, but become devious and corrupt. So in describing the way his wife has treated him, Annable links her behaviour with examples of natural violence and predatoriness—punning on 'groom' he compares his experience as a husband to that of a groom savaged by a vicious horse and his reference to the old verse about the spider and the fly presents the superficial attractiveness of the 'lady' as a device for luring men into a situation ('my lady's parlour') where they can be humiliated and destroyed. The notion of 'refinement' is the social expression of that condemnation of the fundamental natural urges as 'low' or 'sinful' which Nietzsche believed to be central to our Christian ethical tradition. But the repression of powerful urges in this way—a process Nietzsche terms 'introversion'—is often dangerous since it can lead to a kind of inner poisoning when 'Impulses normally expressed in relations with the outer world ... turn inward and act upon other elements in the self'. These impulses may finally find expression in actions which have far more serious consequences than those which would have resulted if the impulse had been expressed immediately. Like Nietzsche, Lawrence links such repressive idealism with the Christian tradition; both tend to see Christianity primarily (though not exclusively, or without qualification) as an ascetic creed which counsels the extirpation or emasculation of the passions and both think, too, that Christian moral values are still dominant, despite the fact that few people now believe in the supernatural framework on which they are founded.

The connection between the dangers of repressing impulse and the Christian tradition is explicitly—and amusingly—made in *The Rainbow* when the young Ursula Brangwen, attempting to live according to New Testament precepts, literally turns the other cheek when her younger sister slaps her in a quarrel—

> Ursula, in a mood of Christian humility, silently presented the other side of her face. Which Theresa, in exasperation at the challenge, also hit. Whereupon Ursula, with boiling heart, went meekly away.
>
> But anger, and deep, writhing shame tortured her, so that she was not easy till she had again quarrelled with Theresa and had almost shaken her sister's head off.
>
> 'That'll teach you,' she said grimly.
>
> And she went away, unchristian but clean.
>
> (R p 285)

The incident is rather like a comic version of Blake's 'The Poison Tree'; despite its brevity and the light tone, it conveys a great deal, revealing for instance, the provocative claim to spiritual and moral superiority which lies behind the initial gesture, the duplicity which the moral tradition encourages ('with boiling heart went meekly away') and the inner 'poisoning', the 'deep writhing shame' which results from introversion. And although it is only briefly repressed, Ursula's anger grows considerably during the time it is denied expression, finally issuing in far more vigorous retaliation than the slap which would have settled the original dispute.

This sequence of repression, of inner poisoning and increased violence of response is not always associated with experiments in Christian living; it is also linked with the kind of contemporary idealism which, although originating in religion, has lost its religious affiliations. Hermione Roddice in *Women in Love* is described as a 'woman of the new school'; her ideas of social and political reform, like the socialism of the local miners, derive from the religious tradition and represent 'a religious creed pushed to its material conclusion'. Lawrence came to believe, like Nietzsche that modern socialist and 'progressive' ideals are a secularised version of the Christian ethic, a 'new religious impulse'. The outlook Hermione represents is the direct descendant of Christian idealism and retains both its depreciation of the physical and high regard for the intellectual and 'spiritual'. These priorities are reflected in the fact that Hermione moves heavily and awkwardly, with a 'strange unwilling motion' as if unable to trust her physical and instinctive self. Committed to ideals of peace and harmony, Hermione has suppressed much in her nature, including its frustrations and latent violence, but the impulses have not disappeared— they remain as 'a strange mass of thoughts coiled in the darkness within her' and because they are never allowed expression they hold her in permanent bondage, 'she was never allowed to escape'. The sinister image of the thoughts as coiled snakes, not only makes her a Medusa-like figure, but suggests that repression brings a kind of inner poisoning in its wake, while the traditional associations of the snake indicate that when they do emerge, her impulses will do so in some devious, treacherous and extremely destructive fashion.

The degree of latent violence in Hermione's nature is hinted at a little later in a conversation among the wedding guests at the Crich home. The discussion centres on race, nationality and war, with the participants using the homely analogy of whether one's hat is worth fighting for if someone else tries to take it. In view of her rejection of Gerald's picture of human nature as essentially competitive and acquisitive and her commitment to cooperation and harmony, Hermione's reaction to one of the questions put to her is unexpected:

> 'But would you let somebody come and snatch your hat off your head?' the bride asked of Hermione.
>
> The face of the tall straight woman turned slowly and as if drugged to this new speaker.
>
> 'No', she replied, in a low inhuman tone, that seemed to contain a chuckle. 'No, I shouldn't let anybody take my hat off my head.'
>
> 'How would you prevent it?' asked Gerald.
>
> 'I don't know,' replied Hermione slowly. 'Probably I should kill him.'
>
> There was a strange chuckle in her tone, a dangerous and convincing humour in her bearing.
>
> (WL p 32)

As the narrative makes clear, Hermione's response is not merely jocular, indeed the 'chuckle in her tone' is evidence of the deep satisfaction the idea brings her; and the fact that the tone of her answer is 'low' and 'inhuman' indicates that it comes not from the superficial conscious fact of her self, but from some much more fundamental area of the psyche.

The craving for violence which this reveals—and for violence of the most extreme kind—does not remain simply a forceful but unfilled desire, because her answer foreshadows her attempt later in the novel to kill Birkin, the lover who is now discarding her. Lawrence's description of the attack makes it quite clear that Hermione does indeed want to kill Birkin, that the impulse comes from deep in the unconscious part of her psyche, and that acting on it gives her the most intense fulfilment she has ever experienced. By employing imagery drawn from powerful forces operating in nature, the narrative underlines the awesome nature of the energies present in the unconscious and indicates how limited and ineffectual the conscious and human part of the self is when confronted by them. Hermione's conscious self is like a struggling swimmer borne down by rushing water or like someone being subjected to powerful electric shocks—images Lawrence often employs in similar contexts. But afterwards, in a demonstration of the shallowness and mendacity of consciousness, Hermione convinces herself that what she has done is quite ordinary and unexceptional—'she had only hit him, as any woman might do'. Not only is Hermione's violence of quite exceptional intensity, it is also described in unmistakeably sexual terms—it is 'her voluptuous consummation', she feels 'a delirium of pleasure' anticipating 'her consummation of voluptuous ecstasy at last'.

Violence and sexuality are linked in the Nietzschean concept of introversion, because impulses which are repressed not only grow in intensity, but may also change in character becoming warped and destructive rather than creative; Nietzsche often links the cruelties practised throughout European history with the more ascetic expressions of Christianity, rather as Lawrence does in his 1912 letter to Edward Garnett, in which he discusses the cruelty which both priests and soldiers show:

> Cruelty is a form of perverted sex ... Priests in their celibacy get their sex lustful, then perverted, then insane, hence Inquisitions—all sexual in origin. And soldiers, being herded together, men without women, never being *satisfied* by a woman, as a man never is from a street affair, get their surplus sex and their frustration and dissatisfaction into the blood, and *love* cruelty. It is sex lust fermented that makes atrocity.[20]

The identification of a certain kind of violence with a perverse and corrupted sexuality is even clearer in Gerald Crich's attack on Gudrun near the end of the novel. Like Hermione, Gerald is aware that his lover is rejecting him, and in his frustration attempts to strangle her in an episode which seems to be describing some grotesque and murderous parody of sexual intercourse:

> ... her throat was beautifully, so beautifully soft, save that, within, he could feel the slippery chords of her life. And this he crushed, this he could crush. What bliss! Oh what bliss, at last, what satisfaction, at last! The pure zest of

satisfaction filled his soul. He was watching the unconsciousness come into her swollen face, watching the eyes roll back. How ugly she was! What a fulfilment, what a satisfaction! How good this was, oh how good it was ... He was unconscious of her fighting and struggling. The struggling was her reciprocal lustful passion in this embrace, the more evident it became, the greater the frenzy of delight, till the zenith was reached, the crisis, the struggle was overborne, her movement became softer, appeased.

(WL p 531)

Neither Hermione nor Gerald are celibates of course, but they are both inheritors of a cultural tradition in which—Nietzsche and Lawrence would argue—an idealism and a depreciation of the senses, which is religious in origin, has shaped our experience over many centuries. Despite its rejection by many intellectuals and its general dilution in the population as a whole, idealism has dominated the lives of Europeans for so long that it has become part of the psyche and no mere intellectual rejection of it will end its influence. Hermione's reforming enthusiasm is a secularised continuation of religious ideas and even Gerald, despite his rejection of his father's faith, is, in a sense, a product and consequence of it. As Birkin recognises, his character and likely fate have a general and not just a personal quality, representing the logical culmination and conclusion of the history of Northern Europe; he is one of the 'strange white demons fulfilled in the destructive frost mystery', perhaps an omen of a general dissolution of North European culture, which will disintegrate in the further development of consciousness and the acquisition of more and more abstract knowledge. The link between this general crisis and the influence of Christianity is directly made at the end of the novel when, lost in the Alpine snows after the flight which followed his attack on Gudrun, Gerald sees a half-buried crucifix and in his delirium links it with the idea that he is going to be murdered:

> There was something standing out of the snow. He approached with dimmest curiosity. It was a half-buried crucifix, a little Christ under a little sloping hood at the top of a pole. He sheered away. Somebody was going to murder him. He had a great dread of being murdered ...
>
> Yet why be afraid? It was bound to happen. To be murdered! He looked round in terror at the snow, the rocking, pale, shadowy slopes of the upper world. He was bound to be murdered, he could see it. This was the moment when the death was uplifted, and there was no escape.
>
> Lord Jesus, was it then bound to be—Lord Jesus! He could feel the blow descending, he knew he was murdered.

(WL p 533)

Gerald is not, of course, in a rational frame of mind at this point but, for Lawrence, it is in extraordinary and extreme states rather than normal ones that awareness and insight are at their greatest. The readers first reaction to Gerald's flight from the scene of his assault on Gudrun is likely to be that confused, and remorseful, he has simply fled without thinking and found himself accidentally in difficulties. But few situations in Lawrence's fiction are accidental in this sense and it is generally the least considered actions of his characters which convey their deepest motivations; Gerald dies because he has deliberately, if unconsciously, *sought* death. Yet the account of his final moments suggests that what has happened is not so much suicide as murder and murder in which the crucifix and what it stands for are somehow involved. If Gerald's death is not just the death of a particular individual but the metaphorical 'death' of the present phase of our culture, then Christianity is fundamentally implicated in, even responsible for, that catastrophe.

The serious, indeed catastrophic, consequences which appear to follow from the culturally maintained repression of instinct seem to support Annable's claim that 'When a man's more than nature he's a devil' and he himself has reacted into a militant naturalism and materialism which is the antithesis of idealism. He refuses to accept that any social or cultural distinctions have a real basis: 'gentility' is simply an affectation and 'ladies' and 'gentlemen' indistinguishable from coarser human material, except in the perversity of their instincts and their failure to be honest about them. When he confronts the two couples in the squire's woods, he is reprimanded by Leslie for suggesting in front of the 'ladies' that they are there to make love. The keeper's ironic apology makes it clear that so far as he is concerned there is no difference between the delicate lady and the common woman—'Very sorry, sir! You can't tell a lady from a woman at this distance at dusk.' Annable not only refuses to recognise the distinctions made within society, he also refuses to concede that men differ in any fundamental way from the lower animals—so, for instance, he asserts that Leslie's own attention to his appearance is designed, as much as the plumage of the male chaffinch, to attract a mate. Underneath such 'cultural' phenomena lie the elementary natural interests of sex and procreation:

> 'See that spink:' he raised his voice for the girls to hear. 'Pretty, isn't he? What for?—And what for do you wear a fancy vest and twirl your moustache, sir! What for, at the bottom!'
>
> **(WP** p 178)

Leslie's initial indignation suggests that Annable is justified in seeing his own experience as representative because it indicates that, among the 'genteel' classes at least, certain natural impulses are not mentioned in mixed company—a convention which indicates both that the impulses themselves are regarded as 'low' and that women are thought of as delicate and exalted creatures, who must not be exposed to such things. And the link the keeper makes between the power of such perverse idealism and the influence of women themselves is supported by the reaction to him of the two women in the group, who keep 'aloof from the man they instinctively hated'. At the same time the contrast in character between Lettie and Emily has been so firmly established and their respective (and very different) attitudes to the body and senses so clearly depicted, that if their reaction to the unaccommodatedly and reductively natural is the same, we are aware that their view of the relation of the physical to the conventionally 'higher' qualities is quite different. If Lettie feels that George could develop considerably in intellectual and aesthetic awareness it is precisely because she is aware that the kind of ample physical vitality he possesses is the precondition of 'higher' achievements.

In *The White Peacock* the anti-natural values of Christianity are linked with the sense of uncertainty and inner conflict which troubles many of the characters. In the scene which immediately precedes the confrontation with Annable, the two couples come upon a mass of snowdrops in blossom which they associate with the pagan past and with the 'old wild lost religion' of the 'strange-hearted Druid folk'. In everyone except the unimaginative Leslie, the experience arouses the feeling that some important knowledge possessed by men in pre-Christian days, has been lost. Lettie, who is most powerfully affected by the place, implies that her own unsureness and indecision are somehow related to this loss:

> 'Look at all the snowdrops'—they hung in dim, strange flecks among the dusky leaves—'look at them—closed up, retreating, powerless. They belong to some knowledge we have lost, that I have lost and that I need.'
>
> **(WP p 175)**

The wisdom embodied in the Druidic paganism which preceded the Christianisation of Britain has vanished, because the later religion represents not a development or refinement of what has gone before, but its ideological opposite. The advent of Christianity represented a revolutionary, rather than an evolutionary, change in religious outlook. It is the meeting and struggle of these two antagonistic faiths (will to power manifests itself in the 'highest' as much as in the 'lowest' activities) which is suggested in the reference to the snowdrops—and therefore what they stand for—as 'closed-up, retreating, powerless'. The narrator's use of 'wild' suggests that the old religion was orgiastic in character and the surmise that the snowdrops were 'the symbol of tears' indicates that the tragic sense of life was an important element in the vanished faith.

These characteristics are closely associated in Nietzsche's treatment of pagan religion and like Lawrence, he saw paganism as the antithesis of Christianity summing up their essential antagonism in *The Will to Power* in the phrase 'Dionysus versus the "Crucified".' The phrase opposes the tragic affirmation embodied in the Dionysus myth of Greek religion to the negation of life which, Nietzsche maintains, finds expression in the story of Christ crucified. At the centre of both kinds of cult is the fact that 'life itself, its eternal fruitfulness and recurrence, creates torment, destruction',[21] but the two religious tendencies are the products of two contrasting kinds of sensibilities, or, more fundamentally, of two different degrees of power, each of which arrives at a very different valuation of the suffering endemic in existence. Paganism accepts and celebrates life despite the conflict and suffering inseparable from it and the pagan cult is therefore 'a form of thanksgiving and affirmation of life'. The tragic disposition courageously accepts a reality constituted by the ramifying activity of will to power, but despite this look at the worst is able to go on and make a joyful affirmation of being. The pagan spirit 'takes into itself and *redeems* the contradictions and questionable aspects of existence'.[22] So the snowdrops are not simply symbolic of pain as Emily suggests, limiting their significance because her own over-sensitivity makes life largely a matter of suffering for her, but—as the more vigorous Lettie can see—symbolise something positive, 'More than tears . . . Something out of an old religion, that we have lost'. Nietzsche links the capacity to affirm life to the fullest with a condition of exuberant vitality; it is the fact that the pagan is 'The type of a well-constituted and ecstatically overflowing spirit'[23] that allows him to make his affirmation and so he associates pagan religious practices with an orgiastic, 'Dionysian' state and generally with a 'wildness' which distinguishes them from Christian ceremonies. Conversely, the Christian suffers from diminished vitality and is too weak to face and affirm the natural world; turning from it he creates a compensatory, wish-fulfilling afterworld, a supernatural place, a heaven, in which all the distressing characteristics of real experience are negated. This present life is seen as not finally real and as having significance not in itself, but as a preparation and probation for a real and eternal life, which will begin after death.

The dell itself is described in terms we would usually associate with a Christian place of worship and with Christian observances—the snowdrops, which are 'scattered like manna' resemble 'a holy communion of pure wild things'; the hazels form a 'light tracery' beneath the canopy of oaks; Lettie picks the blossoms 'as if it were a rite'. The references remind us that in Druidic religion the holy place was a natural location, the sacred grove, rather than an edifice built by man to shut out nature and symbolise, as Lincoln Cathedral does in *The Rainbow*, a superior, supernatural reality. In the later novel, the Cathedral, its stones 'leaping up from the plain of earth' expresses the aspiration towards a unity, order and permanence which are presumed to lie in the supernatural realm; it represents an attempt to deny the reality of the becoming and passing away, the arbitrariness, confusion and conflict, which are the primary characteristics of the natural world and to suggest a place where 'there was no time nor life nor death but only . . . this timeless consummation'. But it is clearly a wish-fulfilling reaction to the chaos of the real and what it symbolises is something Will Brangwen would like to believe rather than what really is:

> His soul would have liked it to be so: here, here is all, complete, eternal: motion, meeting, ecstasy and no illusion of time, of night and day passing by, but only perfectly proportioned space and movement . . .
>
> **(R** p 203)

But even within the cathedral itself, because it is a human creation, there are, in the grotesque carvings which delight Anna, reminders of those aspects of experience which the building as a whole tries to deny.

The victory of Christianity brought about a radical reversal of man's attitude to the natural and with it the loss of the wisdom embodied in pagan religion. The most important consequence of the change was the change in man's view of his own nature, for in denying that a world constituted as the natural world is can be real, Christianity also denies the ultimate value and significance of these characteristics in man which link him with nature. In Christian ethics, man is thought of as a divided creature who incorporates within himself two warring natures—one is animal and links him with the 'merely' natural, the other is 'spiritual' deriving from and drawing him towards supernatural reality. But it is precisely the despised animal element in human nature which Nietzsche regards as having ensured human survival in the competitive natural world. It is evident in all his work that Lawrence shared the view that the natural world was one in which a multitude of competing species struggle for the space and sustenance to grow: in such a world, man owes his survival to his ability to exploit other forms of life for his own ends. In a world in which 'Life always lives at the expense of other life' man has needed his animal impulses to survive, and they have been reinforced so often and strongly that they now constitute the strongest forces in his nature. In other words the impulses which Christianity has branded as base and has attempted to destroy are these which have been crucial for man's success and which are most strongly developed in him.

In *The White Peacock*, it is largely the distrust for the instinctive engendered by centuries of Christian culture which prevents Lettie from following her impulses and acting on the powerful physical attraction she feels towards George; it is in this sense that the disappearance of the old pre-Christian religious knowledge 'creates' her predicament. As George himself recognises she is more strongly drawn to him than to Leslie and in becoming engaged to the latter has denied her deepest feelings. When he hears of her engagement to his rival he says he has expected it because 'she'd made up her mind to it' so that 'It didn't matter—what she wanted—at bottom'. Lettie's conscious, rational self, her mind, has directed her and she has ignored the instinctive, directly physical interest which has drawn her to George from their first meeting. Culturally, she belongs to an ethos in which such an attraction is likely to be seen as 'merely' physical. This fear of instinct, both in the individual and in the culture as a whole, is explained by the frightening power our basic urges have—a power illustrated in the second meeting between George and Lettie, when the attraction has become mutual. Sitting looking at a picture, the pair

> gazed at each other for a moment before they hid their faces again. It was a torture to each of them to look thus nakedly at the other, a dazzled, shrinking pain that they forced themselves to undergo for a moment, that they might the moment after tremble with a fierce sensation that filled their veins with a fluid, fiery electricity.
>
> (**WP** p 73)

The use of words like 'torture' and 'pain' to describe the lovers' state conveys the discomfort such intense feelings create and it is this, Nietzsche argues, which lies behind the Christian attitude to the 'animal' element in human

nature. Those who are weak are unable to face and transform such prodigious energies and therefore set out to deny and repress them. Throughout
the Christian era, this decadent fear of instinct has been the basis of the dominant morality and has influenced even those with the innate strength to
transform their impulses. It is this inherited fear which makes Lettie avoid
George after she has become aware of the full force of her feeling for him
and it also lies behind her reaction to the snowdrops which, she says, make
her 'feel afraid'. The flowers and what they signify have been associated with
a creed in which the senses have accepted and affirmed. Since Lettie is one
of the 'strong' rather than the 'weak' however, her reaction to the snowdrops, like her reaction to George, is not simply one of rejection—instead
she is divided, both yearning for and fearing the natural.

Although Christianity has its origins in the denial of the natural, recognition of the conflict between value and fact which this has created is a recent
development—only now have we become aware that 'Insofar as we believe
in morality we pass sentence on existence'.[24] The ultimate consequence of
this realisation is an attitude Nietzsche calls 'nihilism' which involves a
radical rejection of traditional values and a reaction into a thorough-going
materialism:

> The time has come when we have to pay for having been Christians for two
> thousand years: we are losing the centre of gravity by virtue of which we lived;
> we are lost for a while. Abruptly we plunge into the opposite valuations, with
> all the energy that such an extreme overvaluation of man has generated in
> man.[25]

Annable's personal experience of the effects of 'idealistic' attitudes—he has
been a victim of notions of 'refinement' which are the debased descendants
of Christian standards—has provoked him into rebellion against 'idealism'
in all its forms and he has espoused materialism with a fervour which is the
mirror-image of religious enthusiasm. The keeper's attitudes are further
illuminated by Nietzsche's description of what he calls the 'nihilism of the
strong'. Strong natures are not content simply to observe the human decline
which their philosophy predicts:

> Nihilism does not only contemplate the 'in vain!' nor is it merely the belief that
> everything deserves to perish: one helps to destroy.—This is, if you will,
> illogical; but the nihilist does not believe that one needs to be logical.—It is the
> condition of strong spirits and wills, and those do not find it possible to stop
> with the No of 'judgement': their nature demands the No of the deed. The
> reduction to nothing by judgement is seconded by the reduction to nothing by
> hand.[26]

Although the keeper sees the history of civilised man as a decline into 'folly
and weakness and rottenness', with 'culture' no more than a cosmetic surface
concealing decay, he does not confine himself merely to observing the
inevitable progress to final catastrophe, but actively contributes to the
process of disintegration. As the main agent of the squire's destructive

policies, he does his job with relish, aiding the destruction done by the rabbits by protecting them against natural predators, as well as defending them 'heroically' against poaching miners and angry farmers. He throws himself into his task enthusiastically because he knows that by doing so he is undermining the local community and so helping to destroy a corner of the civilisation he hates.

This destructive impulse is evident in his personal relationships as well as in his social role because, unhappy himself, he is drawn to Cyril the sensitive narrator, because he is able to infect the younger man with his misery. Despite his motto, 'Be a good animal, true to your animal instinct'—which suggests that he has withdrawn from the tormenting and perverse complexities of human experience into a primitive insouciance he is, we learn, 'fundamentally very unhappy' and—the narrator adds—'made me also wretched':

> It was this power to communicate his unhappiness that made me somewhat dear to him, I think.
>
> **(WP** p 208)

If his exposure to culture and refinement has made Annable frustrated and unhappy, his rejection of them does not seem to have brought him fulfilment. The keeper's wretchedness casts doubt on the claim that he is the first example in Lawrence's fiction of a kind of character who embodies Lawrencian positives in a straightforward way. Keith Sagar, for instance, links him with Lawrence's last fictional gamekeeper, seeing both as examples of the 'pagan or demonic outcast' who embodies 'both the destructive element in his vision—his hatred of materialism and society—and also the whole range of Lawrencian positives ...'[27]

R E Pritchard, too, associates the keeper with paganism and suggests that he represents more than the naturalism his own motto would suggest, that he is 'associated with the ancient savage religious mystery'.[28] But despite the fact that he appears 'like some malicious Pan', Annable is not associated with pre-Christian religion or the lost wisdom it represents—we are told quite explicitly that he is a 'thorough materialist' who 'scorned all religion and all mysticism'—his outlook is in fact a thoroughly contemporary one, deriving as Jessie Chambers shrewdly saw, from nineteenth century scientific rationalism. As she remarks, 'his character was created out of Lawrence's despair over the materialist view of life'. **(PR** p 117)

The choice of the snowdrop as its symbol suggest that the lost wisdom of pagan religion depended on the idea of the spiritualisation of instincts and not on their unfettered expression. Furthermore the life which the keeper advocates and endeavours to follow brings no more happiness or fulfilment than the previous phase of his existence and in one of his long autobiographical exchanges with the narrator he describes his own situation in a way which links it with that of the decaying local community, as if he saw his own state as a symptom of the general decline, rather than as an exception to it. Aware of his present misery, Cyril asks him if the future seems more exciting and the keeper replies

'No—about as exciting as this rotten old place—just rot off—Oh, my God!—
I'm like a good house, built and finished, and left to tumble down again with
nobody to live in it.

(**WP** p 210-11)

The image Annable uses is an unexpected choice for someone who usually
expresses such a hatred for the 'human' and 'cultured'—it suggests, among
other things, that just as a house is meant to be lived in, so a fine physique
is of no importance in itself without some 'higher' dimension of being to
'inhabit' it. Cyril is naturally puzzled by the fact that the keeper has chosen
a mode of life he finds impoverished and unsatisfying and his questions
prompt Annable to tell the story of his marriage to the refined Lady
Chrystabel. While he recognises that a life which lacks the 'human' element
cannot be satisfying, his marriage seems to have demonstrated that any
attempt to go beyond the animal leads to perversity. Annable is indeed
'trapped between culture and nature' but this does not mean that Lawrence
thought of the natural and cultural as inevitably opposed. The kind of conflict described in *The White Peacock* and in many of his other works is less
an expression of the 'fundamental dualism of his mind'[29] than an illustration
of the fundamental dualism in contemporary life which derives from the
Christian-idealistic foundations of our culture.

In *The White Peacock* Lawrence continually emphasises the precarious-
ness of animal existence—creatures die by accident, perish in the fight for
food or a mate, or are victims of man, who lives by exploiting the natural
environment. In the conflict-ridden natural world, animals are vulnerable
because they are at the mercy of their instinctive appetites and largely lack
the control, caution and prudence of which human beings are capable.
When, on a walk, Cyril and Lettie find one of the Shelley Mill cats caught
in a trap, its flight is linked with its predatory habits ('It had no doubt been
bounding forward after its prey when it was caught'). Because of its hunting
instinct, any cat is vulnerable in this way and when George's mother sees it
she says 'This is how they all go'. In the fierce competition for space and
sustenance which pervades nature, man owes his commanding advantage to
the subtlety, refinement and control of his responses—the traps he sets for
competing predators show his superior intelligence in action—and it follows
that the possession of cruder and less sublimated urges will expose human
beings to many of the risks and dangers which beset less developed creatures.
In the exchange between Annable and the group of young people in the dell,
the keeper's praise of the uncorrupted animal natures of his 'litter' of offspring prompts Cyril to predict that 'They'll get nicely trapped, one of these
days'. The keeper's reply, that 'they can fend for themselves like wild beasts
do' is scarcely reassuring in view of the number of cases in the novel of
animals being injured or meeting a violent death. And what happens to
Sam—the only member of the keeper's brood to be individualised—bears out
Cyril's forecast. On the two occasions on which he appears between his
father's death and his adoption by the Saxtons he has landed in difficult and
potentially dangerous situations while trying to supplement the family diet

by unorthodox means. After Annable's family is resettled in a house in the village, Cyril and his friends find Sam perched on the ridge of the roof, the target of abuse and even missiles from a hostile crowd of neighbours. The unrestrained naturalness encouraged by his father has led the boy to steal a neighbour's tame rabbit and offer it to his mother as one he has caught. Taking refuge from the hue and cry on the roof, he is only saved from injury by the intervention of George and Cyril. Shortly afterwards, one of the farm dogs at the Mill catches Sam raiding the Saxton's hen-house for eggs and in the scramble gives the boy 'a sharp grab on the thigh'. The riskiness of his mode of life is underlined by the fact that when Emily strips him to clean the bite 'On the boy's body were several scars and bruises—evidently he had rough times'.

But it is not only these incidents which show the consequences of Annable's naturalism. Just after the scene in the dell in which the keeper voices his credo, we see, in a significantly juxtaposed episode, something of the practical implications of his beliefs. Leaving the wood, the four young people hear hysterical shouting from the Kennels where the Annables (appropriately) live and find the mother belabouring Sam with a saucepan because he has bitten one of his sisters on the cheek. The violence of the mother's reaction is a result of exhaustion; she is 'desperately weary and foredone' because of her efforts to control her unruly offspring and her predicament is made more difficult by the fact that she gets no help from the keeper. Believing as he does in unmodified impulse, Annable makes no attempt to control or discipline his children because any such civilising effort would pervert their pristine wholeness and naturalness. The sheer number of children in the household is one of the mother's major problems—reacting against Chrystabel's refusal to have children, Annable now makes no attempt to regulate the size of his family. As he says to Lettie when she reproaches him for failing to exert any paternal authority—

'Duties of parents!—tell me, I've need of it. I've nine—that is eight, and one not far off. She breeds well, the owd lass—one every two years—nine in fourteen years—done well, hasn't she?'

'You've done pretty badly, I think.'

'I—why? It's natural! When a man's more than nature he's a devil.'

(**WP** p 191)

Lack of sexual restraint is defended because it is natural, whereas the attempt to modify impulse, to be 'more than nature' leads—or so the keeper's experience has seemed to show—to corruption. The result is that the Annable household is almost like a kind of epitome of the natural order itself, displaying both the abundance and extravagance which predominate in it and also the conflict and violence which occur if there is no organising force. It is by means of scenes like these, in which 'The strain of such a life upon wife and children is forcefully portrayed'[30] that Lawrence criticizes the keeper's championship of the wholly impulsive life.

It is not only his family who suffer for Annable's militant naturalism: the keeper himself meets a violent and premature end, killed by a fall of rock in an abandoned quarry. His fall may be accidental—a result of being too physically self-confident or it may be an act of revenge by the miners, whose poaching the keeper has resisted vigorously; in any event, it is a natural outcome of the kind of life he has adopted. In regressing to the animal level, Annable has chosen to abandon the highly developed 'foresight and cunning', the intelligence which has ensured man's success, and has exposed himself to the kind of dangers that threaten animals with their importunate and undeveloped urges.

Nietzsche links the development of intelligence in man with his relative physical vulnerability compared to many of his competitors—finding direct modes of satisfaction more difficult, human beings are 'compelled to adopt foresight and cunning, in short to become intelligent'.[31] But within the human species itself, individuals are endowed with markedly different degrees of physical strength and because those who are physically strong can satisfy their desires easily and directly in a physical way, they are less likely to develop intelligence to a high degree than these who are weaker. In Lawrence's fiction, intellect is invariably less fully and spontaneously developed in those who are physically strong than it is in those who are weaker—that is why it is often associated with women. Those whose being is largely physical, whose natures are, like that of the miner Walter Morel in *Sons and Lovers*, 'purely sensuous', tend to show the 'disinclination to self-doubt or to consider alternatives' which 'explains why the strong tend to be less prudent than the weak'.[32] In Morel's case it is this imprudence which explains his constant mishaps at work; being 'rather a heedless man, careless of danger', the miner has 'endless accidents'. Annable is, of course, an educated man—who has been to Cambridge—and is far more intellectually developed than Morel, but his experience of marriage has led him to adopt a mode of life which is a willed and self-conscious equivalent of the one the miner leads and which carries the same element of risk and danger. If the consequences in his case are more serious, this is because his reaction has taken him back beyond even the elementary stage of development represented by Morel.

In *The Rainbow*, both Tom Brangwen and his father die as a result of accidents; the latter falls from a stack and breaks his neck, while Tom is drowned when the canal which runs across the Marsh farm bursts its banks. Like Walter Morel, Alfred Brangwen has a wholly sensuous nature—his generation of Brangwen men is unaffected by the social and intellectual aspirations of the women—and his accident, like those Morel suffers, is a consequence of this fact. His son Tom is influenced by feminine aspirations, but his attempt to fulfil them by marrying the Polish lady fails because, disillusioned by the suffering she has experienced in 'the far-off world of cities and governments', Lydia Lensky wants nothing more for her husband and herself than the secure and stable traditional life of the Marsh. Under her influence, Tom gradually abandons that part of his youthful dream which had been concerned with refinement and subtlety of feeling, with the articulate and the social, and lapses with her into a 'potent, sensuous intimacy', a 'deep, inarticulate interchange' which resembles the 'drowse of blood intimacy' in which his forebears had lived. Because interests not present in his ancestors have been awakened in him, however, his state is presented as a diminishment of his being, as a condition to which Lydia has 'reduced her husband'. Like Annable, although in a much less extreme way, Tom has turned his back on the conscious and articulate and like him dies suddenly and prematurely.

In *The White Peacock*, the Annable episode which is prominent in the second part of the novel is paralleled by the 'lost father' story in the first. Frank Beardsall, the father of Cyril and Lettie who had deserted his family many years ago, reappears 'worn with sickness and dissipation' just before his death. His history offers another illustration of the imprudence and extravagance of unsublimated impulse and significantly his manner of life is associated with animal existence and particularly with the suffering which afflicts wild creatures. George and Cyril come upon him sleeping in the woods, groaning in the grip of some tormenting dream, just after the discovery of the trapped and mutilated cat, and a number of other references also link his fate with the violent and predatory, natural world: he is awakened by 'the scream of a rabbit caught by a weasel' and later the effect his death has on his family, their sense of 'the unanswered crying of failure' is linked with the 'cruel pitiful crying' of trapped creatures which Lettie notices. Beardsall is like an animal because he is undeveloped: 'always wanting, craving' he is the slave of importunate and extravagant appetites which ultimately cause his decline and death. The doctor who attends him in his last illness draws the moral—

> '... there are two ways. You can burn your lamp with a big draught, and it'll flare away, till the oil's gone, then it'll stink and smoke itself out. Or you can keep it trim on the kitchen table, dirty your fingers occasionally trimming it up, and it'll last a long time, and sink out mildly.'
>
> **(WP** p 84)

Beardsall is not a self-conscious primitivist like Annable, but his fate illuminates the more sudden and spectacular end of the keeper and helps to drive home the point that to yield to impulses in their unsublimated form is to court disaster.

If involvement in the social and cultural world, pervaded as it is by a 'woman administered idealism' leads to perversity, corruption and the humiliation of the sensual male, the direct assertion of physical and sensual appetites seems no more satisfactory because those who, by nature or deliberate choice, follow that path fail equally to find fulfilment. Like the Annable episode, the lost father story shows that the reversion to an animalistic existence which might otherwise seem—and indeed has seemed to some critics—a desirable alternative to corrupt 'civilised' life, is unsatisfactory and even destructive.

In *Twilight of the Idols*, Nietzsche argues that the ascetic character of many moralities is due to the fact that in their primitive state the fundamental human urges are extravagant and dangerous. When they first develop, 'urges' are imprudent and short-sighted, sometimes threatening the success and even the survival of their possessor. At this early stage, Nietzsche concedes, the rigorous control imposed by ascetic beliefs may have been necessary, but in the course of human development over generations, organic memory and natural selection work together to 'educate' the impulses so that they gradually become more refined, economical and 'intelligent' in their operation and they become, in Nietzsche's word—'spiritualised'. This transformation of crude 'impulse' into subtle 'instinct' (to borrow Morgan's terms) depends on fortunate heredity: in those who are unlucky in this respect, 'urges' remain immoderate and ill-organised and for such people extreme measures continue to be necessary to ensure self-preservation. It was largely among such ill-constituted individuals that Christianity developed but its success has meant that a morality appropriate to a certain kind of nature has been imposed on everyone and it is only now that this unhealthy state of affairs is being questioned:

> Formerly one made war on passion itself on account of the folly inherent in it: one conspired for its extermination—all the old moral monsters are unanimous that 'il faut tuer les passions'. The most famous formula for doing this is contained in the New Testament, in the Sermon on the Mount, where, by the way, things are not at all regarded from a *lofty* standpoint. There, for example, it is said, with reference to sexuality, 'if thine eye offend thee pluck it out': fortunately no Christian follows this prescription. To *exterminate* the passions and desires merely in order to do away with their folly and its unpleasant consequences—this itself seems to us today merely an acute form of folly ... On the other hand, it is only fair to admit that on the soil out of which Christianity grew, the concept 'spiritualization of passion' could not possibly be conceived. For the primitive Church, as is well known, fought *against* the 'intelligent' in favour of the 'poor in spirit'.[33]

If Nietzsche roundly condemns the extirpation of the passions attempted by Christianity, he also stresses the 'folly' inherent in the passions in their primitive state and recognises the need for their transformation if man is to survive and flourish:

> There is a time with all passions when they are merely fatalities, when they drag their victim down with the weight of their folly—and a later, very much later time when they are wedded with the spirit, when they are 'spiritualised'.[34]

The 'improvement of man'—an enterprise Nietzsche sees as central to all moral codes—need not depend on rejecting his animal nature. Moralities less perversely idealistic than the Christian one might be and have in the past been, the means of genuine and healthy human advance. In the section of *Twilight of the Idols* entitled 'The "Improvers" of Mankind', Nietzsche discusses the contrasting conceptions of and strategies for 'improvement' associated with Christianity and with the paganism which preceded it, remarking that 'one word can conceal the most divergent tendencies'. While

Christianity sets out to weaken the fierce animal energies of man, other more enlightened kinds of morality strive to harness their force in the service of some higher aim, opposed methods which Nietzsche terms 'taming' and 'breeding' or 'training' respectively. The claim that barbarian populations converted to Christianity were thereby 'improved' seems to Nietzsche analogous to the claim that the wild animal is 'improved' by captivity—

> To call the taming of an animal its 'improvement' is in our ears almost a joke. Whoever knows what goes on in menageries is doubtful whether the beasts in them are 'improved'. They are weakened, they are made less harmful, they become *sickly* beasts through the depressive emotion of fear, through pain, through injuries, through hunger.[34]

Like the wild creature, the pagan barbarian was caught and caged, although psychologically rather than physically and lay 'imprisoned ... behind nothing but sheer terrifying concepts', his innocence about his instincts and the integrity of his being undermined by the idea of sin. So he became 'sick, miserable, filled with ill-will towards himself: full of hatred for the impulses towards life, full of suspicion of all that was still strong and happy. In short, a "Christian"...'[36]

But not all moral codes weaken men by creating guilt and inner conflict and Nietzsche goes on to discuss the code which, above all, epitomises the opposite tendency—the ancient Hindu Law of Manu. Like Christianity, the ancient Indian code has its harsh aspects, but these are not directed against the animal instincts—

> Here we are manifestly no longer among animal-tamers; a species of human being a hundred times more gentle and rational is presupposed even to conceive the plan of such a breeding ... How paltry the 'New Testament' is compared with Manu ... But this organization too needed to be *dreadful*—this time in struggle not with the beast but with its antithesis, with the non-bred human being, the hotch-potch human being, the Chandala.[37]

The horrifying edicts concerning the Chandala, the untouchables, are essentially measures of social hygiene, directed at the reduction, segregation or elimination of sickly, ill-constituted or corrupt members of society and in this determination to weed out the 'unfit' lies one of the crucial differences between Hindu and Christian morality. As well as breaking the strong, Christianity has urged compassion for the weak and unfortunate, so that during the Christian centuries they have multiplied and now constitute that significant pathological element which both Lawrence and Nietzsche claim to detect in contemporary European society. In condemning the elimination of the unfit, Christianity is opposing what is natural and endangering the survival of man as a healthy species—

> Nature is not immoral when it has no pity for the degenerate: on the contrary, the growth of physiological and moral ills among mankind is the consequence of a pathological and immature morality. The sensibility of the majority of men

is pathological and unnatural ... The right to altruism cannot be derived from physiology; nor can the right to help and to an equality of lots: these are prizes for the degenerate and underprivileged. There is no solidarity in a society in which these are sterile, unproductive and destructive elements.[38]

The most direct statement in Lawrence's fiction of the link between the subversive influence of the ill-constituted and the ethic of compassion which has allowed them to survive and multiply is made by Lou Witt, the heroine of *St Mawr*. In one of the pivotal passages in the novella, she suddenly realises that the whole of developed American and European civilisation has become infected with a disintegrative, life-denying spirit. Despite the superficial characteristics of our society—like the surface friendliness which is such a marked feature of modern life—it lacks any real solidarity and is indeed pervaded by 'sterile, unproductive and destructive elements'. The apparent attractiveness of contemporary society, Lou realises, is no more than the 'pseudo-handsome' mask of evil. In rather the same way, Hermione's country house, Breadalby, seems to stand, in *Women in Love*, for beauty, serenity and continuity, but its immunity from the destruction and disintegration characteristic of the twentieth century is only apparent. In the conversations about social and political issues among the guests the talk, we are told, 'went on like a rattle of small artillery, always slightly sententious with a sententiousness that was only emphasised by the continual crackling of a witticism, the continual spatter of verbal jest'. In the context established by 'artillery', onomatapoeic words like 'crackling' and 'spatter' inevitably suggest gunfire and so, in an audacious simile, Lawrence links the apparently peaceful setting and civilised exchanges with the violence and destruction of modern warfare, suggesting that the spirit which has caused events like the Great War is also active here, if in subtler form.

In *St Mawr*, Lawrence links this kind of situation quite directly with the influence of the unnaturally compassionate and altruistic morality which has long been dominant; the ways of man have diverged radically and damagingly from the ways of nature—'Creation destroys as it goes, throws down one tree for the rise of another. But ideal mankind would abolish death, multiply itself million upon million, rear up city upon city, save every parasite alive, until the accumulation of mere existence is swollen to a horror. But go on saving life, the ghastly salvation army of ideal mankind.' (**CSM** p 342) Christian idealism favours the weak because it is an expression of their values (and of their will to power). The victory of Christianity has meant that the extreme measures which are expressions of, and appropriate to, weakness have been imposed even on those who have naturally disciplined instincts and do not require them. This is a consequence of the absolute claims of the Christian ethic which is based on the idea of 'the equal value of men before God' and so 'forbade actions and attitudes that were in themselves among the prerogatives of the strongly constituted—as if they were in themselves unworthy of men'. And Nietzsche goes on to say that 'the entire tendency of the strong' was brought into disrepute by the erection of 'the protective measures of the weak ... as a norm of value'.[39]

This oppressive imposition of a single law on both the lion and the ox is seen by Nietzsche as a subtle revenge inflicted on the hitherto dominant strong members of the community by the victims of their 'morality of breeding'. Christianity is the expression of the will to power of the ill-constituted, directed at weakening those healthier than themselves by infecting them with guilt about their own strongest impulses. In place of the existing social hierarchy, Christianity puts an inverted one, in which the humble, lowly and ignorant are accorded the highest moral and spiritual status. The clearest illustration of these processes and their consequences in Lawrence's work is in the treatment of old Mr Crich in *Women in Love*. Wealthy, powerful and—in his younger days—capable and energetic, Thomas Crich is nonetheless convinced of his moral and spiritual inferiority to the miners he employs, believing the Gospel warning that 'He, the rich man ... would hardly enter Heaven because of his possessions' while the poor are 'nearer Christ than himself', being 'humble and despised and closer to perfection ...' Out of his sense of guilt he is charitable and compassionate, but the beneficiaries, far from being morally better than he, are the feckless and degenerate members of the community, the 'whining, parasitic, foul human beings who come crawling after charity and feeding on the living body of the public like lice'. It is because the values of weakness rather than those of strength have prevailed, even with many of those who are dynamic and creative, that our civilisation is faced with catastrophe.

The pagan creeds which preceded Christianity did not differ from it simply in accepting and affirming nature. Pagan morality too aimed at the 'improvement' of man, but realised that aim through 'training' rather than 'taming' animal impulse. The wisdom which was lost with the victory of Christianity was concerned with the task of harnessing the instincts and it is this lost knowledge, symbolised in the snowdrops, which Cyril and Lettie yearn for, with a longing which reflects the desire felt by alienated modern man to recover wholeness of being. The pagan wisdom is not identical with Annable's materialism; as his misery suggests, the keeper is himself a victim of the anti-natural values which are still dominant rather than an embodiment of or spokesman for some healthy alternative to them. He has rejected the idea of 'improving' the natural man because he has experienced the destructive effects of one kind of strategy for improvement; with the loss of the pagan wisdom, no other way of human advance seems possible. As Annable sees it, man is condemned to choose between perverse idealism and remaining on the animal level.

For Nietzsche, the kind of contemporary naturalism Annable espouses is not a genuine alternative to the prevailing idealism, but simply a reaction against it illustrating the general rule that—

> Extreme positions are not succeeded by moderate ones but by extreme positions of the opposite mind. Thus the belief in the absolute immorality of nature, in aim—and meaningless, is the psychologically necessary affect once the belief in God and an essentially moral order becomes untenable. Nihilism appears at that point ... One interpretation has collapsed; but because it was considered

*the* interpretation it now seems as if there were no meaning at all in existence, as if everything were in vain.[40]

Annable's materialism has developed in just that way, as a reaction against his wife's attitudes and, as a result, it is still conditioned by and bound to the things he is reacting against. While he is convinced that the traditional means for improving man serve only to diminish him, he continues to accept the claim implicit in the traditional moral scheme, that such means are the *only* ones available. Because the Christian-idealist interpretation has been considered '*the* interpretation' it now 'seems as if there were no meaning at all in existence'.

In all this Annable is not so much a forerunner of positive characters like Mellors in *Lady Chatterly's Lover* as of those characters in *Women in Love* like Halliday or, in his more complicated way, Gerald Crich, who are locked into an uncreative action-reaction pattern of behaviour. Because Annable is a strong character, his reaction against idealism and into naturalism is complete and final; weaker characters like Halliday are incapable of such decisiveness, and are swept first one way and then the other by irresistible and opposite tides of feeling. Impelled at one moment towards an extravagant 'spirituality', at the next Halliday plunges into an extreme and debased sensuality. The psychological split from which he suffers, and which prevents him from making any genuine advance in his development is linked, as Birkin makes clear, with the influence of religious idealism—

> On the one hand he's had religious mania, and on the other he's fascinated by obscenity. Either he is a pure servant, washing the feet of Christ, or else he is making obscene drawings of Jesus—action and reaction—and between the two, nothing ... He wants a pure lily, another girl, with a Botticelli face, on the one hand, and on the other, he *must* have Minette to defile himself with her.
> (**WL** p 106)

Since Christianity condemns the body and its functions, particularly the most assertive of them—sexuality—as animal or unclean or evil and defines purity and spirituality in terms of emancipation from the senses, those influenced by it strive to be spiritual by repressing their sensual being. But since it is the strongest and most fundamental forces in human nature which are being repressed, they inevitably force their way to the surface at regular intervals, appearing in an extreme and perverse form as a result of the attempted supression. The result is the kind of Jekyll and Hyde alternation of spirituality and defilement which Halliday displays. For Lawrence, as for Nietzsche, such introversion alters the character of the impulses themselves; something naturally creative like sexuality becomes gross and violent while spirituality, detached from its sources in the sensual, becomes abstract and disembodied.

Gerald's case is more complicated because there is at least a possibility that given the right sort of stimulus he could escape the essentially static condition to which Halliday is condemned. But in taking Gudrun as his mistress, he too is conforming to the action-reaction pattern which Birkin sees as characteristic of the uncreative existence of modern man. Conservative in his politics and social attitudes, concerned with propriety and good form, Gerald nevertheless has spells of dissipation like the one described early in *Women in Love* where he mingles with decadent bohemians and artists and has a brief liaison with the promiscuous Minette. His case is far less extreme than Halliday's, but there is the same kind of psychic split in his nature and in taking up with Gudrun he is not trying to forge some new sort of relationship with a woman which will contribute to the development of each, but simply reacting against a conception of marriage which has lost its vitality. It is this kind of response which Birkin implicitly criticises in his own reflections on matrimony—

> ... the thought of love, marriage and children, and a life lived together, in the horrible privacy of domestic and connubial satisfaction, was repulsive ... True he hated promiscuity even worse than marriage, and a liaison was only another kind of coupling, reactionary from the legal marriage. Reaction was a greater bore than action.
>
> (**WL** p 223)

Even Birkin has not managed to shake off the influence of centuries of Christian belief and is himself in danger of falling into the same kind of unproductive oscillation between idealism and sensuality. Hermione, who is incapable of imagining creative possibilities, sees her lover's growing interest in Ursula Brangwen as no more than a natural swing of the pendulum away from an intellectual and spiritual relationship towards a more earthy and sensual one—

> he had now reacted towards the strongly female, healthy, selfish woman—it was his reaction for the time being—there was no helping it all. It was always a foolish backward and forward, a violent oscillation that would at length be too violent for his coherency and he would smash and be dead ... This violent and directionless reaction between animalism and spiritual truth would go on in him till he tore himself in two between the opposite directions ...
>
> (**WL** p 334)

Certainly Hermione is trying to assure herself that Birkin will come back to her in time, but what Ursula says in the pivotal 'Excurse' chapter at least partly bears out her diagnosis. Ursula can see that Birkin has not managed to emancipate himself fully from old patterns of living and relationship, and denounces him as a coward and hypocrite, who wants to keep Hermione as a 'spiritual bride' while coming to her for 'daily use'. Birkin recognises that there is a substantial element of truth in her allegations and—as is often the case in Lawrence's work—the conflict is an important stimulus to breaking with the old ways and encouraging the risky commitment to the new and untried.

As Hermione's reaction to her lover's apostasy shows, it is easy to confuse the uncreative action-reaction pattern of behaviour in Lawrence's work with real creative development, both because of superficial similarities between the two and because different possibilities may be latent in a character at the same time. 'Development' in the proper sense is never linear and straightforwardly progressive in Lawrence, but always proceeds—for reasons I will discuss later—by rhythmic alternations, by a sequence of advances toward a new state of being and of retreats back towards the old. An oscillating, to-and-fro motion is common both to 'creative', mobile living and to uncreative, 'static' existence: where both possibilities are present, as in the two couples in *Women in Love*, it is sometimes difficult to tell one from the other, as Middleton Murry's well known assertion that the major relationships in the novels are indistinguishable indicates.

In the lost pagan tradition, the improvement of man depends on that 'spiritualisation of passion' which was impossible to imagine for those to whom Christianity appealed. As a result of this 'spiritualisation' or 'sublimation', the fundamental human urges develop 'increased sensitiveness and considerateness of action' and find expression 'in thought and imagination rather than in mere muscular response alone'.[41] Passions like cruelty and lust are refined and subtilised in this way and appear as 'the highest things in human culture', as 'religion, philosophy, art', activities which, ironically, may come to be contrasted with and seen as opposed to, the 'base' passions which are their unseen source—

> When an urge becomes more *intellectual* it gets a new name, a new charm and new valuation. It is often contrasted to the urge on the older level, as its contradiction ...[42]

Lawrence often uses flowering plants, like the snowdrop in *The White Peacock* as symbols of 'spiritualisation' in this sense. The processes of plant growth and particularly the relation of root and blossom, offered him—as they offered Yeats in the final stanza of 'Among School Children'—apt analogues both for the transformation of natural impulse and for the interdependence of body and spirit. And such parallels are more than figurative, for in formulating his definition of the essential character of life, Nietzsche had insisted 'that a generalisation intended to cover all life must apply to plants as well as animals' and examples from plant life form an important part of his evidence because in these, the simplest living things, the essential aspects of the life processes are easier to identify and because plant growth takes place without the intervention of even the elementary degree of consciousness which animal life might be assumed to involve. So when he sets out to discuss the question of purpose in organic life, Nietzsche notes that 'one should start from the "sagacity" of plants'[43] and in rather the same way, Lawrence begins his consideration of the meaning of existence in *Study of Thomas Hardy* by invoking the 'sagacity' of the poppy. Like Nietzsche, Lawrence often uses such examples from the plant world to illustrate processes and relations which are obscured by the sheer complexity of higher life-forms and in his work frequently links plant growth and human development to make the fundamental patterns in the latter clear.

This kind of comparison finds elaborate expression in the revised version of 'Discipline',[44] one of a group of poems which grew out of Lawrence's experiences during the time he taught in Croydon. The revised 'Discipline' which appeared in *Amores* (1916), Lawrence's second volume of verse, has little in common, apart from its subject and the two opening stanzas, with the original poems of that title printed in *The English Review* in 1909.

Both poems record the antagonism Lawrence faced from his pupils when he tried to teach through love, rather than in a conventionally authoritarian way—

> I came to the boys with love, dear, and only they turned on me;
> With gentleness came I, with my heart 'twixt my hands like a bowl,
> Like a loving-cup, like a grail, but they spilt it triumphantly
> And tried to break the vessel, and violate my soul.

In the earlier version, the poet has no doubts about the rightness of his approach and the boys' reaction is seen as an example of a general human fear of and resistance to new possibilities—

> Ah, my Darling, when over the purple horizon shall loom
> The shrouded Mother of a new idea, men hide their faces,
> Cry out, and fend her off, as she seeks her procreant groom,
> Wounding themselves against her, denying her great embraces.
>
> And do I not seek to mate my grown, desirous soul
> With the lusty souls of my boys?—yet they hide their faces,
> And strike with a blindness of fury against me ...45

In the revision, in contrast, the pupils' resistance has come to seem justified. The offer of love now seems an attempt to dominate in an undesirable way, a 'trespass' on the being of others and the boys' antagonism, an instinctive attempt to preserve their integrity as individuals and freedom to develop in their own way—

> ... perhaps they were right, for the young are busy deep down at the roots,
> And love would only weaken their under-earth grip, make shallow
> Their hold on reality, enfeeble their rising shoots
> With too much tincture of me, instead of the dark's deep fallow.

The young are likely to be right in their responses because they are close to the unconscious sources of being, to the 'roots' which 'In the night where we first have our being', instinctively seek, grasp and transform the raw materials we need for our development. Our 'roots'

> ... blind themselves to the dark,
> And drawing the darkness together, crush from it a twilight, a slow
> Dim self that rises slowly to leaves and the flower's gay spark.

The unconscious roots of human nature are the 'urges' of Nietzsche's dynamic psychology, reaching out to appropriate and assimilate what is needed for growth. Since the urges are 'intelligent' and 'interpret' the world around they are able to recognise what a particular individual needs and reject what is inappropriate; the hatred with which the boys greet their teacher's offer of love is at once an instinctively expressed judgement that his offer will endanger their integrity and an instinctive revulsion from it. At this fundamental level of being, effort, struggle and conflict rather than love are the main forces—the will to power naturally 'seeks that which resists it' striving, as 'bind' and 'crush' suggest, to overwhelm what it grasps and reshape it. The effort is carried on in a world full of living things engaged in the same enterprise—the 'deep soil' is crowded with roots all grappling for sustenance—so at the most fundamental level, life is ruthlessly competitive, depending on an unconscious egoism rather on the altruism associated with love—

> And there in the dark, my darling, where the roots are entangled and fight
> Each one for its hold on the concrete darkness, I know that there
> In the night where we first have being, before we rise on the light,
> We are not lovers, my darling, we fight and we do not spare.

Yet it is this Dionysian substratum of being which is the source and support of the more 'human' and 'spiritual' qualities in our nature. The 'flower' of the 'soul' in man's creative activities like art, religion and philosophy grows from the roots of his unconscious urges; they are not gifts from some higher realm of being as the Christian tradition suggests. It is because they want to emphasise that the elements in man traditionally regarded as good and valuable have their origins in the natural and earthly, in the physical and animal nature of man, that Lawrence and Nietzsche constantly employ horticultural metaphors. Summarising his view of the relation between nature and culture in an early essay, Nietzsche says—

> When one speaks of *humanity*, there lies behind it the idea that humanity is that which *separates* and distinguishes mankind from nature. But in reality there is no such separation: the 'natural' qualities and those called specifically 'human' are inextricably entwined together. Man is in his highest and noblest powers entirely nature and bears in him nature's uncanny dual character. Those capacities which are dreadful and accounted inhuman are ... the fruitful soil out of which alone all humanity in impulse, act and deed can grow.[46]

Zarathustra makes the same point more briefly, saying to his hearers 'Once you had passions and called them evil. But now you have only your virtues: they grew from out your passions.'[47] In Lawrence's words it is 'that which is physic—non-human, in humanity'[48] which is the source of the 'human' element in us.

It is this kind of transmutation which explains Lettie's insistence in *The White Peacock* that the snowdrop stands for 'more than tears'. Although it does indeed stand for effort and struggle, it also, in its blossoming, symbolises their transformation into beauty and serenity. So it is the 'stillness' of the flowers which indicates to Lettie that Emily's idea of their significance is too narrow and negative. The snowdrop is particularly appropriate for Lawrence's symbolic purposes because, as the first flower to appear after the winter, its beauty emerges in hard conditions, suggesting the challenge involved in the pagan affirmation of life in all its harshness and also perhaps hinting at the beginning of a new and healthier era in man's moral history.

Graham Hough sees *The White Peacock* as a catalogue of failures and disappointments, arguing that in it 'no one even points the way to fulfilment'. But in the novel, the possibility of a creative transformation of sense into spirit is not exclusively associated with the vanished pagan past. The image of the growing, blossoming plant is used in connection with the development of Lettie and also, more importantly, with that of George. Early in the novel, Lettie uses such an image to describe the young farmer's immaturity, saying to him 'You never grow up, like bulbs which spend all summer getting fat and fleshy, but never wakening the germ of a flower'. George's life is an accummulative, power-getting existence, lacking the natural complement of an expressive, power-spending phase: in terms of the contrast developed at the beginning of *Study of Thomas Hardy* he lives like the cabbage instead of like the poppy. The process of 'flowering' has gone further in Lettie, but is not complete—as she says 'the flower is born in me, but it wants bringing forth'. The contrast between the pair lies in the fact that Lettie can imagine a fulfilling life but cannot, by herself, act to realise it while George, trapped in a traditional outlook, cannot even conceive of a more satisfying existence without outside stimulus. A little later in the novel, when Lettie and Leslie come upon George working in the fields with his father, she sees him as a 'great firm bud of life'. Since 'spiritual' potential depends on the strength of the physical life from which it derives, the image is an appropriate one suggesting that George's abundant vigour could be the source of an impressive 'flowering'. Will Brangwen in *The Rainbow* is also described as budding but failing to flower but, more self-aware than George, is himself conscious of this deficiency—

> As he sat sometimes very still, with a bright, vacant face, Anna could see the suffering among the brightness. He was aware of some limit of himself, of something unformed in his very being, of some buds which are not ripe in him, some folded centres of darkness which would never develop and unfold whilst he was alive in the body. He was unready for fulfilment. Something undeveloped in him limited him, there was a darkness in him which he *could* not unfold, which would never unfold in him.

> (**R** p 210)

Late in *The White Peacock*, when George has become aware of his unfulfilled potential, he remarks to Cyril that his full 'flowering' would have needed either the stimulus of a lasting relationship with the more developed Lettie, or the additional strength provided by another generation of living. Despite the fact that he is a wealthy and successful businessman, George does not feel that he has found fulfilment and he goes on to explain the nature of his failure using the now familiar metaphor of plant growth. He has come to realise that his real vocation was artistic but that he lacked sufficient inherited strength spontaneously to choose this very demanding kind of life—

> 'I think, really, I ought to have made something of myself—a poet or something, like Burns—I don't know. I shall laugh at myself for thinking so, tomorrow. But I am born a generation too soon—I wasn't ripe enough when I came. I wanted something I hadn't got ... I'm like corn in a wet harvest—full, but pappy, no good. I s'll rot.'
>
> (**WP** p 371)

Will is unready for fulfilment in the same way—the 'unripe buds' of his being will not develop, but the qualification 'whilst he was alive in the body' suggests that they will come to fruition in a future generation and points forward to the greater degree of self-realisation attained by his daughter Ursula. What is suggested in both novels is a process of storing, then releasing, strength which extends over several generations, but which is not dependent on any conscious acquisition and transmission of knowledge. The imagery Lawrence uses points instead to the action of organic memory passing on embodied experience so that each generation finds itself further along the road to the expansive, outgoing, 'flowering' phase of being which for Lawrence, as for Nietzsche, is the true end of life.

Reflecting on his predicament, George feels that he might have reached fulfilment himself if he had had a sufficiently strong stimulus and he links his interest in Lettie with this possibility, implying that it expressed an instinctive recognition of the part she could play in his growth—'I wanted something that would ha' made me grow fierce. That's why I wanted Lettie ...' And Lettie herself, in her analysis of George's deficiencies early in the story, says that his development has been arrested because he has never faced real challenge or discomfort or difficulty, while she is more developed because she has:

> If you'd ever been sick; if you'd ever been born into a home where there was something oppressed you, and you couldn't understand; if ever you'd believed, or even doubted, you might have been a man by now. You never grew up, like bulbs which spend all summer getting fat and fleshy, but never wakening the germ of a flower. As for me, the flower is born in me, but it wants bringing forth. Things don't flower if they're overfed. You have to suffer before you blossom in this life. When death is just touching a plant, it forces it into a passion of flowering. You wonder how I have touched death ... There's always a sense of death in this house. I believe my mother hated my father before I was born.
>
> (**WP** p 46)

In Nietzschean terms, maximum growth needs the stimulus of severe conditions:

Examine the lives of the best and most fruitful people and peoples, and ask yourselves whether a tree that is supposed to grow to a proud height can dispense with bad weather and storms: whether misfortune and external resistance, some kinds of hatred, jealousy, stubbornness, mistrust, hardness, avarice and violence do not belong among the favourable conditions without which any great growth even of virtue is scarcely possible.[49]

Because conflict and difficulty are conditions of continuing growth, it is when the bitter struggle with his wife Anna has largely ceased that Will Brangwen becomes aware of a limitation in himself that he will never be able to transcend. Partially emancipated from his religious idealism by his wife's constant insistence on the reality and significance of the material world, Will's further development is interrupted by the fact that after Ursula's birth, Anna loses her intellectual and spiritual adventurousness and becomes 'willing ... to postpone all adventures into unknown realities'. Since she no longer wants to participate through her husband in such realities, she stops trying to influence him:

> Anna was absorbed in the child now, she left her husband to take his own way.
> (**R** p 206)

She has made Will realise that his beloved Lincoln Cathedral and the idealism it symbolises are not absolute; that the Cathedral does not point to a higher world beyond, but is part of this one, 'a world within a world, a sort of sideshow'—but without continuing stimulus from her, he cannot go beyond this negative realisation to a new affirmation. As a result, he remains loyal to traditional forms and beliefs, even while he recognises their limitations. Will chooses 'to continue in the old form' even though he feels slightly ashamed 'like a man who has failed, who lapses back for his fulfilment'.

For Nietzsche 'Spiritualisation' involves the expression of urges 'in thought and imagination rather than in mere muscular response alone'. In creative individuals like Siegmund and Hampson in *The Trespasser* (both are musicians) the 'looking for intensity in life', for 'vivid soul experience' is—as Hampson himself says—the sublimated expression of more elementary kinds of desire for excitement and challenge; it 'takes the place ... of the old adventure and physical excitement'. This kind of transformation is the result of the long exercise of firm discipline over the naturally antagonistic, imprudent urges and so in, *Beyond Good and Evil*, Nietzsche emphasises the importance of 'cruelty' in the genesis of culture. Since the strong man seeks not to extirpate or weaken his instincts but 'to [put] them into service: which may also mean subjecting them to a protracted tyranny',[50] the task of spiritualisation demands that man should direct his cruelty inward, against his own unregenerate nature. Elsewhere, Nietzsche emphasises the importance of another of man's urges, his sexuality, to his 'higher' achievements, asserting that 'The degree and kind of a man's sexuality reaches up into the topmost summit of his spirit'.[51]

It is his sense of the interdependence of body and spirit which lies behind Lawrence's continuing interest in human sexuality, an interest so prominent in some of his novels, that one early reviewer of *The Rainbow* described it as 'mainly a prolix account of three generations of sexual crises in the Brangwen family'.[52] The novel *is* very much concerned with sexual success or failure, but this is because Lawrence is interested above all in the struggle to attain a wholeness of being in which both physical and spiritual satisfaction are achieved. It is this state which is symbolised by the rainbow in the novel's title. In a letter to an American enquirer, Lawrence said he had 'called it "The Rainbow" in reference to the Flood', the rainbow, the bow joining heaven and earth which appears when the waters of Noah's flood have receded, serving as an apt symbol for the union of sensual and spiritual sought by successive generations of Brangwens. If sexuality is a major concern in *The Rainbow*, then this is because Lawrence sees sexuality as the most powerful urge in adult experience and since spiritual potential depends on vigour of impulse, sexual success or failure is of central importance for 'higher' human activities. That is why, from the time when Tom Brangwen meets the cultivated foreigner and his mistress at Matlock early in the novel, the quest for sexual fulfilment and the aspiration towards some more refined and civilised mode of being are inextricably linked. As a result of the meeting, Tom

> dreamed day and night, absorbedly, of a voluptuous woman and of the meeting with a small, withered foreigner of ancient breeding. No sooner was his mind free, no sooner had he left his own companions, than he began to imagine an intimacy with fine-textured, subtle-mannered people such as the foreigner at Matlock, and amidst this subtle intimacy was always the satisfaction of a voluptuous woman.
>
> (R p 25)

Although sexual fulfilment and creative, spiritual effort are linked in this way, the fact that after its transformation an 'urge is often contrasted to the urge on the older level, as its contradiction ...' has given rise to the idea that sense and spirit are opposite and opposing forces. This idea is of central importance in the main love relationships in both *The Trespasser* and *Sons and Lovers*, for in both these novels the principal female characters, influenced by ascetic Christian attitudes, think of their lovers as fundamentally divided in their natures. For Helena there is a 'dream' Siegmund and a more ordinary—and less 'real' one; for Miriam there is 'her' Paul, intense and spiritual, and his 'lesser self'. In both cases, the woman endangers the man's creative capacities through her distrust and depreciation of the sensual energies in which these capacities have their origin. This inability to recognise the relation between sense and spirit is dramatised directly in Helena's reaction to the change in Siegmund which follows their first love-making. The transformation is so radical that her lover seems like an entirely different person:

> She wondered at him; he was so different from an hour ago. How could he be the same! Now he was like the sea, blue and hazy in the morning, musing by itself. Before, he was burning, volcanic, as if he would destroy her.
>
> She had given him this new soft beauty. She was the earth in which his strange flowers grew. But she herself wondered at the flowers produced of her. He was so strange to her ...
>
> (**Tr** p 36)

In fact, as the familiar flower image makes clear, the spirituality of the gentle poetic Siegmund has been created by their passion; the two apparently contradictory aspects of his nature are continuous and interdependent.

This unawareness or misunderstanding of the relation between sense and spirit can happen within, as well as between, individuals, because conscious awareness is an inadequate reflection of inner reality. Although he himself is not consciously aware of it, Will Brangwen's intense religious feeling has its roots in his powerfully sensual nature. Seated next to him in church and looking at his absorbed 'dark-rapt, half-delighted face' his wife senses that he was 'conveying to strange, secret places the love that sprang in him for her'. In the book about Bamberg Cathedral which he brings back from Nottingham after one of their quarrels, and which gives him 'thrills of bliss', it is, significantly, the pictures of sculptured female figures which excite Will most—

> The book lay in his hands like a doorway. The world around was only an enclosure, a room. But he was going away. He lingered over the lovely statues of women. A marvellous, finely wrought-universe crystallised out round him as he looked again, at the crowns, the twining hair, the woman faces.
>
> (**R** p 165)

Will believes in a really existing 'crystalline' world which is finer, more orderly, more coherent than the limited material 'enclosure' of ordinary reality and the ordinary world is largely important for him as something which can symbolise, or provide intuitions of, a more comprehensive spiritual realm which is the primary reality. But what the narrative makes clear is that Will's spirituality is rooted in his sexuality, that the physical and sensual is primary and the apparently autonomous spiritual world an oblique expression and articulation of it. This is clearest of all in *The Rainbow* in the description of Will's response to Lincoln Cathedral. Passing the 'lovely unfolding of the stone' he enters 'the perfect womb' in which his soul, leaping up into the gloom 'quivered in the womb, in the hush and the gloom of fecundity, like the seed of procreation in ecstasy':

> Here the stone leapt up from the plain of earth, leapt up in a manifold, clustered desire each time, up, away from the horizontal earth, through twilight and dusk and the whole range of desire, through the swerving, the declination, ah, to the ecstasy, the touch, to the meeting and the consummation, the meeting, the clasp, the close embrace, the neutrality, the perfect swooning consummation ...
>
> (**R** p 202)

The whole description of the building is pervaded by erotic imagery in this way and its structure is marked by a pattern of partial repetition, of advance and retreat, in both words and rhythm, designed to suggest the sexual act, and thereby to reveal the true origins, not only of Will's religious feeling, but of the part played by sexuality in general in creating what is, ostensibly, a symbol of the order which lies beyond the world of the senses.

In *Sons and Lovers*, the experience which means most to Miriam is a kind of spiritual ecstasy which resembles Will's response to the Cathedral, and the description of her rapt state before the wild rose tree in the 'Lad and Girl Love' chapter of the novel suggests that her 'spirituality' like his, is an indirect expression of sexuality. She takes Paul to see the tree, feeling that the most valuable kind of contract between them lies in things like shared contemplation of the beauty of the blossoms. But despite the fact that there is no 'inferior' physical contact in the experience, it is described in a way which suggests that her apparently 'exalted' feelings have their roots in a sensuality which, on a conscious level, she rejects and represses:

> Paul looked into Miriam's eyes. She was pale and expectant with wonder, her lips were parted, and her dark eyes lay open to him. His look seemed to travel down into her. Her soul quivered. It was the communion she wanted.
>
> (**SL** p 198)

What takes place is presented as a kind of visual equivalent of sexual penetration and implicit in the description is a contrast between a cold and detached communion based on sight (linked with light and consciousness) and a warm, healthy contact based on touch (linked with darkness)—a contrast which is recurrent in Lawrence's writing. In *Thus Spake Zarathustra*, Nietzsche devotes a chapter to those who value and seek such 'passionless' contemplation and 'spiritual' communion. In it he argues that what he jocularly terms 'immaculate perception' originates among those who, because they feel guilty about their desires, are afraid to express them openly. In such people, the impulses find oblique and devious modes of expression, but behind their apparent 'spirituality', the psychologist is able to detect that they too 'love the earth and the earthly' although 'shame and bad conscience is in [their] love'. Summarising their creed, Nietzsche emphasises the way in which physical coldness is accompanied by intense emotion:

> 'For me, the highest thing would be to gaze at life without desire and not, as a dog does, with tongue hanging out'—thus speaks your mendacious spirit to itself:
> To be happy in gazing, with benumbed will, without the grasping and greed of egotism—cold and ashen in body with intoxicated moon-eyes! For me, the dearest thing would be to love the earth as the moon loves it, and to touch its beauty with the eyes alone'—thus the seduced one seduces himself.[53]

Miriam's conception of what is valuable in human nature and human relations is linked with the attitude to the natural world she displays here. Just as she regards only certain elements in Paul's nature as worthy and looks on others as unimportant or even base, so here her reverence is for the blossoms, which she touches 'in worship'. The gesture is significant because night has fallen, hiding the tree itself and leaving only the great, white luminous roses visible, so that they seem to have fallen like 'great spilt stars' from some higher realm, rather than to have grown out of the earth. The bush becomes a visual symbol of that dissociation of the spiritual from its roots in the physical and sensual which is characteristic of Miriam's attitude to both human nature and nature in general; unable to accept that spirituality and beauty, in man or the natural world, originate in forces which frighten and repel her, she thinks of them as having a different origin, in some transcendent sphere of things. Though the relationship of flower to stem and root is obscured by the dusk, the roses have, of course, grown up out of the earth and the grappling roots, just as her 'spirituality' has developed out of the 'lower' elements in her nature.

As Mark Spilka points out, the meaning of the 'communion' between Paul and Miriam is thrown into sharper relief by being juxtaposed with a similar incident a few pages further on in which he is again invited to admire some flowers—this time by his mother, who has discovered some scyllas growing beside the garden fence:

> 'Now, just see those!' she exclaimed. 'I was looking at the currant-bushes, when, thinks I to myself, "There's something very blue; is it a bit of sugar bag?" and there, behold you! Sugar-bag! Three glories of the snow, and *such* beauties! But where on earth did they come from?'
> 'I don't know', said Paul.
> 'Well, that's a marvel, now! I *thought* I knew every weed and blade in this garden. But *haven't* they done well? You see, that gooseberry-bush just shelters them. Not nipped, not touched!'
> He crouched down and turned up the bells of the little blue flowers.
> 'They're a glorious colour!' he said.
> 'Aren't they!' she cried. 'I guess they come from Switzerland, where they say they have such lovely things. Fancy them against the snow! But where have they come from? They can't have *blown* here, can they?'
> Then he remembered having set here a lot of little trash of bulbs to mature.
> 'And you never told me', she said.
> 'No; I thought I'd leave it till they might flower.'
> 'And now, you see! I might have missed them. And I've never had a glory of the snow in my garden in my life.'
> She was full of excitement and elation.
>
> (SL p 203)

As Spilka says 'The vitality, the animation, the healthy glow of the life-flame, is typical of Mrs Morel'[54] and the exuberance of mother and son here forms the sharpest possible contrast to the intense and silent contemplation into which Paul has been drawn by Miriam. It is significant too, that while the girl's interest is focussed on the blossoms, Mrs Morel is eager to know where the flowers have come from; she is interested in the whole cycle of growth and not just in the end product, and her interest is ymptomatic of her recognition that sense and spirit, the 'higher' and 'lower' in life, are interdependent.

And as if in illustration of Nietzsche's reiterated claim that the most beautiful and valuable things in nature derive from and grow out of those which are much less so, the 'glories of the snow' have sprung from 'a lot of little trash of bulbs' which Paul has planted. As a whole the episode serves as a warning against the easy identification of what the two women stand for and tells against the contention that they are direct rivals for Pauls' love, in bitter competition because each wants essentially the same kind of relationship with him. Mrs Morel's sensuous responsiveness is not, after all, inconsistent with her Puritan nature or firmness of moral principle, and she is presented as responding to Morel's physical vitality in a way that Miriam can never bring herself to respond to Paul.

CHAPTER 4

# Consciousness, Language and the Unconscious Self

The activity of our urges in recognising and engaging with what is required for growth proceeds on the unconscious level and accounts for that fluctuating and apparently motiveless pattern of advance and retreat, attraction and aversion, which marks the behavior of Lawrence's major characters at crucial stages of their development. What is reflected in the play of alternating feelings is the sequence of judgements made at a deeper level, where an unconscious power struggle is going on in the psyche. In the struggle, an impulse to seek fresh experience wrestles with a conservative urge to continue engaging with the kind of challenge which, because of its familiarity, can readily be mastered. What we, as subjects, are aware of, on the conscious level, is a mere epiphenomenon of these fundamental processes: to use an illustration from physics which both Lawrence and Nietzsche employ, we see the visible trace of complex unconscious movements, rather as the experimenter using Chladni's apparatus sees how on 'a fine tray, delicately sanded, the sand takes lines unknown' when a fiddle-bow is drawn across the metal. Nietzsche argues that we normally lack any sense of this inner complexity and dynamism because we 'lack any sensitive organs for the inner world' and as a result 'sense a thousandfold complexity as a unity',[2] thinking of our reactions as 'caused' by a single entity, a unitary and stable ego. So for Nietzsche, as for Lawrence, the essential reality of being requires for its detection and articulation 'a deeper sense than any we've been used to exercise',[3] an intuition through which we became aware of the psyche as a complex and dynamic entity, in which the relations between the elements may change, giving rise to new 'allotropes', new dimensions of the personality, as different from one another as diamond is from coal, but still essentially 'states of the same radically unchanged element'.[3] A change in conditions, like that experienced by the Brangwens or Saxtons, will produce a change in character because 'we contain the *sketch* for *many* persons in ourselves ... Circumstances bring out one shape in us: if the circumstances change very much, one also sees two, three shapes in himself'.[4] But however protean the individual transformations may appear to be, we are not free to change in just any sort of way—the basic outline, the sketch which is worked up, is given and unalterable and so only certain shapes are possible. The 'element' remains 'radically unchanged'. As Nietzsche says

> We do not believe that a man will become another if he is not that other already; i.e. if he is not, as is often the case a multiplicity of persons, at least the embryos of persons. In this case, one can bring a different role into the fore-ground ... The aspect is changed, not the essence.[5]

In normal circumstances, the experiencing subject has less awareness and understanding of things than a sensitive outside observer might have, precisely because he is closest to, and most implicated in, his psychic processes. It is this fact which lies behind Lawrence's consistent use of the third-person narrative form and his apparent lack of interest in the more innovative and subjective narrative strategies exploited by writers like Virginia Woolf and James Joyce. Convinced that human development is governed by forces and movements deep in the unconscious, Lawrence employs a narrative voice which, if not omniscient, registers far more, even about self-aware characters like Birkin, than Birkin's own consciousness could do.

The self consists of a group of urges, each of which, as a specialized form of will to power, desires to 'rule' and so the natural state of the psyche is one of constant strife. The attainment of a degree of unity among the struggling urges is a gradual one, the result of the combined action of organic memory and natural selection. Nietzsche sees the firmly integrated personality, in which a large measure of harmony subsists between rulers and ruled as the exception rather than the rule—it is a consequence of fortunate heredity which has created a psychic community ruled by a single enlightened passion which directs and organises the whole. The dominant impulse works, for the most part, unconsciously, directing the individual towards certain kinds of experiences and away from others, in accordance with instinctive judgements about what is useful or harmful for development at a particular stage of growth. Reflecting on his own development, Nietzsche concludes that

> Our distant future destiny rules over us, even when we as yet have no eye open for it; for a long time we experience only riddles. The choice of men and things, the selection of events, the shoving aside of what is most agreeable, often what is most revered—it terrifies us ... but it is the higher reason of our future task. Meantime the organising 'idea' which is called to rule grows and grows in the depths—it begins to command, it leads slowly *back* from by paths and wrong paths, it prepares *single* qualities and abilities which will one day prove themselves indispensable as a means to the whole ... before it lets anything be known of the dominating task.[6]

Nietsche stresses that this complex process of development is best left to unconscious forces, to what he terms 'the higher reason' of the dominant urge. To bring it to consciousness would endanger its successful progress:

The whole surface of consciousness—consciousness *is* a surface—must be kept clear of all great imperatives. Beware even of every great work, every great pose! So many dangers that instinct comes too soon to 'understand itself'.[7]

In *Sons and Lovers*, when Paul Morel realises that his dominant urge may be an artistic one (and even at the age of fourteen he thinks that 'he might make a painter'), he makes no conscious effort to cultivate this tentative sense of vocation:

> he was proud within himself, measuring people against himself and placing them, inexorably. And he thought that *perhaps* he might also make a painter, the real thing. But that he left alone.
>
> (**SL** p 113)

Wisely, Paul leaves the growth of his artistic sensibility to the government of his instincts which, possessing greater intelligence, foresight, and organising capacity than the superficial conscious part of the self, can be trusted to bring his potentialities to fruition. Paul's intuitive faith in the wisdom of the unconscious is shared by his mother, who is confident that he will achieve something of significance precisely *because* he is not aware of the extent of his own capacities; his mother 'had a great belief in him, the more because he was unaware of his own powers'. The confidence in instinct which mother and son share contrasts with Miriam's conviction that consciousness is pre-eminent and her constant stimulation of Paul to further degrees of conscious awareness. Paul himself instinctively recognises the danger such excessive stimulation represents for his healthy growth and it is one of the things which leads him to make the final break with her.

In the integrated individual, the dominant passion does not rule alone but is balanced and complemented by a subsidiary group of impulses which act as a counterweight, preventing it from tyrannising over the psychic community and creating a one-sided and obsessive personality. Nietzsche offers Benvenuto Cellini as an example of this kind of ideally integrated individual in whom

> everything—knowing, desiring, loving, hating—gravitates towards a centre, a root force, and where precisely through the compelling and dominating ascendancy of this living centre there is formed a harmonious system of motions to and fro, up and down.[8]

It is this kind of pattern of growth which is invoked by George Saxton when, in the elegaic 'Poem of friendship' chapter of *The White Peacock*, he tries to explain to Cyril what loss of contact with Lettie will mean for his development:

> 'You see that sycamore', he said 'that bushy one beyond the big willow? I remember when father broke off the leading shoot because he wanted a fine straight stick, I can remember I felt sorry. It was running up so straight, with such a fine balance of leaves—you know how a young strong sycamore looks

about nine feet high—it seemed a cruelty. When you are gone, and we are left from here, I shall feel like that, as if my leading shoot were broken off. You see, the tree is spoiled. Yet how it went on growing. I believe I shall grow faster.'

(**WP** p 293)


Rather as the tree had a main direction of growth which, allowed to proceed, would have created 'a fine balance of leaves', so George has a dominant interest round which the other elements in his nature might be harmoniously organized. The continued development of this central impulse depends on remaining in contact with the more developed Beardsalls, and particularly Lettie, so George predicts that their impending departure will interrupt his growth and distort his subsequent development, in rather the way that his father's action had affected the growth of the young tree. The sycamore has continued to grow vigorously but the removal of its leading shoot has given rise to an unsightly profusion of small branches; despite lacking the stimulus offered by Lettie and Cyril, George does continue to develop rapidly, extending his interests and exploring fresh areas of experience. But his later life has no consistent pattern—it is marked by constant changes of direction as George seeks fulfilment in domesticity, inn-keeping, horse-dealing or politics. In all these diverse activities, George is at first enthusiastic and successful then rapidly and thoroughly disillusioned; like the proliferating shoots of the young tree, the several interests he pursues represent subsidiary directions of growth and the vital centre of his being remains dormant. On his visit to his friend in London, George tells Cyril about his failure to find satisfaction and goes on to suggest that the undeveloped central impulse may have been an artistic one. He links his unrealised impulse to be 'a poet or something' with the idea of shaping and forming the self which Nietzsche stresses in his account of the dominant impulse, saying regretfully 'I ought to have made something of myself'. The attainment of psychic wholeness depends largely on the 'benevolent despotism' exercised by an organising and integrating instinct. Without its regulating influence, 'the antagonism of the passions' in cases where 'two, three, a multiplicity of "souls in one breast"' is 'very unhealthy' and leads to 'inner ruin'.[9] So, lacking a living centre, George rapidly falls victim to the inner disintegration which Nietzsche sees as endangering those in whom the passions are powerful but uncoordinated, and his decline is both reflected in, and accelerated by, his increasingly heavy drinking.'

As Nietzsche's account of his own development makes clear, the process of self-realisation is a difficult one involving the 'shoving aside of what is most agreeable' and even of 'what is most revered'. Despite his emphasis on instinct, Nietzsche does not think of the development of the self as proceeding automatically and effortlessly. He argues, indeed, that the task of creating the self is so forbidding that most people are unable to sustain the effort by themselves and need the support and stimulus of another or others to succeed. Without contact with George, Lettie cannot 'bring forth' the 'flower' which is born in her, while he, on his side, needs her help to develop the artistic impulse which is potentially the strongest force in him.

Nietzsche's ideal pattern of integration is, then, one in which one particular passion exercises an 'enlightened despotism', providing a centre and focus for the entire personality. He associates the gradual evolution of crude and wasteful 'impulse' into subtle and intelligent 'instinct' which this presupposes with just the kind of stability which both Saxtons and Brangwens have experienced over many generations. In such conditions, constant repetition of the same activities allows a steady increase in skill which is embodied and passed on:

> How do men attain great strength and a great task? All the virtues and effi-
> ciency of body and soul are acquired laboriously and little by little, through
> much industry, self-constraint, limitation, through much obstinate, fruitful
> repetition of the same labours, the same renunciations; but there are men who
> are the heirs and masters of this slowly-acquired manifold treasure of virtue
> and efficiency.[10]

This association between a long-established mode of life and the transformation of impulse into instinct means that characters like George Saxton or Tom and Alfred Brangwen are far from representing 'turbulent and anarchic energies'. In fact, each is endowed with a significant degree of instinctive measure and control. When, early in *The White Peacock*, George visits the Beardsalls, the difference between his way of life and theirs is certainly emphasised, but the contrast is not an absolute one, between refinement and crude vitality, organisation and energy, civilized and primitive—it is, rather, one which involves different degrees of order and organisation. Lettie may be 'elegant' but George we are told has also 'a grace of his own' even if it is out of scale with his present surroundings. His vigorous dancing is an expression of the same natural, instinctive grace—like Morel in *Sons and Lovers*, he dances as if it were 'natural and joyous in him' rather than something learned. In Alfred Brangwen in *The Rainbow* the same innate integration and measure is evident in his natural talent for drawing in which the 'big bold lines, rather lax' which his hand traces parallel the large grace George Saxton displays. And Tom Brangwen also has a natural subtlety and sensitivity, though of a rather different kind; at school, 'his feelings were more discriminating than those of most of the boys ... He was more sensuously developed, more refined in instinct than they'. Since they have inherited urges which now embody a considerable degree of 'intelligence' and which together form a potentially integrated self, George, Tom and Alfred have each considerable capacity for development towards creative expression although only the last makes much progress towards his goal. Tom and George are awakened—both become dissatisfied with their present narrow lives and aspire to richer fuller being—but neither can find the support and stimulus needed to complete his development.

Since the fluctuating feelings which flow and recoil to shape our growth are essentially 'embodied' judgements which, given fortunate heredity, represent the accumulated wisdowm of many generations, neither Lawrence nor Nietzsche is, in the strict sense, an irrationalist thinker. Graham Hough's claim that Lawrence's philosophy is a 'non-moral and anti-intellectualist'[11] one, inspired by his own emancipation, through passion, from the restraints and inhibitions implanted by his upbringing, demands considerable qualification. Nietzsche is sometimes thought to have enjoined men to reject morality and live 'beyond good and evil', but what he in fact recommends is the adoption of a contrasting kind of morality, of which the poles are 'good' and 'bad'.

The Nietzschean analysis of contemporary morality is complex, but essentially he rejects the claim of any morality to be true (as the Christian moral code claims to be true) for any time, place, or person and suggests instead that our judgements of right and wrong should take account of all the individual circumstances of the act. In place of an absolute morality we should put one that is dynamic, personal and situational. In such a scheme, the worth of an action would not be judged by how it fitted in to some pre-existing ethical framework, but on what sort of person performed it and whether it expressed and added to vitality, or testified to diminished energies, or disintegrative and destructive ones. Like Nietzsche, Lawrence rejects the idea of a single, invariable ethical framework, valid for all judgements of value, linking the idea of a 'certain moral scheme'[12] with a stability and consistency which is fundamentally false to the dynamism of natural life. And such rigid schemata are associated with the simplifying activities of the conscious mind, which can turn against the unpredictable life-flow and attempt to impose its own crude and inflexible order on it. So if both Lawrence and Nietzsche are critical of the moral (and intellectual) conclusions arrived at by the conscious mind this is not because they feel that reason ought to be defied or violated, but because they believe that the 'feelings' which in normal circumstances direct our lives are often the expression of a more comprehensive, though unconscious, intelligence.

In his celebrated letter to Ernest Collings which, in the words of Harry T. Moore, 'contains the first full statement of [his] "blood-knowledge" philosophy',[13] Lawrence declares his faith in the intelligence of the 'flesh', the physical self—

> My great religion is a belief in the blood, the flesh, as being wiser than the intellect. We can go wrong in our minds. But what our blood feels and believes and says, is always true.[14]

Here the contrast is not one between rational intellect and irrational impulse, but between the comparatively shallow and fallible intelligence of the conscious mind and the profounder 'wisdom' of the unconscious. Since we 'lack any sensitive organs' for the complexities of inner experience we are more likely to arrive at an understanding of this wisdom through observing physical, behavioural facts than through introspection—although both Lawrence and Nietzsche accept that some exceptional individuals have in developed form 'a deeper sense than any we've been used to exercise' which allows them more direct access to profounder levels of being. Nevertheless, it is largely through 'external phenomenology' that we are appraised of 'an activity which would have to be ascribed to a far higher and more comprehensive intellect than we know of';[15] using this method, even these things in human experience which seem to be random or chance occurences, which have nothing to do with conscious motive or deliberate action, are seen to be the consequences of unconscious motives and choices and to reveal more about the essential being of an individual than the kinds of evidence usually regarded as important.

Early in *Women in Love* we learn that when Gerald Crich was a boy, he killed his brother in an accident with a shotgun. Ursula remembers the story of the tragedy while discussing Gerald with her sister after the pair have seen him swimming in a local lake and, significantly, the recollection is not directly prompted by anything that has been said, but seems to come into Ursula's mind in an accidental and unmotivated way. The sisters have been discussing Crich's abundant energy and puzzling about its direction, but Ursula does not consciously offer the shooting as evidence that it is directed towards destruction—it is clear however that on the subconscious level, she has seen the significance of the 'accident' and recognised its evidential value for the problem they are considering. There is no suggestion that Gerald had any conscious intention to kill, but Ursula argues—convincingly one feels—that even allowing for youth and ignorance, no one with sound instincts would be able to point even an empty gun at someone else and pull the trigger. In other words, actions are a more reliable guide to fundamental impulses than any conscious motive (or absence of motive) and the incident demonstrates that Gerald has a powerful *unconscious* will to destruction. Things like his organisation of the mines later in the story indicate that Ursula's intuition was sound:

> As soon as Gerald entered the firm the convulsion of death ran through the old system. He had all his life been tortured by a furious and destructive demon, which possessed him sometimes like an insanity. This temper now entered like a virus into the firm, and there were cruel eruptions. Terrible and inhuman were his examinations into every detail: there was no privacy he would spare, no old sentiment but he would turn it over.
>
> (**WL** p 257)

And when he has destroyed the old system, Gerald goes on to establish a new industrial regime which, in its exclusion of the human element, actually embodies his will to destruction. In the original conversation, Gudrun had sharply rejected the suggestion that Gerald was responsible—if unconsciously—for his brother's death: the vigour of her denial not only reflects her growing, though largely unrecognised, interest in him, but also, more generally, her deep instinctive fear at the suggestion that our 'accidental' actions have meaning. Her resistance is the resistance of someone who is afraid that if their own actions were judged in this way their inner destructiveness would become evident.

Ursula's tentative conclusion about the importance of unconscious as against conscious motives in accounting for actions is anticipated by Birkin in the second chapter of the novel. Attending a wedding party at the Crich mansion, Shortlands, Birkin remembers the story of the shooting and speculates on the significance of such 'accidental' events. His conclusions are similar to Ursula's; beginning in the same tentative way, as if he finds it difficult to break with our ordinary habit of emphasising conscious intention, he arrives at the same verdict, although he expresses it more firmly than she does:

> There was such a thing as pure accident, and the consequences did not attach to one, even though one had killed one's brother in such wise. Gerald as a boy had accidentally killed his brother. What then? Why seek to draw a brand and a curse across the life that had caused the accident. A man can live by accident, and die by accident. Or can he not? ... Or is this not true, is there no such thing as pure accident? Has *everthing* that happens a universal significance?
> He did not believe that there was any such thing as accident. It all hung together in the deepest sense.
>
> (**WL** p 28)

It is not only in such obviously portentous events that unconscious motives are involved; later when Birkin breaches etiquette at the wedding reception by driking his champagne before the toasts begin—a breach of decorum reminiscent of the earlier incident where the bridegroom pursues the bride outside the church—he considers whether his action is deliberate or not and decides that 'according to the vulgar phrase, he had done it "accidentally on purpose".' The phrase expresses a piece of folk-wisdom, a traditional recognition that it is possible for things which appear to be accidental to be, in some deep sense, purposeful and deliberate.

In his autobiography, *Ecco Homo*, Nietzsche had remarked on the order and purpose retrospectively apparent even in the apparently trivial or accidental events in his own life and had seen this as evidence that his development had been directed by an intelligence more far-sighted and profound than that consciously at work. In *The Will to Power*, he expresses the same idea in more general terms in a note on the 'Theory of Chance' in which he suggests that the things which seem simply chance occurrences, in which no conscious choice is present, are caused by unconscious forces and show that the 'soul'—a term both Lawrence and Nietzsche use for the ruling group of impulses—is 'a selective and self-nourishing entity, perpetually extremely shrewd and creative'.[16] As a result of insights like these we are compelled to revise our attitude to the conscious self which can no longer be seen as the centre and focus of being and cause of all significant action:

> We learn to think less highly of all that is conscious; we unlearn responsibility for ourselves, since we as conscious, purposive creatures, are only the smallest part of us.[17]

As a corollary of this, we realise that 'What one used to call "body" and "flesh" is of such unspeakably greater importance: the remainder is a small accessory'.[18]

Because of the primacy of the physical and the inadequacy of the 'inner sense' as a reflector of its activity, for Nietzsche what someone says or consciously believes about themselves is usually a less reliable guide to fundamental impulses and values than apparently inconsequential details of appearance or behaviour. Such an emphasis creates problems for the writer, and in particular for the novelist, because it implies that many of the conventional techniques for revealing character are of limited utility; the novelist who adopts a Nietzschean perspective and strives to explore and express, as Lawrence did, the 'dark presence of the otherness that lies behind man's conscious mind' is compelled to modify traditional forms and develop new ones so as to render 'this immediately perceived otherness in terms of conscious literary art'.[19]

Early in the 'Strife in Love' chapter of *Sons and Lovers*, Paul Morel complains to Miriam that she somehow forces him to be intense and serious whenever he is with her. She replies that she does not consciously intend to do so—

> 'Oh, you make me knit the brows of my very soul and cogitate.' Slowly she shook her head despairingly.
> 'I'm sure I don't want to,' she said.
> 'I'm so damned spiritual with *you* always,' he cried.
> She remained silent thinking, 'Then why don't you be otherwise?'
> But he saw her crouching brooding figure, and it seemed to tear him in two.
> **(SL** p 232)

Miriam does not consciously set out force Paul to be 'spiritual' when he is with her and even seems prepared to accept a different sort of relationship with him so that, on the face of it this seems to be one of the several places in the story where, in the words of Louis Martz, the portrait of Miriam that 'lies behind the overpainted commentary of the Paul-narrator'[20] is momentarily visible. Martz argues that details like this reveal the essential normality of Miriam's love and indicate that the difficulties in the relationship are due not to her life-denying idealism, but to the unnatural character of the bond between Paul and his mother. Such a reading of the scene, and other similar scenes, depends on two related, but—in the context of Lawrence's fiction—mistaken assumptions: that actions are caused by conscious motives and that introspection is a source of accurate information about determining attitudes and values. In fact, what Miriam herself believes about the nature of her feelings is contradicted—as the use of 'but' suggests—by the more reliable physical evidence of bearing and posture. Her 'crouching, brooding figure' communicates to Paul an instinctive depreciation of the body which is more fundamental than her conscious 'acceptance' of it and this revives the conflict of feeling in him. Deeply influenced by her mother's religious idealism and revulsion from the physical and sexual, Miriam is full of 'self-mistrust', deeply suspicious of her own spontaneous feelings and of the promptings of her physical nature. Her attitudes are reflected in the tense 'clenched' manner in which she habitually moves—as if she felt it necessary to keep her body under rigid control—and in the way in which she always seems to be trying to diminish herself physically so that she is almost invariably described as 'bowed' or 'crouched'. The systematic repression of the physical which her ascetic outlook imposes sets up a psychic conflict which is a constant source of inner discomfort and, as a result, she is never able to feel whole-heartedly joyous. Paul links her fundamental physical traits with this inability when, earlier in the same scene, he askes her—

> 'If you put red berries in your hair ... why would you look like some witch or priestess and never like a reveller?'
>
> (SL p 231)

Even festively adorned, Miriam's physical appearance would still express her fundamental solemnity and 'spirituality'. And Paul goes on to claim that even her laughter is not the expression of real gladness but rather something which springs from and reflects the inner discomfort created by her 'self-mistrust':

> 'Why can't you laugh?' he said. 'You never laugh laughter. You only laugh when something is odd or incongruous and then it almost seems to hurt you.'
>   She bowed her head as if he were scolding her.
>   'I wish you could laugh at me just for one minute—just for one minute. I feel as if it would set something free.'
>   'But'—and she looked up at him with eyes frightened and struggling—'I do laugh at you—I *do*.!
>   'Never! There's always a kind of intensity. When you laugh I could always cry; it seems as if it shows up your suffering.'
>
> (SL p 232)

Paul is particularly sensitive to the kind of physical evidence Nietzsche associates with 'external phenomenology' because, as his talent for painting shows, he posseses unusual sharpness of perception and, as a result, he is constantly made aware of the nature of Miriam's unconscious feelings through the involuntary physical 'symptoms' she displays. In a later scene between the pair, he himself states directly what the episode just discussed seems to imply, claiming that Miriam *unconsciously* demands that he should always be 'spiritual' with her. Paul has been 'urged to an intensity like madness' by her desire 'to draw all of him into her' (a phrase which reflects how will to power acts as much on the high spiritual or intellectual plane as in the simpler physical one) and he exhausts himself in intellectual activity:

> He was discussing Michael Angelo. It felt to her as if she was fingering the very quivering tissue, the very protoplasm of life, as she heard him. It gave her her deepest satisfaction. And in the end it frightened her. There he lay in the white intensity of his search, and his voice gradually filled her with fear, so loud it was, almost inhuman, as if in a trance.
>
> (SL p 239)

Disturbed by his state, Miriam urges him to stop talking, only to be told that she is responsible for what is happening—

'. . . you always make me like it,' he said.

'I don't wish to,' she said, very low.

'Not when you've gone too far, and you feel you can't bear it. But your unconscious self always asks it of me.'

(**SL** p 239)

The narrative supports Paul's claim because it is indeed in the contact with his 'white intensity' that she finds her deepest satisfaction, seeing in intellectual activity 'the very quivering tissue, the very proplasm of life'—an image which makes it clear that while Miriam thinks of the life of ideas as primary and central to existence, it is the physical which really occupies that place.

Paul first complains to Miriam about the effect she has on him soon after his first meeting with Clara Dawes, because it is that encounter which brings to a head his dissatisfaction with the 'blanched and chaste' intimacy he shares with the younger woman. Paul detects in Clara an acceptance of the body and the senses which is the antithesis of Miriam's idealism and as a result he becomes aware of the possibility of a different, less physically inhibited kind of relationship. As with Miriam, Clara's fundamental impulses are expressed not in what she says, or even what she thinks, about her feelings, but by apparently involuntary physical things, so despite the fact that she is dintinctly uncommunicative on their first meeting, Paul is able to arrive at an estimate of her character which later experience will show to be accurate. When they discuss Mrs Dawes later, he surprises Miriam by the confidence with which he pronounces on the older woman's personality. On the basis of one brief, and on the face of it, unhelpful meeting, he seems to be claiming to know Clara better than her friend Miriam does. She, on her side is naturally skeptical about his assertions and asks him for his evidence. His response is to invoke involuntary, physical facts. Evidently his conclusions have been shaped by his observation of details of Clara's appearance and bearing. He asks whether Clara is disagreeable and Miriam replies:

'I don't think so. I think she's dissatisfied.'

'What with?'

'Well—how would *you* like to be tied for life to a man like that?'

'Why did she marry him, them, if she was to have revulsions so soon? . . . And I would have thought she had enough fight in her to match him,' he said.

'Ay?' she queried satirically. 'What makes you think so?'

'Look at her mouth—made for passion—and the very set-back of her throat . . .' He threw his head back in Clara's defiant manner.

(**SL** pp 230-1)

Meeting the two women in Nottingham, Paul had immediately noticed the contrast in bearing:

One day, as he was going up Castle Gate, he met Miriam. He had seen her on the Sunday, and had not expected to meet her in town. She was walking with a rather striking woman, blond, with a sullen expression, and a defiant carriage.

> It was strange how Miriam in her bowed, meditative bearing, looked dwarfed
> beside this woman with the handsome shoulders.
>
> (SL p 227)

Miriam's hostility to the body and the senses is reflected in her physically self-
effacing carriage and so she appears 'dwarfed' by the other woman who
walks with a defiant and assertive bearing which reflects her pride in her
physical self.

The superiority of external phenomenology to inner sense, which allows
Paul to recognise motives and impulses in Miriam of which she herself is
not aware, is also strikingly illustrated in the contrast between his confident
conclusions about Clara and what Clara herself imagines are her real feelings. As with Miriam, conscious introspective awareness is superficial and
misleading, giving a less reliable picture of the self than the involuntary
physical symptoms observed by others. Disappointed in her marriage, Clara
has left her husband and believes that she has rejected the entire male sex,
but from her first appearance in the novel it is clear that there is a conflict
in her between her superficial conscious contempt for men and her strongly
passionate nature:

> She had scornful grey eyes, a skin like white honey, and a full mouth, with a
> slightly lifted upper lip that did not know whether it was raised in scorn of all
> men or out of eagerness to be kissed, but which believed the former.
>
> (SL p 228)

And when Paul meets her later at Willey Farm, the same kind of ambiguity
is apparent in her greeting:

> To shake hands she lifted her arm straight, in a manner that seemed at one to
> keep him at a distance, and yet to fling something to him.
>
> (SL pp 281–2)

Because he is able to interpret the physical evidence, Paul concludes that
Clara has a passion and sensuality which are more fundamental than her conscious rejection of men, and in conversation with Miriam's brother Edgar
about the visitor he underlines the contrast between conscious and unconscious attitudes he has detected in her Edgar asks—

> 'You think she's a man-hater?'
> '*She* thinks she is,' replied Paul.
> 'But you don't think so?'
> 'No,' replied Paul.
>
> (SL p 284)

Ironically, at the beginning of his association with Clara, Paul misunderstands his own feelings in rather the same way. Although the real nature of
his interest in her is unambiguously expressed in things like the way in which
he looks at her and so is quite evident to the girls at Jordans and to Clara

herself, their relationship develops at first without concealment because all the women recognise that Paul is not aware of the true state of his feelings—

> The other girls noticed that when Paul met Mrs Dawes his eyes lifted and gave that peculiar bright greeting which they could interpret. Knowing he was unaware, Clara made no sign, save that occasionally she turned aside her face from him when he came upon her.
> They walked out together very often at dinner-time; it was quite open, quite frank. Everybody seemed to feel that he was quite unaware of the state of his own feeling, and that nothing was wrong.
>
> **(SL** p 334)

Paul's conscious attitude is summed up a page or two later:

> ... she was a married woman, and he believed in simple friendship. And he considered that he was perfectly honourable with regard to her. It was only friendship between man and woman, such as any civilized persons might have.
>
> **(SL** p 337)

'Considered' suggests that Paul is mistaken about the nature of his interest and it is noticeable that if in the early stages of their intimacy, the new relationship resembles the old—Paul talks to Clara at first 'with some of the old fervour with which he talked to Miriam'—intellectual exchange is now less important to him and so 'he cared less about the talk; he did not bother about his conclusions'. Clearly his interest in Clara is—at the deepest level—of a different kind from his interest in Miriam.

The same kind of pattern had earlier been evident in the relationship between Paul and Miriam itself. At first neither had acknowledged that love was developing between them, but their conscious understanding of themselves is described in a way which indicates that it is superficial and mistaken—

> That there was any love growing between him and Miriam neither of them would have acknowledged. He thought he was too sane for such sentimentality, and she thought herself too lofty. They were both late in coming to maturity, and psychical ripeness was much behind even the physical.
>
> **(SL** p 201)

But clearly love is growing, if in an unacknowledged way, between the pair and the confidence both feel in their immunity to it is misplaced. The final sentence links their misunderstanding of themselves with the fact that in both, physical and psychic development are out of step, with the former more advanced than the latter. This situation suggests the Nietzschean conception of the conscious part of the psyche as an agent of the 'flesh', the more extensive, powerful and dynamic physical self, so that physical change is normally primary, preceding and accounting for psychic change. It is Miriam who first comes to psychic ripeness and recognises the real nature of her feelings for Paul. She first becomes aware that she wants him physically when challenged by her worldly sister Agatha, but from the beginning her desire is complicated by the profound sense of guilt and shame engendered by her religious upbringing and she does her best to repress it. At the same time she realises that for all his conscious rejection of the idea, Paul is unwittingly coming to love her. As in the later relationship, the true nature of his feelings is apparent not only to the woman concerned but also to the couple's friends and acquaintances. Again the judgement of those not directly involved, based on involuntary and physical evidence, is more reliable than Paul's view of his own state:

> He would not have it that they were lovers. The intimacy between them had been kept so abstract, such a matter of the soul, all thought and weary struggle into consciousness, that he saw it only as a platonic friendship. He stoutly denied there was anything else between them. Miriam was silent, or else she very quietly agreed. He was a fool who did not know what was happening to himself; by tacit agreement they ignored the remarks and insinuations of their acquaintances.
>
> 'We aren't lovers, we are friends,' he said to her '*We* know it. Let them talk. What does it matter what they say?'
>
> (**SL** p 213)

Clearly Lawrence believes, like Nietzsche, that conscious awareness is derivative, simplifying and fallible, that it is 'a more or less fantastic commentary on an unknown text, one which is perhaps unknowable, but yet felt'. The existence of such an apparently superfluous capacity presents a problem for the German philosopher who constantly emphasises in a Lamarkian way, the part played by need in the creation and development of vital functions—

> The problem of consciousness (more precisely, of becoming conscious of something) confronts us only when we begin to comprehend how we could dispense with it ... For we could think, feel, will, and remember, and we could also 'act' in every sense of that word, and yet none of all this would have to 'enter our consciousness' ... The whole of our life would be possible without, as it were, seeing itself in a mirror. Even now, for that matter, by far the greatest portion of our life actually takes place without this mirror effect; and this is true even of our thinking, feeling and willing life, however offensive this may sound to older philosophers. *For what purpose*, then, any consciousness at all when it is in the main superfluous.[21]

Nietzsche concludes that 'it is our relation with the "outer world" that evolved it'—

> ... it is evolved through social intercourse and with a view to the interests of social intercourse—'Intercourse' here understood to include the influences of the outer world and the reactions they compel on our side; also our effect upon the outer world.[22]

It is because it has grown up in this way that consciousness registers 'outer' experience far more fully and accurately than 'inner' events. The conscious mind has developed because of our need to recognise and relate to the things and people around us and the most important part of what goes on inside us normally does not enter consciousness at all—'the direction or protection and care in respect of the co-ordination of the bodily does *not* enter our consciousness'.[23] In his 1913 letter to Ernest Collings, Lawrence associates the conscious intellect with the world around us in just this way, emphasising at the same time the mystery and fascination of the 'body', the physical self, of which intellect is an emanation—

> I conceive a man's body as a kind of flame, like a candle flame, forever upright and yet flowing: and the intellect is just the light that is shed on to the things around. And I am not so much concerned with the things around—which is really mind—but with the mystery of the flame forever flaring, coming God knows how from out of practically nowhere, and being *itself*, whatever there is around it, that it lights up.[24]

If self awareness involves a kind of internal mirroring in which inner events are only partially and selectively reflected, then the common belief that 'thoughts as they succeed one another in our mind stand in some kind of causal relation'[25] must be rejected. We have to realise, in fact, that everying we become conscious of in ourselves, whether thoughts or feelings 'is a terminal phenomenon, an end—and causes nothing; every successive phenomenon in consciousness is completely atomistic'.[26] The sequence of conscious states is discontinuous, marked by sudden transitions and reversals of a kind familiar in Lawrence's fiction; one allotropic state succeeds another, sometimes involving a change as radical as that from diamond to graphite. In the often-quoted letter to Garnett, Lawrence tries to explain his reasons for abandoning in the surface consistency and gradual, logical and progressive change we usually expect fictional characters to show, using the 'allotrope' analogy to argue that such apparently abrupt and 'illogical' movements are more accurate representations of the way in which human beings actually behave. This is not to say that we have no distinct identity, simply that the 'carbon' of which we are composed, the 'single radically unchanged element' which is our true individuality lies far below the conscious level and it would take 'a deeper sense than any we've been used to exercise' to explore it.

The development of conscious awareness is closely linked with the genesis of language—indeed Nietzsche insists that 'we think only in the form of language'—and language is a social product created by man's circumstances. Man's complexity made him an extremely vulnerable creature, and so he needed to communicate with those around him:

> Consciousness has developed only under the pressure of the need for communication; that from the start it was needed and useful only between human beings ... and that it also developed only in proportion to the degree of this

utility. Consciousness is really only a net of communication between human beings ... that our actions, thoughts, feelings and movements enter our own consciousness—at least a part of them—that is the result of a 'must' that for a terribly long time lorded it over man. As the most endangered animal, he *needed* help and protection, he needed his peers, he had to learn to express his distress and to make himself understood: and for all of this he needed 'consciousness' first of all, he needed to know himself what distressed him, he needed to 'know' how he felt, he needed to 'know' what he thought. For, to say it once more: the thinking that rises to *consciousness* is only the smallest part of all this—the most superficial and worst part—for only this conscious thinking takes the form of words, which is to say signs of communication ...

In brief, the development of language and the development of consciousness—go hand in hand ... It was only as a social animal that man acquired self-consciousness.[27]

Consciousness is not the centre of being then, but an instrument of the greater inscrutable purposes of the unconscious self. Because of their social origins, both consciousness and language are generalising, simplifying functions which do not 'really belong to man's individual existence but rather to his social or herd nature' and it follows from this that they have 'developed subtlety only insofar as this is required by social or herd utility'.[28] So neither is capable of adequately reflecting what is distinctive in us and 'Fundamentally all our actions are altogether incomparably personal, unique and infinitely individual ... [though] as soon as we translate them into consciousness *they no longer seem to be*'.[29]

The inability of language to cope with characteristics unique to a particular person is brought out very clearly in *The Trespasser* when Siegmund, realising he does not fully understand Helena concludes that 'She can't translate herself into language. She is incommunicable; she can't render herself to the intelligence. So she is alone and a law unto herself'. Language and conscious awareness are linked and the social—therefore generalising and simplifying nature of both is seen as condemning those who are genuinely individual to ultimate isolation. In his mature works, Nietzsche takes a pessimistic view of human potentialities (in early essays like 'Schopenhauer as Educator' he had been more hopeful, arguing that everyone is at least potentially unique) and he thinks of the small number of real individuals as cut off from the great mass of their fellows by the distinctiveness of their experience and the consequent inability of ordinary language to transmit it. Since language has developed because human vulnerability makes communication necessary, the true individual is more vulnerable because of his isolation than those whose experience is routine and commonplace; this is the reason for Nietzsche's curious insistence that in human societies, exceptionally, it is the 'unfit' rather than the 'fit' who flourish. Expressed in less provocative terms, this simply means that because they are able to understand and help one another, the unexceptional are more successful than their vital superiors.

Like Nietzsche, Lawrence moved from relative optimism about human possibilities in his early work to a much bleaker and more pessimistic view in the aftermath of the Great War. *The Rainbow* ends with Ursula's vision of industrial society regenerated, transformed into a real human community. During her convalescence after losing Skrebensky's child, she looks from her bedroom window into one of the dingy streets of the small industrial town where she lives with her parents. There she sees the people of the district—housewives, miners, schoolchildren—and these quite ordinary individuals become the inspiration for a Blakean vision of individual and communal regeneration in which the inhabitants of the contemporary industrial world are transformed into free, fulfilled and joyful beings:

> As she sat at her window, she saw the people go by in the street below, colliers, women, children, walking each in the husk of an old fruition, but visible through the husk, the swelling and the heaving contour of the new germination.
>
> (**R** p 494)

She has already used the same image to describe her own development, seeing herself as 'the naked clear kernel thrusting forth the clear, powerful shoot', and the 'smoky landscape' around as 'all husk and shell lying by'. The emancipated and self-aware heroine is not fundamentally different from the ordinary people around her, just more developed than they are. Ursula does not belong to a privileged, specially-endowed elite, an aristocracy of the spirit, but is simply further on in the direction of a new phase of living than the majority. And Lawrence's choice of ordinary working people as the inspiration for her vision is deliberate, reflecting that sympathy for some aspects of socialism which he felt early in his career. So the vision is a general and democratic one, foreseeing the transformation of society as a whole. Underneath the hard shell created by modern urban and industrial conditions, the fluid, changeable organic life survives and will grow, until, with the irrestible force of a plant pushing aside formidable obstacles to reach the light, it breaks through the unliving carapace of the old form. The metaphor of the growing seed inside the hard outer casing is a characteristic Lawrencian one; it indicates that the process is both inevitable and unwilled—that conscious and deliberate action play no part in the change, which will be brought about in us by forces which we share with all living and growing things. It suggests too, that the fundamental vitality and capacity for creative growth which most people possess has not been damaged in any fundamental way by the tyranny of the machine and the ugliness of contemporary life: the hard, distorted shell is just a shell and what lies underneath is essentially healthy.

In contrast, in *Women in Love*, Birkin and Ursula seem to be the only characters capable of new growth; the rest of British society is either corrupt, like the bohemian artists and intellectuals of the Cafe Pompadour or conformist like the young working-calss couple Birkin and Ursula meet in a street market in the chapter entitled 'Chair'. The couple represent the semi-educated urban masses who with the advent of political democracy are able to shape the social order; they are the 'meek' who have inherited the earth and although they are not presented in a wholly hostile way, Birkin sees them as having a social rather than an individual identity in contrast to the 'proud' few. Imitative and gregarious, they will create a society in which there can be no significant social role for the exceptional individual, who will become marginal and irrelevant. Disturbed by Birkin's prediction that those like the young couple, the 'children of men', as he calls them (recalling his own contrasting designation as a 'son of god'), Ursula asks what place is left for them:

> 'Then what are we going to do?' she asked. 'We're not like them, are we? We're not the meek?'
> 'No. We've got to live in the chinks they leave us.'
> 'How horrible!' cried Ursula. 'I don't want to live in chinks.'
> 'Don't worry,' he said. 'They are the children of men, they like market-places and street-corners best. That leaves plenty of chinks.'

> (**WL** p 407)

The unindividual, the 'unfit' in Nietzsche's sense, have triumphed politically, finally displacing the 'fit', the genuinely individual, from whatever residual influence they exerted in society. The confidence Lawrence expressed in *The Rainbow* in the capacity of ordinary men and women to participate in a new creative life has vanished and in its place is a much bleaker vision which sees the majority as incapable of achieving individual being. It was the Great War which made him adopt a more pessimistic view of contemporary humanity and the change is reflected in the elitism of *Women in Love* and the vision of an authoritarian, corporatist social organisation expressed in *Aaron's Rod*, *Kangaroo* and *The Plumed Serpent*.

Helena in *The Trespasser* is a member of the small group of true individuals and so is an isolated, alien figure in a world composed of these who are more ordinary. When the lovers are travelling back to London by train after their holiday, their compartment is invaded by eight large German tourists. Siegmund sees Helena's situation at this point—she is squeezed uncomfortably into a corner of the compartment, surrounded by people talking a language she cannot understand—as a kind of epitome of her life as a whole. Solitary and fastidious, she must live in a world largely populated by people with whom she has nothing in common, constantly and inevitably exposed to discomfort, inconvenience and misunderstanding. The fact that their fellow travellers are foreign serves to underline the fact that it is Helena whom Siegmund sees as the alien. Foreign-ness in the oridinary sense is of less significance than her incommunicable individuality. Her inability to follow the rapid, colloquial German of her companions dramatises her inability to understand or communicate with her fellows and at the same time the sheer volubility of the tourists is stressed, together with the fact that they all seem to share the same attitudes and opinions, and act as a group rather than separate individuals:

> The whole party began to talk in German with great animation. They told each other of the quaint ways of this or the other ... they questioned each other, and answered each other concerning the places they were going to see ... They were pleased with everying; they extolled things English.

> (**Tr** p 131)

As the passage suggests, language reflects the routine responses of the majority and so is an alien medium for Helena whose distinctive selfhood cannot be expressed through it. As a result she seems to Siegmund like 'a member of an unknown race that can never tell its own story' and he realises that 'he knew nothing of ... her real inner life. She has a book written in characters unintelligible to him and to everybody'. Nor will further contact between them bring fuller understanding—'There was something in her he could never understand ...'

Helena's situation illustrates Nietzsche's idea that though the exceptional are more isolated and vulnerable than the majority, this very fact can lead them to acquire great strength. The events in the train have made Siegmund sharply aware of Helena's inescapable isolation and he begins to worry about her ability to face an uncomprehending world alone (he has already decided to kill himself, although the decision has been subconscious), asking himself

> what would become of her when he had left her, when she was alone, little foreigner as she was, in this world ... Helena would be left behind; death was no way for her. She could not escape thus with him from his house of strangers she called 'life'. She had to go on alone, like a foreigner who cannot learn the strange language.
>
> (Tr p 132)

However we are made aware that this view of Helena is a one-sided one; she is certainly sensitive, vulnerable and isolated, but she also possesses unusual strength—'She was very small. Her quiet ways, and sometimes her impetuous clinging made her seem small; for she was very strong. But Siegmund saw her now, small, quiet ...' The involuntary 'evidence' offered by the physical self, rather than the 'knowledge which comes from apparently more intimate sources, is the best guide to what is fundamental in the personality.

Closely linked with conscious awareness, language normally shares its shallow and derivative character, and in Lawrence's work what is said is no more reliable as a guide to a character's real values and inclinations than what is consciously felt or thought. Miriam's physical attributes reveal more about her deepest feelings than what she herself believes and says about them; during her affair with Paul, when Clara wants to find out what is troubling him, she does not begin by asking him how he feels, but attends instead to seemingly trivial features of his behaviour, aware that she is likely to learn more from these than from anything he might say:

> One evening they were walking down by the canal, and something was troubling him. She knew she had not got him. All the time he whistled softly and persistently to himself. She listened, feeling she could learn more from his whistling than from his speech. It was a sad dissatisfied tune— a tune that made her feel he would not stay with her.
>
> (SL p 428)

The value of the kind of evidence on which Clara relies here is suggested by things like the contrast described earlier in the novel between Paul's conscious scorn for the music of the sea-side minstrels and the fact that he nevertheless 'knew all their songs, and sang them along the roads roisterously'. The occasion is the holiday at Mablethorpe described at the end of the 'Lad-and Girl Love' chapter. There, while the rest of the family go off to the 'Coons', Paul and Miriam who feel that the entertainment is 'insufferably stupid' stay behind at the holiday cottage. The judgement is Miriam's and reflects the fact that in her idealistic creed, only the conscious and intellectual is accounted valuable; she despises the minstrels' music because it is wholly unintellectual, appealing simply and directly to the senses. Paul thinks he agrees with her, but his belief illustrates the fallibility of introspective awareness, because other kinds of evidence make it abundantly clear that on another and deeper level of being, he responds enthusiastically to the immediate, sensuous quality of the music:

> Coons were insufferably stupid to Miriam, so he thought they were to himself also, and he preached priggishly to Annie about the fatuity of listening to them. Yet he, too, knew all their songs, and sang them along the roads roisterously. And if he found himself listening, the stupidity pleased him very much. Yet to Annie he said: 'Such rot! there in't a grain of intelligence in it. Nobody with more gumption than a grasshopper could go and sit and listen.'
>
> (**SL** p 219)

The episode is one of several which illustrate how Miriam's influence makes Paul priggish and censorious, encouraging in him a contempt for oridinary physical interests and pleasures which he does not naturally and spontaneously feel. And the fact that the rest of the family enjoy the minstrels underlines the fact that his conscious attitude is alien to his real nature. In the later scene with Clara, there is no such opposition between conscious and unconscious, and what Paul says confirms what Clara has learned from his whistling:

> She walked on in silence. When they came to the swing bridge he sat down on the great pole, looking at the stars in the water. He was a long way from her. She had been thinking.
> 'Will you always stay at Jordan's?' she asked.
> 'No,' he answered without reflecting. 'No; I s'll leave Nottingham and go abroad—soon.'
> 'Go abroad! What for?'
> 'I dunno! I feel restless.'
>
> (**SL** p 428)

Clara has sensed that Paul is dissatisfied with his present circumstances and wants to change them. He answers her 'without reflecting' so his words are not associated with the unreliable workings of the 'inner sense' and the process of mirroring which it involves but, exceptionally, come directly from the subsonscious and reveal what is going on at that level, confirming rather than contradicting the other physical signs Clara has picked up. Paul himself can offer no rational explanation for the sudden desire to go abroad, because the inclination does not originate in consciousness—instead it is the expression of an unconscious judgement that at this stage of his growth, his experience should be extended and new challenges sought. Essentially the desire to travel is the expression of a desire to seek larger 'resistances' in the interests of gaining greater 'power'. It is the clash between this powerful impulse to break with the familiar and his equally strong love for his mother which is the source of Paul's present trouble. And although he is not fully aware of the reasons for his frustration and discomfort, what he says to Clara indicates clearly enough to the reader what lies behind his present predicament. While he feels that the urge to extend his experience cannot be denied, he recognises that so long as his mother remains alive any escape from a familiar—and now limiting—situation can only be temporary; he says 'I shall hardly go for long, while there's my mother.'

As this example suggests, in Lawrence's writing what is said is generally most revealing when least premeditated. It is therefore not possible to argue in connection with things like the harsh words Paul uses to Miriam in the difficult late stages of their relationship, that a character's unconsidered words can be discounted because they do not represent his real feelings. Discussing the episode in the 'Defeat of Miriam' chapter in which Paul criticises the girl for the way she responds to the daffodils in the farm garden, Stephen Miko says

> Mrs Van Ghent has described Miriam's attitude in this scene as one of 'blasphemous possessorship', interpreting Paul's accusation that Miriam wants only to absorb as Lawrence's accusation as well. There is certainly some force in this view, especially when we remember that, whatever his difficulties, Lawrence resisted through his first two novels attitudes regarding nature as a possession. Miriam's lavish fondling, her fervent kisses, her swaying and stroking are all a bit disgusting, and this heavy quality, reminiscent of Helena and strongly foreshadowing Hermione in *Women in Love*, cannot be altogether dismissed as an expression of Paul's point of view. But at the same time his responses are excessive and petulant, and we are told that his 'fretted soul' has caused him to speak without 'the faintest notion of what he was saying'.[30]

Lawrence does emphasise strongly that Paul's words are not deliberate and calculated, telling us that 'He scarcely knew what he was saying. These things came from him mechanically ... He had not the faintest notion of what he was saying'; his words came from his 'fretted tortured soul run hot by thwarted passion' which 'jetted off these sayings like sparks from electricity'. But, as in the previous case, the fact that what is said does not originate in the consciousness makes it more, not less, significant. Paul's angry words rise directly from the unconscious self, the 'soul' and express the turmoil created in it by 'thwarted passion'. And here too physical and verbal evidence are in agreement because the hostility in Paul's words is matched by the hostility expressed by his body which appears to Miriam like 'one weapon, firm and hard against her'. The unconscious conflict which Paul is suffering is created by Miriam's constant, though subconscious, demand that he should always be 'spiritual' when he is with her. As a result of it, his physical interest in her is repressed almost before he himself is aware of its existence—and this 'introversion' if it continues is likely to lead to psychic disintegration. Further, the more powerful the urge involved the more likely it is that its continual frustration will seriously damage the individual concerned. Miriam's idealistic separation of sense and spirit and her depreciation of the physical threaten Paul's psychic wholeness in just this way, and her influence becomes particularly dangerous when his sexual impulse begins to grow in strength. He himself unconsciously recognises the increasing danger and his growing and apparently irrational hostility to her is essentially the expression of this instinctive judgement.

This is why the tension between the pair, although evident before, increases sharply after the curious incident at the end of their Mablethorpe holiday. Although Paul is not consciously aware of its significance, the intense state he experiences marks the awakening in him of physical desire—

> He did not know himself what was the matter. He was naturally so young, and their intimacy was so abstract, he did not know he wanted to crush her to his breast to ease the ache there. He was afraid of her. The fact that he might want her as a man wants a woman had in him been supressed into a shame.
>
> (**SL** pp 220-1)

But the suppression is not spontaneous; it is a response to Miriam's revulsion from the idea of sexual contact—

> When she shrank in her convulsed, coiled torture from the thought of such a thing, he had winced to the depths of his soul. And now this 'purity' prevented even their first love-kiss. It was as if she could scarcely stand the shock of physical love, even a passionate kiss, and then he was too shrinking and sensitive to give it.
>
> (**SL** p 221)

Paul is well aware that Miriam is an unusually sensitive girl, that she is very easily hurt and under normal circumstances takes great care not to do or say anything which might upset her. However, in the later stages of their relationship he has subconsciously realised that she is doing him harm and that if he wants to prevent more serious damage he will have to break with her, though it is only when he is under stress that the subconscious revulsion from her finds expression. At other times his more superficial conscious affection, gentle and protective in character governs his behaviour.

In *The Rainbow* as in *Sons and Lovers*, unpremeditated utterance is important because it expresses unconscious judgements and decisions. Early in the novel, Tom Brangwen is travelling home from Nottingham when he passes a woman who looks up when she hears his cart:

> Her face was pale and clear, she had thick dark eyebrows and a wide mouth, curiously held. He saw her face clearly, as if by a light in the air. He saw her face so distinctly that he ceased to coil on himself, and was suspended.
>
> 'That's her,' he said involuntarily.
>
> (**R** p 29)

Since his meeting with the girl and the foreigner at Matlock, Tom has been possessed by a dream of a more fulfilling kind of life which would involve both a 'voluptuous woman' and contact with 'fine-textured, subtle-mannered people'. A Polish aristocrat by birth and a widow, Lydia Lensky embodies in her own person both the social distinction and sexual sophistication which Tom seeks and as soon as he sees her, he instinctively recognises her significance for him and expresses it in the sudden but decisive 'That's her'. At the same time the tension which has been increasing in him as his desire to escape from the Marsh reasserts itself, stops growing; he ceases to 'coil on himself' like a tightening spring and is 'suspended'. Before his meeting with Lydia, the frustration of his intense longing to extend his experience by the inherited 'inertia' created by generations of life at the Marsh has lead to periodic crises which Tom has relieved by drinking. When he encounters her, he has been approaching one of these crises:

> It was a time when he was getting ready for another bout of drinking, so he stared fixedly before him, watchful yet absorbed, seeing everything and aware of nothing, coiled in himself.
>
> (**R** pp 28-9)

The build-up of tension in him is interrupted when he sees the woman on the road, because he is intuitively aware from the moment he sees her that she offers the chance of an escape from his present predicament. Though Tom cannot free himself from the Marsh to venture into the wider, more challenging world beyond, that world, in the person of Lydia Lensky, has come to him. Capable of interpreting instantaneously the subtlest physical indications (and Tom is highly developed in feeling if not in intellect), the unconscious self is more sensitive in its observations and more rapid in its deliberations than the clumsily rational conscious mind; the judgements are expressed in the form of sudden intuitions like that which Tom experiences when he sees the stranger. The result is that on the basis of a brief and wordless encounter with someone he has never seen before, Tom is able to recognise that she represents his chance for fulfilment. And that intuitive recognition is expressed in words which have nothing to do with the conscious will but which spring 'involuntarily', from the deepest level of being and which express its profounder wisdom.

Conversely, deliberate or considered utterances are often misleading in Lawrence's fiction. In the 'Class-Room' chapter of *Women in Love*, the ultra-conscious Hermione launches a prolonged attack on the way in which modern education destroys children's spontaniety and encourages in them the development of an unnatural degree of conscious awareness. Although her criticisms echo the charges that Birkin—and Lawrence—levelled against contemporary schooling, Birkin is infuriated by what he sees as a distortion of his beliefs and attacks her fiercely, claiming that her defence of instinct is 'merely making words', because fundamentally she attaches most importance to consciousness and knowledge—she is, in his harsh words, 'the most deliberate thing that ever walked or crawled'. Birkin's accusation is borne out in the revealing and ironic juxtaposition of Hermione's vindication of instinct as opposed to formal education with her own lack of physical spontaniety and grace. Her gestures and movements, like those of Miriam, are awkward, tense, 'convulsed', testifying to a lack of inner integration and control which is the antithesis of instinctive ease; it is these physical symptoms rather than her deliberate words which tell us about her state. Birkin's counterattack suggests that her 'primitivism' is self-conscious, that she does not want genuinely to revert to a wholly instinctive state, but wants to exploit her animal impulses consciously, to see them reflected in the mirror of consciousness in a voyeuristic way:

> It's all that Lady of Shalott business,' he said, in his strong abstract voice. He seemed to be charging her before the unseeing air. 'You've got that mirror, your own fixed will, your immortal understanding, your own tight conscious world, and there is nothing beyond it. There, in the mirror you must have everything.'
>
> **(WL p 45)**

In saying all this Birkin is aware of Hermione's vulnerability and of the pain he is causing her, as Paul Morel had been aware of Miriam's sensitivity. It is only in states of intense emotion that the superficial conscious considerateness displayed by both men is swept aside and more fundamental feelings of hostility and rejection revealed. In both cases, it is these 'irrational' outbursts which represent the real wisdom of the psyche, since they are the expressions of an unconscious instinct for health and sanity attempting to repudiate a relationship which is now limiting, or even dangerous. And like Paul's words to Miriam which 'came from him mechanically', what Birkin says to Hermione arises straight from a level of being below consciousness, so that his voice is impersonal and 'abstract'; at the height of his anger, it is as if his conscious self has disappeared entirely—

> But a bitterer red anger burned up to fury in him. He became unconscious of her, he was only a passionate voice speaking.
>
> **(WL p 46)**

Normally our complex unconscious life does not enter our consciousness at all; it is only when there is some upheaval or crisis in the 'society' of which we are made up that we become aware of ourselves as a multiplicity rather than a unity. As Nietzsche puts it, every 'apperception' is a symptom of inner maladjustment indicating that the stable psychic hierarchy with established patterns of command and obedience has broken down. Like Nietzsche, Lawrence thought of the development of conscious thought as a symptom of inner difficulty—

> ... Man is stirred into thought by dissatisfaction, or unsatisfaction, as heat is born of friction. Consciousness is the same effort in male and female to obtain perfect, frictionless interaction ...[31]

In *The Trespasser*, Siegmund becomes directly, if dimly aware, of his self as a multiplicity as a result of sharing in Helena's ecstatic mood. The experience has temporarily weakened his inner organisation so that he is aware of the increased independence—and resistance—of the separate elements in the self and becomes aware that command and obedience are involved in all action. In all this, it is emphasised that, though Siegmund says nothing to Helena, his effort to understand his strainge condition is made using language:

> He shuddered lightly now and again, as they stepped lurching down the hill. He set his jaws hard to suppress this shuddering. It was not in his limbs, or even on the surface of his body, for Helena did not notice it. Yet he shuddered almost in anguish internally.
> 'What is it?' he asked himself in wonder.
> His thought consisted of these detached phrases, which he spoke verbally to himself.
>
> (Tr p 75)

This inner verbalising occurs while his consciousness is 'unnaturally active' and when this conscious activity, the symptom of his temporary sickness, begins to diminish, it too ceases:

> ... his consciousness, which had been unnaturally active, now was dulling. He felt the blood flowing vigorously along the limbs again, and stilling his brain, sweeping away his sickness, soothing him.
> 'I suppose,' he said to himself for the last time, 'I suppose living too intensely kills you, more or less.'
>
> (Tr p 77)

Evidently for Lawrence, as for Nietzsche, conscious awareness and language have grown up together so that conscious thought is always mediated through words.

Although we have some awareness of fundamental vital processes when we experience a psychic crisis, the full complexity of what goes on in us at the unconscious level is never reflected in consciousness; what appears there is at best merely a symptom, a dim and fragmentary indication of unseen events. Siegmund's conscious thoughts do not constitute a coherent and logical series—they consist of 'detached phrases'—because, in Nietzsche's phrase, 'each successive phenomenon in consciousness is completely atomistic'; because reflection is incomplete, 'thoughts as they succeed one another in our minds' do not stand in any kind of casual relation. Siegmund's attempt at self-analysis illustrates another limitation in conscious awareness: his consciousness is not only fragmentary, it is also vague and imprecise so he cannot arrive at a clear understanding of his state—he is 'vaguely aware' of the activity inside him and his effort to understand what is going on is a 'dim searching' in which no definite answer is found as he 'struggled to diagnose his case of splendour and sickness'.

The same kind of association between a breakdown of authority in the self and the reflection in consciousness of things which are normally unconscious occurs in *Sons and Lovers*, in the more serious psychic crisis which Paul

Morel experiences after his mother's death. At first he has reacted to his loss by rejecting the world around him as unreal and without significance, but the will to live survives in him and gradually reasserts itself. His recovery begins one evening when he comes home late to his lodging:

> The fire was burning low; everybody was in bed. He threw on some more coal, glanced at the table, and decided he wanted no supper. Then he sat down in the arm-chair. It was perfectly still. He did not know anything, yet he saw the dim smoke wavering up the chimney.
>
> (**SL** p 499)

Both Paul's body and his conscious mind are completely inactive at this point:

> The time passed ... He had not moved a muscle. He did not want to move. He was not thinking of anything. It was easier so. There was no wrench of knowing anything.
>
> (**SL** p 499)

But the impression of complete passivity is only superficial for beneath the conscious level, the unconscious life-processes continue unceasingly; although Paul's voluntary mental activity is in abeyance, 'some other consciousness' in him, which is independent of his conscious will, continues to work 'mechanically'. The word is not used here with the hostile implications which it tends to have in Lawrence's later fiction—Paul's 'other consciousness' is mechanical simply in the sense that, like his angry words to Miriam, which are descibed in the same way, it is not governed by the conscious will. The involuntary activity of the other consciousness is unceasing, but its operations are only occasionally evident to what might be called the 'reflexive consciousness' and these fragmentary indications take verbal form:

> He was not thinking of anything. It was easier so. There was no wrench of knowing anything. Then, from time to time, some other consciousness, working mechanically, flashed into sharp phrases.
>
> (**SL** p 499)

The phrases make up an inner dialogue, an argument between two voices, one nihilistic and despairing, the other more hopeful and determined. The exchange represents Paul's necessarily incomplete awareness of the conflict in him at the unconscious level, of the oscillation of his 'soul', 'first on the side of death, then on the side of life'. His recent suffering has undermined the integrity of his 'self' so that instead of being a single, united entity, it has split into two antagonistic parts. And, as in Siegmund's case, it is this weakening of the hierarchical structure and the consequent resistance to authority from normally subordinate elements in being, which reveals that the self is a power-structure in which command and obedience, rulers and ruled, are necessary for action.

Since consciousness is generated by difficulty and conflict, the degree of conscious awareness naturally increases as the underlying crisis intensifies. At first despair is dominant in Paul and the 'live feeling' which 'resisted his own annihilation' is 'dull' and 'gone in an instant'. But as that feeling grows in strength and the inner struggle becomes proportionately more intense, his awareness of what is going on inside him becomes fuller and more precise— so, after a short pause 'quite mechanically and more distinctly, the conversation began again inside him'. In this second part of the involuntary 'inner' conversation, Paul's will to live, which at first was evident only in the vague and transitory feeling of opposition to his self-destructive behaviour, has become a second, opposing 'voice', arguing stubbornly against despair and urging the resumption of active, creative life. The argument, which centres on the significance of his mother's life, reveals that there are two contrasting elements in Paul's nature—with one part of himself, he sees Mrs Morel's suffering and death as an argument against existence, and is attracted by death because it offers an escape from the struggle and pain which are inseparable from living. In other words, one side of his nature responds to the facts of suffering, change and death in the way that Nietzsche characterises as 'weak' or 'decadent'; like the decadent originators of Christianity and other ascetic creeds, Paul concludes that a world which includes such things must be worthless and unreal and that death is desirable. But, with the other and 'stronger' side of himself he is able to find in his mother's 'struggle' a reason for living, rather as, in Nietzsche's account of the life-affirming 'tragic disposition', suffering and death serve as a stimulus to fresh effort:

> Then, quite mechanically and more distinctly, the conversation began again inside him.
> 'She's dead. What was it all for—her struggle?'
> That was his despair wanting to go after her.
> 'You're alive.'
> 'She's not.'
> 'She is—in you.'
> Suddenly he felt tired with the burden of it.
> 'You've got to keep alive for her sake,' said his will in him.
> Something felt sulky, as if it would not rouse.
> 'You've got to carry forward her living, and what she had done, go on with it.'

(SL p 500)

This contrast within Paul clearly resembles and is related to the contrast between his parents. He has inherited both his mother's doggedness and his father's tendency to avoid difficulty and while the former is normally dominant in him, his recent suffering has weakened its authority, increasing the degree of conflict in his 'self' to the point where the struggle is reflected in consciousness.

The inner clash, in which the recalcitrant, 'sulky' part of Paul's being is challenged by his 'will' strongly resembles the clash of wills between Paul and Baxter Dawes when the latter is convalescing after his bout of typhoid. The smith too is described as 'sulking', for, although his physical recovery is complete, he is reluctant to leave the sheltered and comfortable world of the hospital and return to ordinary life. Paul feels responsible for the other man and helps him to 'move forward towards convalescence' but, significantly, the therapeutic methods he employs depend less on sympathy than on challenge and criticism. Like the 'sulky' part of Paul's self, the 'sulking' Dawes is urged back to fuller life through conflict rather than collusion. The relevance of this to the division in Paul's nature and the question of heredity is suggested not only by the generally acknowledged fact that Dawes strongly resembles the elder Morel, but also by the close parallel between Paul's role in the smith's recovery and the part played by his mother much earlier in the novel when Morel had made himself ill by sleeping in the sun on a trip to Nottingham with Jerry Purdy. On that occasion the miner had quickly recovered, thanks to his 'fine constitution', but, used to being indulged during his illness, had wanted this comfortable existence to continue, so 'He often put his hand to his head, pulled down the corners of his mouth, and shammed pains he did not feel'. Mrs Morel had responded to the pretence first with amusement, then with impatience and contempt, and, reluctantly, the miner had been 'forced to resume a normal tone and to cease to whine'. Paul embodies in his own person the contrasting attitudes evident in these clashes between different individuals although, of course, the inner conflict he experiences after his mother's death is far more intense and prolonged than either.

The 'mechanical' conversation marks the beginning of his recovery because it indicates that the self-destructive urge which has been dominant to him so far is now being challenged by his reviving will to live. But, as its indecisive character suggests, the inner argument does not end in the decisive victory of either element in his being and the oscillation of his 'soul' between life and death continues and intensifies in the weeks that follow, as his will to live struggles to gain the ascendancy. The intense conflict which follows is not reflected directly in consciousness, but emerges rather in sudden and quite unpredictable changes in mood and behaviour, as one or another of the contending impulses gains a temporary advantage.

The pattern evident in the succeeding weeks first becomes apparent at the end of the scene under discussion when, after sitting motionless for some hours, apparently without the energy to move, Paul moves swiftly and decisively—'He rose suddenly, went straight to bed'. The move is significant because, if Nietzsche associates consciousness with psychic crisis and sickness, he also tends to link forgetting and sleep with recuperation. Siegmund's temporary 'sickness' ends when his consciousness ceases to be active—the paragraph which describes his return to his normal state begins 'Then Siegmund forgot ...'—and, in *Sons and Lovers*, the wholly unpremeditated character of Paul's action indicates that it is caused by the temporary dominance in him of the healthy side of his being. But before he has carried out his intention, the other impulse momentarily reasserts itself, and he feels again the longing to follow his mother:

When he got inside his bedroom and closed the door, he stood with clenched fists.

'Mater, my dear ...' he began, with the whole force of his soul. Then he stopped. He would not say it. He would not admit that he wanted to die, to have done. He would not own that life had beaten him, or that death had beaten him.

(**SL** pp 500–1)

Despite the force of the death-wish, it is the determination not to give in which is finally dominant and its victory is reflected in the fact that immediately after he has made his resolution 'Going straight to sleep, he slept at once, abandoning himself to the sleep'. The issue has not been decided, of course; the warring impulses are too evenly matched for their struggle to end quickly and so sudden alternations of feeling of the kind experienced here continue in the days that follow:

So the weeks went on. Always alone, his soul oscillated, first on the side of death, then on the side of life, doggedly.

(**SL** p 501)

Nietzsche considers that individuality depends on the successful integration of the group of 'wills' which makes up the 'self'. It is an achievement in which individual effort supplements the effects of fortunate heredity, rather than something which is simply given. Conversely, lack of any distinct individuality, weakness of 'will', involves 'the antagonism of the passions', the 'multiplicity of "souls in one breast"', and this is a state which is 'very unhealthy' and which will lead to 'inner ruin ... unless one passion at last becomes master'. At this point in the novel, Paul's being is dominated by two powerful and opposing impulses, neither of which is able, for the moment, to impose its will. The result is that he is unable either to go forward with life or to abandon the struggle and because he is unable to release his impulses in action, tension and frustration accumulate inside him and threaten his survival:

Where could he go? There was nowhere to go, neither back to the inn, or forward anywhere. He felt stifled. There was nowhere for him. The stress grew inside him; he felt he should smash.

(**SL** p 501)

But, as before, the determination to go on is marginally stronger and prevents the disintegration which threatens: 'I mustn't,' he said; and, turning blindly, he went in and drank.' Like Tom Brangwen who, divided and frustrated for different reasons, becomes a bout-drinker, Paul finds relief for his inner discomfort in the temporary anaesthesia produced by alcohol.

The fluctuations of the battle below conscious level are reflected directly in sudden changes in how reality is perceived, like that which Paul experiences on one of the occasions when he goes to have a drink:

> Sometimes he stood before the bar of the public-house where he had called for a drink. Everything suddenly stood back away from him. He saw the face of the bar-maid, the gabbling drinkers, his own glass on the slopped, mahogany board, in the distance. There was something between him and them. He could not get into touch.
>
> (SL p 501)

These changes occur unexpectedly and are clearly independent of the conscious will, issuing rather from some alteration in the unconscious balance of power. Since Nietzsche thinks of our perceptions as part of that 'apparatus of knowledge' which has developed as an instrument of the ruling urges, it follows that our awareness of the world is shaped by the impulses currently dominant in us and that any significant change in the power relations in the self will find expression in a corresponding change in the nature of the 'reality' we experience. The impulse to go forward with life inevitably involves 'wanting' things, and while it is dominant, Paul sees the world normally. The other powerful force in him is an impulse of the opposite kind, an urge to abandon the difficult business of growing, a lapsing of all desire and it is the temporary ascendancy of this second impulse which causes the sudden change in perspective described above. In the period immediately following his mother's death, this negative impulse had been the single most powerful element in his being and its steadily increasing force had found expression in his growing sense of the remoteness, meaningless and unreality of existence. This influence is at its strongest just before the 'mechanical' conversation takes place, when Paul has almost completely lost any sense of time, place or individual identity:

> The days passed, the weeks. But everything seemed to have fused, gone into a conglomerated mass. He could not tell one day from another, one week from another, hardly one place from another. Nothing was distinct or distinguishable. Often he lost himself for an hour at a time, could not remember what he had done.
>
> (SL p 499)

The description of the evening in his lodgings follows this, and, as the detail with which it is presented suggests, it marks the point at which Paul recovers his ability to discriminate and distinguish. The will to live gathers strength beneath conscious level and its progress is reflected not only in the increasing authority of the 'mechanical' voice which counsels renewed effort, but also in the way in which the things around Paul, which at first seem distant to him, come to reassume their normal places:

> One evening he came home later to his lodging. The fire was burning low; everybody was in bed. He threw on some more coal, glanced at the table, and decided he wanted no supper. Then he sat down in the arm-chair. It was perfectly still. He did not know anything, yet he saw the dim smoke wavering up the chimney. Presently two mice came out, cautiously, nibbling the fallen crumbs. He watched them as it were from a long way off. The church clock

> struck two. Far away he could hear the sharp clinking of the trucks on the
> railway. No, it was not they that were far away. They were there in their places,
> but where was he himself?
>
> (**SL** p 499)

The mice in the room seem a long way off, and the noises from the railway
too seem remote at first, but then Paul realises that the impression of distance
is illusory. After this his perceptions are normal—there is no suggestion that
he repeats his error about the railway trucks when, later, he hears the 'sound
of a heavy cart clanking down the road', and the fact that the noise made
by the electricity meter in the room is described as a 'bruising thud' underlines
the fact that his normal sensitivity has returned. Since, at this point, Paul
cannot find the energy for deliberate mental effort, conscious thought and
will play no more part in the change in his view of reality than they do in the
argument which is simultaneously taking place in him; like the sharp phrases
which flash into consciousness, the alteration in perspective is a symptom of
unconscious changes. In the weeks that follow, the sense of distance from
reality which Paul had consistently felt before only 'sometimes' returns and
when it does it is never so acute as in the period just before the evening of
the mechanical conversation.

If the urge to give in continues to reappear, but with steadily—if slowly—
diminishing force, the impulse to go forward with life gathers strength. When
he had first moved to Nottingham after his mother's death, Paul had found
himself quite unable to begin painting again:

> Everything seemed to have gone smash for the young man. He could not paint.
> The picture he finished on the day of his mother's death—one that satisfied
> him—was the last thing he did. At work there was no Clara. When he came
> home he could not take up his brushes again.
>
> (**SL** p 498)

After the evening on which the mechanical conversation takes place, the
determination to work returns and if, at first, the effort cannot be sustained,
the fact that it is made at all is a sign of returning health—

> For ever restless, he went here, there, everywhere. He determined to work. But
> when he had made six strokes, he loathed the pencil violently, got up, and went
> away, hurried off to a club where he could play cards or billiards, to a place
> where he could flirt with a barmaid who was no more to him than the brass
> pump-handle she drew.
>
> (**SL** pp 501–2)

Later, during his last meeting with Miriam, his reaction to the work in the
sketch-book which she has picked up suggests that he has recovered his
enthusiasm for art. Paul has not been consciously aware of any change in
his attitudes and so before he sees the sketches again, he dismisses them. As
a result, he is surprised to find when he comes to examine the book, that it
contains a good deal that is interesting:

she was curiously examining a sketch-book when he returned with the coffee.
'There's nothing new in it, ' he said, 'and nothing very interesting.'
He put down the tray, and went to look over her shoulder. She turned the pages slowly, intent on examining everything.
'H'm!' he said, as she paused at a sketch. 'I'd forgotten that. It's not bad, is it?'
'No,' she said. 'I don't quite understand it.'
He took the book from her and went through it. Again he made a curious sound of surprise and pleasure.
'There's some not bad stuff in there,' he said.

(SL p 504)

Even at the end of the novel, however, the conflict in Paul's being is not fully resolved. After the final parting with Miriam, he feels again the longing to join his mother in death but, as before, it is the determination to go forward with life which finally prevails:

On every side the immense dark silence seemed pressing him, so tiny a spark, into extinction, and yet, almost nothing, he could not be extinct. Night, in which everything was lost went reaching out, beyond stars and sun. Stars and sun, a few bright grains, went spinning round for terror, and holding each other in embrace, there in a darkness that outpassed them all, and left them tiny and daunted. So much, and himself, infinitesimal, at the core a nothingness, and yet not nothing.
'Mother!' he whispered—'mother!'
She was the only thing that held him up, himself, amid all this. And she was gone, intermingled herself. He wanted her to touch him, have him alongside with her.
But no, he would not give in. Turning sharply, he walked towards the city's gold phosphorescence. His fists were shut, his mouth set fast. He would not take that direction, to the darkness, to follow her. He walked towards the faintly humming, glowing town, quickly.

(SL pp 510–1)

Paul's resolution is the more remarkable in that his final vision of the cosmos is one which has been shaped by the scientific and philosophical revolution which Nietzsche sees as responsible for the pessimism and nihilism characteristic of the age. Since Paul is able to confront a reality stripped of its consoling metaphysical trappings and still find the strength to go on, the conclusion represents rather more than 'a bare and minimal sort of hope'[32] for him. In the idealistic tradition which has dominated western culture, 'reality' and 'truth' have been associated with qualities like stability, distinctness and intelligibility, with the result that the changeable material world in which we live has been thought of as 'unreal', as being, at best, an imperfect copy of some 'true' world, some suprasensible realm in which the clarity and permanence absent from our oridinary experience can be found. But modern man has come to realise that change is, in fact, the only reality, that there is no 'true being' in the traditional sense and that the allegedly superior supernatural world is no more than a wish-fulfilling fantasy, constructed by those who lacked the strength to accept and affirm the dynamic character of existence. For Nietzsche, ultimate reality is flux rather than form; 'truth' is Dionysian rather an Apollonian and lies, so to speak, 'below' the sensible world in a darker, more flowing and changeable area of being, rather than in the higher, clearer realm of the idealist's absolute. Although Nietzschean reality is an 'absolute flow of happening',[33] a chaos of conflict, change and irreducible multiplicity its 'incomprehensible, fluid Proteus-nature'[34] nevertheless gives rise to the world we know because it is perpetually throwing up relatively stable forms, temporary associations of wills, some of which have a relatively slow rate of change and therefore seem permanent to the human eye. Significantly, it is this 'dark' Nietzschean absolute rather than the 'light' absolute of Christian and Platonic tradition which Paul sees as the source and end of all things. The visible universe of light and colour and form is a mere epiphenomenon of the more fundamental 'night', the undifferentiated, creative flow of happening, and the whole of creation from man to the circling stars has issued from, and will ultimately return to, the 'living gloom':

> In the country all was dead still. Little stars shone high up; little stars spread far away in the flood-waters, a firmament below. Everywhere the vastness and terror of the immense night which is roused and stirred for a brief while by the day, but which returns, and will remain at last eternal, holding everything in its silence and its living gloom.

> (**SL** p 510)

The bleak vision is Paul's but, as the change of tense indicates, it is not simply a cosmic projection of his grief, but represents Lawrence's own view of the nature of things.

Related to the traditional belief that there is a 'real' supernatural world above and beyond the changeable world of ordinary experience is the idea that human nature is essentially dual; that man has a perishable animal part which connects him with the mundane, and an eternal, spiritual part which links him with the realm of 'true being'. Since he alone is endowed with this special capacity, man has a unique moral status and occupies a central position in the natural order. One of the consequences of the intellectual revolution of recent centuries has been the steady erosion of this 'faith in the dignity and uniqueness of man, in his irreplacibility in the great chain of being',[35] so that 'The most universal sign of the modern age' is that 'man has lost dignity in his own eyes to an incredible extent'.[36] Nietzsche links this diminishment with the beginnings of the modern view of the universe:

> Since Copernicus, man seems to have got himself on an inclined plane—now he is slipping faster and faster away from the center into—what? into nothingness? into a '*penetrating* sense of his nothingness'?[37]

Nietzsche argues that one of the advantages of 'the Christian moral hypothesis' was that 'It granted man an absolute value, as opposed to his smallness and accidental occurrence in the flux of becoming and passing away' and thus served as an antidote to nihilism. Without its support, man is in danger of being overwhelmed by a sense of his own insignificance and succumbing to despair and paralysis of the will, rather as Paul, feeling that he is merely 'one tiny upright speck of flesh, less than an ear of wheat lost in the field ... could not bear it'. But Paul's failure of resolution is only temporary. In the end he finds the strength to accept reality as it is, and turning from the darkness, walks towards the lights of the town. The rejection of the darkness and the movement back to ordinary life is in sharp contrast to his behaviour immediately after his mother's death, when he had welcomed the dark, because in concealing movement and change it had obscured the dynamic character of reality and thereby satisfied his longing for stability. Because of his mothers death, Paul had been unable to accept and affirm a reality which is essentially process and so had come to see the ordinary daytime world as unreal:

> Everything seemed so different, so unreal. There seemed no reason why people would go along the street, and houses pile up in the daylight. There seemed no reason why these things should occupy the space, instead of leaving it empty.
>
> (**SL** p 498)

The featureless darkness had seemed realer than these:

> The realest thing was the thick darkness at night. That seemed to him whole and comprehensible and restful. He could leave himself to it.
>
> (**SL** p 499)

In Nietzsche's philosophy the degree of reality, of beauty, of significance, apparently present 'in' the world is dependent on the state of the observer. Those who are strong and vital unconsciously project their vitality on to the things around them and so perceive the world as fuller, richer and more meaningful than do those who are weaker. Because Paul possesses exceptional vitality, he normally sees the world with unusual distinctness and vividness. Further, as his success as an artist suggests, he is also able to communicate this finer vision—which is why Miriam had felt that to experience fully the beauty of a wild rose bush in the wood she must see it with him:

> She wanted to show him a certain wild-rose bush she had discovered. She knew it was wonderful. And yet, till he had seen it, she felt it had not come into her soul. Only he could make it her own, immortal. She was dissatisfied.
>
> (**SL** p 197)

Immediately after his mother's death, however, instead of being more vivid for Paul than it is for most people, experience has become less so; he is in the 'anti-idealising' state which Nietzsche associates with reduced vitality, in which reality and significance are taken from rather than given to, the world and, as a consequence, things seem undifferentiated, unreal and purposeless. In fact, Paul's pessimistic view of the world after his mother's death is as much an unconscious interpretation of happening as the vividness and richness it seemed to have before; the contrast between the two perspectives reflects radically different degrees of strength.

For the strong, the recognition that existence is process, that change, death and decay are inseparable from it, is a stimulus to affirmation and celebration. For those who are temporarily or permanently weak or decadent, on the other hand, such a recognition involves intolerable suffering and instead of confronting and accepting it, they turn away from reality, seeking relief from the pain of living in diminished states of consciousness or in imaginary worlds from which the disturbing characteristics of the real world have been banished. Thus Paul escapes temporarily from the pain caused by the fact 'that things had lost their reality' in the hard, mechanical work of the factory, which brings 'pure forgetfulness, when he lapsed from consciousness'. And the attraction of the darkness derives from the fact that in it he is largely undisturbed by reminders of process and can remain in an unconscious fantasy world where time and change are absent and he can still be with his mother:

> The realest thing was the thick darkness at night. That seemed to him whole and comprehensible and restful. He could leave himself to it. Suddenly a piece of paper started near his feet and blew along down the pavement. He stood still, rigid, with clenched fists, a flame of agony going over him. And he saw again the sick-room, his mother, her eyes. Unconsciously he had been with her, in her company. The swift hop of the paper reminded him she was gone. But he had been with her. He wanted everying to stand still, so that he could be with her again.
>
> (**SL** p 499)

Nietzsche argues that the decadent finds the world intolerable because he imposes his own torment on it; the ascetic or pessimistic vision of things is created by the 'tyrranic will of one who suffers deeply, who struggles, is tormented ... who, as it were, revenges himself on all things by forcing the image of his torture on them, branding them with it.'[38] So Paul projects his sense of the tragedy of his mother's life into the world around and the extent to which his view of things is conditioned—if unconsciously—by his loss is illustrated by things like the change in the significance of the first snowdrops, The flowers which once would have seemed to Paul symbols of hope and renewal now signify only transience and meninglessness:

> The first snowdrops came. He saw the tiny drop-pearls among the grey. They would have given him the liveliest emotion at one time. Now they were there, but they did not seem to mean anything. In a few moments they would cease to occupy that place, and just the space would be, where they had been.
>
> (**SL** p 498)

Later when the sight of a scrap of windblown paper arouses in him feelings of extraordinary intensity by indirectly suggesting the loss of his mother, Paul himself becomes aware of the way in which his unconscious preoccupations have coloured even his most trivial experiences. Nietzsche regards this kind of awareness as an end-result and, significantly, the realisation happens at the crisis point of Paul's malady, at the point when he begins to recover.

# CHAPTER 5

# Individual Growth and Human Relationships

After his mother's death, Paul Morel does not move steadily towards recovery, but goes through a series of sudden and involuntary oscillations, first in one direction, then in the other. Within this general pattern, each forward movement takes him a little further towards new life and each recoil back a little less far towards darkness and death. This alternating, wave-like pattern of change, its rhythm determined beneath conscious level, follows naturally from Nietzsche's conception of the self as a hierarchical organisation of dynamic, power-seeking urges. In such an organisation, change involves a struggle between contending impulses, each striving to gain sole authority; if the combatants are equally matched, the conflict will be prolonged and the initative will change hands a number of times as first one, then another, of the warring impulses gains a temporary advantage. In *The Gay Science*, Nietzsche compares this pattern of flow and recoil in the activity of will to power with the movement of the tides—a favourite image, and one often employed by Lawrence in a similar way:

> How eagerly this wave comes hither, as if it were a question of its reaching something! How it creeps with frightful haste into the innermost corners of the rocky cliff! It seems that it wants to forestall someone; it seems that something that is concealed there has value, high value.—And now it retreats more slowly, still quite white with excitement,—is it disappointed? But already another wave approaches, still more eager and wild than the first, and its soul also seems to be full of secrets and of longing for treasure-seeking. Thus live the waves—thus live we who exercise will.[1]

More than most philosophers, Nietzsche based his account of human nature on close observation of human behaviour, laying greatest stress on the affective side of our conduct; for him, our feelings, our desires and aversions are the decisive things in us. This emphasis, which he shares with Lawrence, makes both see human development as a fluctuating pattern of advance and retreat, the resultant of a continuing conflict between subconscious feelings;

the pattern is one which is surely closer to the fluid and often puzzling way in which individuals change than are the tidier and more rational paradigms of development often used by philosophers—and novelists. Lawrence had to warn even a sophisticated reader like Edward Garnett that he had repudiated conventional, literary structure because it was based on the assumption that human development is linear, but he went on to insist that his own work, far from being formless, had patterns and rhythms of its own, based on a more complex understanding of how people change. The image he offers of *his* kind of form is a wave-trace, a visible record of rhythmic, alternating motion caused by invisible forces:

> ... I say, don't look for the development of the novel to follow the lines of certain characters; the characters fall into the form of some other rhythmic form, as when one draws a fiddle-bow across a fine tray delicately sanded, the sand takes lines unknown.[2]

The progress and eventual outcome of the struggle in Paul Morel is determined at the unconscious level. His conscious will is not involved in the process and such conscious awareness as he has of it is at best dim, partial, incapable of causing anything at all. The relation between conscious and unconscious is illustrated in the 'involuntary conversation' which is his conscious awareness of the unconscious battle and signficantly the argument is carried on 'in' him rather than 'by' him; his conscious self is no more than a passive auditor, aware of but not involved in, the dispute. That conversation reveals the existence of conflicting elements in his unconscious self which are clearly related to his divided inheritance and the importance of these elements in determining his fate indicates that Lawrence, like Nietzsche, emphasises 'the body, instinct and heredity' against the stress usually laid on 'mind, reason and consciousness'[3] in explaining human behaviour.

The importance of the physical, instinctive self is evident again at the very end of the novel where the stemming of the 'drift towards death' is linked with Paul's sense of his physical self. Feeling that though his mother has 'gone abroad into the night', he is 'with her still', Paul's longing to join her is somehow resisted by his own physical substantiality:

> Now she was gone abroad into the night, and he was with her still. They were together. But yet there was his body, his chest, that leaned against the stile, his hands on the wooden bar. They seemed something.

> (**SL** p 510)

Julian Moynahan recognises that it is 'The pressure of his body leaning against the stile 'which effectively prevents him from moving toward death and the mother', but he underestimates the importance of the physical in Lawrence's scheme of things and so sees this kind of resistance as offering only the faintest of hopes for Paul's survival—

> It is clear from the passage that if he is somehow to be saved he has only the stubborn physical fact of his own body and its mysterious life with which to resist the night.[4]

Far from having the kind of limited importance this suggests, it is precisely the body which is associated throughout the novel with the decisive forces in human development, so the 'resistance' offered by Paul's physical self is more significant and his prospects better than most critics suppose. Moynahan implies too, in his account of the end of the novel, that Paul's turning towards the town is his first movement in the direction of life—if this were so, Paul's final state would indeed be precarious and the reader would be left unsure whether his resolve will be maintained, but as I have shown, it is only the latest in a number of such advances made as Paul's 'soul' has oscillated between life and death. Several other commentators have simplified the conclusions of the novel in the same way, taking as their cue Lawrence's remark in a letter to Garnett that Paul is left with the 'drift towards death', suggesting uninterrupted movement in a single direction. For Schorer such a negative ending is anyhow implied by what he takes to be the theme of the novel: a tragic denouement is the logical outcome of the perverse and damaging relationship between mother and son. The result is that for him, even a precariously hopeful ending is unsupported by what has gone before and fails to convince—rather as Leavis argues that the hopeful end of *The Rainbow* is unjustified:

> ... in the last four sentences of the novel, Paul rejects his desire for extinction and turns towards 'the faintly humming, glowing town', to life—as nothing in his previous history persuades us that he could unfalteringly do.[5]

The rejection of the darkness is hardly unfaltering in fact since the desire to rejoin his mother asserts itself with considerable force just before the end—nor, as I have shown, is it something which appears suddenly 'in the last few sentences of the novel'. The alternation of two conflicting impulses evident there is part of a pattern of development which has been evident since the time of the involuntary conversation. And it is exactly the strength of the impulse to rejoin his mother which testifies to the now even *greater* power of the contrary urge to rejoin life. If we trust the tale in this instance rather than the artist's correspondence, it is clear that the force in Paul which directs him back to the town is a powerful and enduring one.

Lydia Lensky's recovery after her husband's death in *The Rainbow* has the same complex, prolonged, alternating shape—but is often simplified in the same way. H M Daleski, for instance, summarises the change in her as if it involved a straightforward return from the 'living death' she experienced then:

> Bereaved of her husband, she experiences a sort of living death, in which for a long time she remains 'blotted safely away from living', but her responsiveness to the tenacious existence of some snowdrops which she watches is a prelude to her own spiritual rebirth: she moves 'outside the enclosure of darkness'. It is Tom who is the fertilizing influence in her regeneration. When she meets him, 'the stranger who [is] not a gentleman yet who [insists] on coming into her life', the 'pain of a new birth in herself [strings] all her veins to a new form.[6]

But Lydia's rebirth is not as simple as this suggests. It involves the same kind of oscillation between life and death as Paul's had done, indicating that the same kind of unconscious struggle takes place in her. Because the process is largely an internal one, it is not dependent on Tom in the way that Daleski implies and her regeneration is fairly advanced by the time she first meets him.

Her withdrawal from ordinary life begins with the deaths of her two youngest children after which, for a time

> She walked always in a shadow, silenced, with a strange, deep terror having hold of her, her desire was to seek satisfaction in dread, to enter a nunnery, to satisfy the instincts of dread in her, through service of a dark religion. But she could not.
>
> (**R** p 51)

Her reaction illustrates Nietzsche's claim that 'What really arouses indignation against suffering is not suffering itself but the senselessness of suffering' so that ascetic religions like Christianity have their origins in the need to find a meaning for it. According to Nietzsche, the Christian 'has interpreted a whole mysterious machinery of salvation into suffering'. Lydia makes her own suffering more bearable by accepting the explanation of it offered by the 'dark religion' of her Polish Catholic girlhood—seeing the tragedy as the work of a punishing God, who has visited affliction on her because of her sins. The deep terror she experiences is a result of her sense of sin and guilt and her desire to enter a nunnery is the expression of her sense that she must atone for it. Nietzsche maintains that the kind of meaning ascribed to suffering in Christian doctrine helps the suffering believer to survive, because the doctrine of sin generates extreme emotions, intense feelings of fear, guilt and self-hatred, which act as intoxicants, and paradoxically offer temporary relief from pain. So Lydia wants to 'seek *satisfaction* in dread' and—unexpectedly—would like to *maintain* the 'strange deep terror' which the service of the 'strange dark religion' brings. But if such measures bring temporary relief, their end result is to make the sufferer's condition worse; they are essentially decadent expedients, resorted to by those whose intuitive capacity to judge what will help and what damage them, has broken down. Those who retain some health take the opposite course, and strive to minimize feeling and reaction. So, even in her extremity, some of Lydia's sound instinct has survived and despite her desire to become a nun and immerse herself in the intense feelings generated by the sense of the 'dark religion', she finds she simply cannot take the veil.

By the time of her husband's fatal illness, Lydia has intuitively adopted the other, sounder strategy for survival in the face of great suffering—she retreats from the ordinary world, which comes to seem unreal to her as it had to Paul after his mother's death. Just as he had continued working 'mechanically' so she continues to act automatically, her real life associated, as his had been, with darkness, with the unconscious and with memories of the past before tragedy struck:

> In the superficial activity of her life, she was all English, She even thought in English. But her long blanks and darkness of abstraction were Polish.
>
> (**R** p 52)

Like Paul, who had wanted everything to stand still after his mother's death, Lydia is unable to face the ordinary world of movement and change because of the tragedy associated with it and sees it as 'unreal'. And just as Paul had found (or unconsciously created) an alternative reality, a timeless imaginary realm in which the past with his mother could be recovered and he could remain 'Unconsciously . . . in her company', Lydia retreats into her memories of life in Poland before the loss of her husband and children. Although she does not consciously think of the past very much ('she did not think of Poland, nor of that life to which she had belonged'), the 'real' as against the 'superficial' activity of her life lies not in England where she now lives but in that Polish past which appears as 'a great blot looming blank in its darkness'. For a while, this darkness is the only reality for her, but as she slowly recovers her vitality, the ordinary world comes to seem somewhat more real and substantial, although it is still only dimly apprehended:

> So she lived for some time. Then, with a slight uneasiness, she used half to awake to the streets of London. She realized that ther was something around her, very foreign, she realized she was in a strange place.
>
> (**R** p 52)

Before this point, the English and English life 'did not exist for her'—she had been 'like one walking in the underworld, where the shades throng intelligibly but have no connection with one'.

Lydia's awakening continues with her move to Yorkshire. There she comes into contact with the active, changing natural world and finds herself compelled to attend to it, despite her reluctance on a conscious level to submit to the pain which this involves:

> She was sent to Yorkshire, to nurse an old rector in his rectory by the sea. This was the first shake of the kaleidoscope that brought in front of her eyes something she must see. It hurt her brain, the open country and the moors. It hurt her and hurt her. Yet it forced itself upon her as something living . . .
>
> There was green and silver and blue in the air about her now. And there was a strange insistence of light from the sea, to which she must attend. Primroses glimmered around, many of them, and she stooped to the disturbing influence near her feet, she even picked one or two flowers, faintly remembering, in the new colour of life, what had been.
>
> (**R** p 52)

As her strength returns, the pain which she had experienced in the first stages of her awakening lessens and she begins to respond to the vivid life, the growth and change around her with unease rather than actual 'hurt':

> Summer came, the moors were tangled with harebells like water in the ruts of the roads, the heather came rosy under the skies, setting the whole world awake.

> And she was uneasy—she went past the gorse bushes shrinking from their presence, she stepped into the heather as into a quickening bath that almost hurt.
>
> (**R** p 53)

But this advance into life is followed by another long retreat when 'she shrank away again, back into her darkness, and for a long while remained blotted safely away from living'. After the lapse, Lydia feels a stronger and more active desire to live again although she has not yet recovered enough strength to face the challenge of creating a new mode of existence and instead demands the return of the old:

> ... autumn came with the faint red glimmer of robins singing, winter darkened the moors, and almost savagely she turned again to life, demanding her life back again, demanding that it should be as it had been when she was a girl, on the land at home, under the sky.
>
> (**R** p 53)

But, of course, the life of her youth does not come back and again 'There was a little agony of struggle ... then a relapse into the darkness of the convent, where Satan and the devils raged round the walls, and Christ was white on the cross of victory'. When spring returns, Lydia re-emerges from the darkness and this time sees the growth around her not with pain or even unease, but with 'equanimity'; she is now able to accept, if she cannot yet affirm, life as process—

> ... with curious equanimity the returning woman watched the snowdrops on the edge of the grass below, blown white in the wind, but not to be blown away.
>
> As she rose in the morning, the dawn was beating up white gusts of light blown like a thin snowstorm from the east, blown stronger and fierier, till the rose appeared, and the gold, and the sea lit up below. She was impassive and indifferent. Yet she was outside the enclosure of darkness.
>
> (**R** p 54)

Another recoil follows, but this time it is briefer and associated with 'shadow' rather than 'darkness':

> There passed a space of shadow again, the familiarity of dread-worship, during which she was moved, oblivious, to Cossethay.
>
> (**R** p 54)

When the oblivion passes and Lydia awakens to the world once again, her mere 'indifference' to the life around has given way to a more active and positive response. Hearing the thrushes in the shrubbery, for instance, 'her heart, beaten upon, was forced to lift up its voice in rivalry and answer'. She becomes aware that she will be urged back into active life again despite her conscious unwillingness—

> She was full of trouble almost like anguish. Resistant, she knew she was beaten, and from fear of darkness turned to fear of light. She would have hidden herself

indoors, if she could. Above all, she craved for the peace and heavy oblivion of her old state.

(R p 54)

As the urge compelling her back into activity grows in force, the psychic conflict becomes more evenly balanced until she feels unable to move in either direction—

> She could neither wake nor sleep. As if crushed between the past and the future, like a flower that comes above-ground to find a great stone lying above it, she was helpless.

(R p 55)

She tries desperately to recover 'the old obliviousness' in which she has found escape before,

> But the vicar showed her eggs in the thrush's nest near the back door. She saw herself the mother-thrush upon the nest, and the way her wings were spread, so eager down upon her secret. The tense, eager nesting wings moved her beyond endurance.

(R p 55)

Paul Morel finds himself in a similar predicament towards the end of *Sons and Lovers* when, finding himself unable to go either forward or back and aware that the resulting increase in tension may threaten his survival, he thinks in despair of abandoning responsibility for his life to someone else, of seeking out Miriam and leaving her to make the choices he finds himself unable to make. Lydia's instincts lead her to the same kind of solution; lost and helpless, unable either to 'wake' or 'sleep', she is drawn to Tom because 'the rooted safety of him, and the life of him' makes her feel that she will be able to 'relinquish herself to him'. In the earlier novel, when Paul realises that Miriam cannot 'take him and relieve him of the responsibility of himself' he is able to find the strength in himself to go on alone, but because she is a woman, Lydia is less resilient and is anyhow in a more difficult because less familiar environment; she feels 'she had not the strength to come to life now in England, so foreign, skies so hostile'. As a result, she needs the relationship with Tom if she is to live fully again and the attraction she feels to him is essentially the intuitive recognition of this fact rather than any more personal (and superficial) kind of feeling. Her interest in him is not, as Daleski suggests, the cause of her awakening, instead it is a consequence of it.

But even after the meeting with him the inner struggle between her impulse to go forward and the opposite 'will to save herself from living' continues and is reflected in the fluctuations in her feelings towards him. Lydia is educated, emancipated, cosmopolitan, an aristocrat by birth and the stolid yeoman farmer is emphatically 'not of her own sort'; to enter into a close relationship with him would be a radical new departure for her and with one part of herself she recoils from this risky commitment. The 'will to save herself from living' finds expression in the fact that 'her impulse was strong against him' but, at the same time, the more positive urge draws her to him so that she can find the support she needs to continue into fuller life in such alien surroundings—

> She got to know him better, and her instinct fixed on him—just on him. Her impulse was strong against him, because he was not of her own sort. But one blind instinct led her, to take him, to have him, and then to relinquish herself to him.
>
> (**R** p 55)

Reason and conscious will play no part in this inner battle in which the contending forces are 'instinct' and 'impulse'—feelings with their roots in unconscious judgements. Her opposing feelings are almost equally balanced, with that which leads her to Tom only marginally stronger than that which pulls her away, so the psychic conflict which ensues when her interest is aroused is a prolonged one, in which each impulse in turn assumes a temporary dominance. As the unconscious struggle continues, the conflicting feelings alternate, but the interest in Tom grows in force each time it reappears, while her periods of indifference and withdrawal gradually become less important. When she had first met Tom on the road, she had felt him go by 'almost as if he had brushed her. She had tingled in body as she had gone up the road'. After her second meeting with him, this physical response to him has developed further and she now begins to feel desire for him:

> After she had been with him in the Marsh kitchen, the voice of her body had risen strong and insistent. Soon, she wanted him. He was the man who had come nearest to her for her awakening.
>
> (**R** p 55)

But even after this point, her interest in him does not simply increase continuously—its steady growth is regularly interrupted by the reappearance of her defensive apathy:

> Always, however, between-whiles she lapsed into the old unconsciousness, indifference, and there was a will in her to save herself from living any more.

When the interest in him revives again, simple physical desire has given way to a more complex kind of feeling, to the impulse to enter into a stable relationship which will provide the support she needs. The recoil which follows is less of a retreat into 'darkness' than those which preceded it; this time the lapse seems little more than a prelude to an inevitable reawakening—

> Then she lapsed again to stupor and indifference. This, however, was bound to pass. The warmth flowed through her, she felt herself opening, unfolding, asking, as a flower opens in full request under the sun, as the beaks of tiny birds open flat, to receive, to receive.
>
> (**R** p 56)

The involuntary character of the processes which determine Lydia's fate is underlined by the comparisons with the opening flower and the hungry fledgling. In all this, her conscious self is simply an observer, so that 'she felt herself opening, asking ...', her being involuntarily compelled in a certain direction, as if by magic:

> When she opened and turned to him, then all that had been and all that was, was gone from her, she was as new as a flower that unsheathes itself and stands always ready, waiting, receptive. He could not understand this. He forced himself, through lack of understanding, to the adherence to the line of honourable courtship and sanctioned, licensed marriage. Therefore, after he had gone to the vicarage and asked for her, she remained for some days held in this one spell, open, receptive to him before him.
>
> (**R** p 56)

Lydia's arstocratic sensibility allows her to accept and act on her own impulses without referring them to conventional moral values; Tom has not moved so far in the direction of independence and self-responsibility, so despite the fact that he is 'roused to chaos' by his sense of her receptiveness, he is afraid of his own desires and unable to break with the conventional 'line of honourable courtship'. Inhibited by this 'self-fear' and by his 'conception of honour towards her', Tom is unable to respond and 'after a few days, gradually she closed again, away from him, was sheathed over, impervious to him, oblivious'.

The discontinuous pattern, the alternating flow and recoil of feeling which marks our progress to 'new places' is also characteristic of the opposite motion, of our withdrawal from 'things gone dead'. Mrs Morel's growing estrangement from her husband in *Sons and Lovers* follows essentially the same alternating rhythm as the movement towards new life in Paul or Lydia, the difference lying in the overall direction of motion. Lawrence uses Nietzsche's central image for the action of will to power, the motion of the tides, to describe the change which begins in Gertrude Morel when, after six months of happy marriage, she discovers the unpaid bills for furniture which her husband has hidden from her. From this point, although 'There were many stages in the ebbing of her love for him ... it was always ebbing', until, after the tensions and frustrations of eight years of married life 'her self no longer set towards him, helplessly, but was like a tide that scarcely rose, standing off from him. After this she scarcely desired him'. The end result of the process is summed up in another characteristic metaphor, that of husk and kernel:

> There was the halt, the wistfulness about the ensuing year, which is like autumn in a man's life. His wife was casting him off, half-regretfully, but relentlessly ... Henceforward he was more or less a husk.
>
> (**SL** p 62)

Mrs Morel is educated and articulate, but the fact that crucial stages in her development are described in terms of metaphors like these suggests that critics are mistaken in seeing her as an early version of that recurrent female type in Lawrence's fiction—the woman who personifies the destructive overdevelopment of consciousness and the bullying exercise of deliberate will. Mrs Morel does not anticipate characters like Hermione Roddice in any significant way and claims that she does have more to do with what Lawrence the man later said about the real woman who was his mother than with how Lawrence the novelist presents the fictional Gertrude Morel.

In *Women in Love*, the decisive step in Rupert Birkin's growing estrangement from Hermione Roddice comes with his realisation that the kind of life she represents—and which he has been part of hitherto—offers no really new possibilities. It is like a game of chess in which the number of possible moves is very large but in which the essential rules always remain the same:

> ... how known it all was, like a game with the figures set out, the same figures, the Queen of chess, the knights, the pawns, the same now as they were hundreds of years ago, the same figures moving round in one of the innumerable permutations that make up the game. But the game is known, its going on is like a madness, it is so exhausted.
>
> **(WL** p 110)

The insight comes to Birkin as he watches the guests at Breadalby, Hermione's family home and his rejection of the kind of life they represent is expressed through what is, on the face of it, a very ordinary and undramatic act—Birkin rises and leaves the room. As is often the case in Lawrence's fiction, the fact that his leaving is not the result of any conscious decision, but happens suddenly and unexpectedly, indicates that it has its origin in the subconscious and it is accompanied by words said to himself which are 'involuntary'; they spring from the same deep level of being, reflecting both the tension in him and the self-preserving unconscious judgement which impels him away from the damaging effects of Hermione's kind of life.

Like Mrs Morel's repudiation of her husband, Rupert's rejection of Hermione and the exhausted mode of life she represents is described in terms of a tidal motion by which he, as a conscious being, is carried passively along, with no control over the speed or direction of his journey. Trivial though his act is, its full significance is nevertheless registered by Hermione herself. Unconsciously on the alert because she senses a break may be imminent, she is able through her intuitive perceptiveness and intelligence to sense the larger meaning of Birkin's departure and is aware of its decisive importance for their relationship:

> Suddenly Birkin got up and went out.
> 'That's enough,' he said to himself involuntarily.
> Hermione knew his motion, though not in her consciousness. She lifted her heavy eyes and saw him lapse suddenly away, on a sudden, unknown tide, and the waves broke over her.
>
> **(WL** p 110)

But, as with Mrs Morel's casting adrift of her husband, the image of the tide does not imply a steadily increasing distance following a once-and-for-all break, but a to-and-fro motion, in which the couple will continue to have periods of closeness even if a larger irresistible movement is drawing them apart.

The comparisons Lawrence uses to describe Lydia's or Gertrude Morel's or Rupert Birkin's development illustrate that tendency, which he shared with Nietzsche, to treat events or processes in the human psyche in terms which derive from the natural world. Both tend to avoid the vocabulary and conceptual framework usually associated with the depiction of inner life in philosophical or psychological discourse and employ instead a more metaphorical and poetic idiom. They use this approach not only because they feel that the way in which we usually talk about inner experience derives from and refers to what is present to consciousness—and so is shallow and misleading—but also because, by linking human with natural processes, the centrality of instinct can be emphasised. The fact that Lawrence, like Nietzsche, takes his characteristic metaphors not only from animate nature, but from other aspects of the physical universe as well, suggests that both hold that the same forces, if at different levels of organisation and complexity, act in both man and the cosmos. Both are fond of describing human nature in terms of physical forces like those of wind and tide, of magnetic or electrical flow or of chemical action.

At the beginning of *The Rainbow*, the tidal flow and return of the life-process, the systole and diastole which makes up the 'double rhythm' of the will to power, flows in the Brangwens and in the world around them. The seasonal renewal of life is not something that they simply observe; they experience it within themselves—

> They felt the rush of the sap in the spring, they knew the wave which cannot halt, but each year throws forward the seed to begetting, and, falling back, leaves the young-born on the earth.
>
> (**R** pp 8–9)

Here the advancing, overflowing phase of will to power appears in its simplest form in reproduction which is simultaneously the culmination of individual development and the 'self-overcoming' movement beyond it:

> The impetus of will to power culminates in a thurst which is at once a venture upward and a leap to death. The simplest illustration is animal reproduction: when the animal has grown to full strength it gives its best energies for its young and so brings about its own decline.[7]

Self-overcoming may take subtler forms than procreation. Nietzsche thinks of it as something which also happens in the development of the individual; growth is not a matter of steady, gradual evolution but a discontinuous process, involving—on the surface at least—surprising jumps and qualitative leaps. In describing these, he often uses metaphors of birth, or of death and resurrection, similar to those Lawrence employs; in the work of both writers, such comparisons serve to remind us that the physical and psychical events are expressions of the same essential impulse. Each is, on a different level, an illustration of the truth that life is fundamentally 'that which must overcome itself again and again'. In *The Rainbow*, when Lydia's interest in life first begins to revive, her state is associated with parturition, the metaphor suggesting not that she is 'giving birth' but that she is 'being born'—or reborn—impelled out of womb-like comfort and safety, the 'peace and heavy oblivion' of her former state by forces as much beyond her control as the physical events of labour are beyond the control of an infant coming into the world. And as well as indicating that the process in which she is involved is beyond conscious control, the metaphor of birth—like that of tidal motion— reflects the discontinuous though rhythmic nature of her progress. Her movement towards new life is not merely independent of her consciousness but actually impels her in a direction opposite to that she consciously wants to follow:

> She was full of trouble almost like anguish. Resistant, she knew she was beaten, and from fear of darkness turned to fear of light. She would have hidden herself indoors if she could. Above all, she craved for the peace and heavy oblivion of her old state. She could not bear to come to, to realise. The first pangs of this new parturition were so acute, she knew she could not bear it. She would rather remain out of life, than be torn, mutilated into this birth, which she could not survive. She had not the strength to come to life now, in England, so foreign, skies to hostile. She knew she would die like an early colourless, scentless flower that the end of winter puts forth mercilessly.
>
> (**R** p 54)

In *Sons and Lovers*, when Paul's will to live and grow first begins to reassert itself after the shock of his mother's death, two creative possibilities suggest themselves to him (and in view of the passivity of his conscious choosing self that is the right way of putting it)—going on with his art, or marrying and having children. Each option reflects the Nietzschean idea that those who are vital want to create beyond the self in some way, because will to power is not a principle of endless acquisitiveness but involves an alternation of getting and spending and one in which, if anything, the accumulative phase exists for the sake of the expressive one. If, initially, will to power risks power, so as to get more and store it up, this should be followed by the outgoing, expansive movement which in human contexts, Nietzsche calls 'self-overcoming'—and which, in its most important manifestation, Lawrence calls 'utterance'—just as on the physiological level, sytole is followed by diastole in the action of the heart. For both Lawrence and Nietzsche then, the 'passion to be rich is not merely the greedy wish to be secure within triple walls of brass, along with a huge barn of plenty' but is also, and far more importantly, the contradictory impulse which has driven man since the beginning of his history into wasting himself in 'begetting children, colouring himself and dancing and howling ... scratching pictures on the walls of his cave, and making graven images of his unalterable feelings'. This kind of behaviour is only possible of course if power has been 'stored' in abundance;

looking at the blossoming poppy, the philosophical cave-man in *Study of Thomas Hardy* reflects on the 'labour, the careful architecture, all the chemistry, the weaving and casting of energy, the business of day after day and night after night'[8] which is dissipated in the brief flowering. He recognises that the two aspects of life are inseparable, but also accepts, even if the timidity of age makes him a little reluctant to do so, that the blossoming is the true culmination and fulfilment of the life process; and he goes on to embody his insight in the parable of the phoenix. Lawrence goes on to endorse the cave-man's conclusion more discursively in his own voice:

> The phoenix grows up to maturity and fulness of wisdom, it attains to fatness and wealth and all things desirable, only to burst into flame and expire in ash. And the flame and the ash are the be-all and the end-all, and the fatness and wisdom and wealth are but the fuel spent. It is a wasteful ordering of things, indeed, to be sure; but so it is, and what must be, must be.[9]

Like the urge to get power, the urge to spend it manifests itself in different ways and with different degrees of subtlety. If the most obvious expression is the desire for procreation, it can also be expressed in sublimated forms, notably in artistic creation. For Nietzsche, artistic activity—in common with all human activities traditionally regarded as valuable because essentially 'spiritual'—has the roots in our passions and 'above all [in] the intoxication of sexual excitement' which brings a 'feeling of plenitude and increased energy'.[10] The artist unconsciously projects this feeling on to the world around, enriching it and giving it significance. Art is essentially a sublimated, spiritualized expression of sexuality; as Nietzsche puts it in one of his examples. 'Making music is another way of making children'.[11] It is this association which lies behind Lawrence's insistence in his fiction that forces which distort, damage or weaken sexuality—the influence of Miriam on Paul, for instance, or of Helena on Siegmund—also directly threaten 'higher' kinds of expression as well.

In his Thomas Hardy essay, Lawrence links 'begetting children' with the first stages of man's artistic activity and the two are also associated in the involuntary conversation in Paul Morel which marks the beginning of his recovery after the trauma of his mother's death. Paul does not deliberately choose his options, they are presented to his consciousness from another deeper level of being, and each represents, in its different way a creative possibility. Nietzsche argues that the essential difference between two such apparently unrelated, and even (on a conscious level) contrasting, impulses is not so much one of kind as one of degree. The 'higher' urge is not essentially different from the 'lower', but simply the same one in a more subtle, disciplined and organised form—and in this new form it represents a greater *degree* of power. It follows that the amount of power involved in something like artistic creation is significantly greater than that involved in a physical activity like procreation, and Lawrence and Nietzsche alike stress that the greatest effort, risk and danger are encountered in the 'spiritual' realm rather than the physical. Bother writers often convey this belief by describing

intellectual or artistic effort in terms of things which are physically demanding or dangerous, like exploration or warfare. At the beginning of *The
Rainbow*, the Brangwen women look out beyond the immediate physical
existence of the farm to the distant world of 'utterance', from the
accumulative to the expressive life, straining to see there

> what man had done in fighting outwards to knowledge ... to hear how he
> uttered himself in his conquest ...

because

> her deepest desire hung on the battle that she heard, far off, being waged on
> the edge of the unknown.
>
> (**R** p 9)

If man's thought-adventuring is described in military terms, physical
courage, like that displayed by Anton Skrebensky or Gerald Crich—Gerald
has been both an explorer and a soldier—is not rated very highly. For all his
undoubted physical bravery, Skrebensky lacks the more demanding kind of
courage needed to take emotional, moral or intellectual risks and his lack of
enterprise is underlined by the fact that is juxtaposed with Ursula's more
active exploration of life and its possibilities. In *Women in Love*, there is a
similar kind of contrast between Gerald and Birkin; Gerald's war service and
his expedition to the Amazon Basin testify to abundant physical courage, but
like Skrebensky he lacks more important kinds of resolution. Though he
finds conventional life unfulfilling, he can do no more than react against it
in simple negation, flirting briefly from time to time with a bohemian world
which is a mirror-image of the bourgeois world, a 'gesture of rejection and
negation' against it, rather than a real alternative to it. He cannot face the
radical rejection of contemporary civilisation entailed in the creation of a
genuinely new mode of life just as, on a personal level, he shirks the challenge
of taking his friend Birkin seriously and responding fully to him:

> There was something very congenial to him in Birkin. But yet, beyond this, he
> did not take much notice. He felt that he, himself, Gerald, had harder and more
> durable truths than any the other man knew ... It was the quick-changing
> warmth and vitality and brilliant word utterance he loved in his friend. It was
> the rich play of words and quick interchange of feelings he enjoyed. The real
> content of the words he never really considered: he himself knew better.
>     Birkin knew this. He knew that Gerald wanted to be *fond* of him without
> taking him seriously.
>
> (**WL** p 64)

The contrast between Ursula and Shrebensky, Birkin and Gerald, illustrates the Nietzschean idea of the importance of 'need' in the development
of human traits and the dialectical conception of the growth of power which
is related to it. Skrebensky and Gerald both have that physical fulness and
strength which tends to inhibit spontaneous development towards higher

degrees of power, while the characters they are contrasted with, because physically less substantial—Birkin's slightness, even frailty is constantly emphasised in *Women in Love*—need to develop other and 'higher' kinds of power. And it is Birkin, physically the most vulnerable, who for just that reason is most dynamic, least fixed in personality; his changeableness like his frailty is constantly stressed in contrast to the relative 'inertia' of a character like Gerald Crich or the actual 'fixity' of many of the people in the book, from the wedding guests at the beginning, to the Arab servant employed by Birkin's bohemian acquaintances. Such people—the majority in *Women in Love*, though not in *The Rainbow*—are not capable of any fresh life-initiative and merely repeat old and now outworn patterns.

In *Sons and Lovers*, the effort and difficulty involved in something like artistic creation is brought out in the description of Paul Morel at work; he draws 'with all his soul's intensity directing his pencil', able to maintain the prodigious effort only because he can feel his mother's warmth 'inside him like strength'. Although both the alternatives which present themselves when his recovery begins—marriage and family and continuing with his painting—are creative and so involve, in different ways, a willingness to take risks, at that point it is the less demanding, less 'spiritual' course which attracts Paul most strongly. Marriage and family appeal to him because as yet he lacks the strength to cope with the more formidable challenge which his art presents. The determination to pursue some creative course has its origins in that part of his nature which he has inherited from his mother; she does, quite literally, live on in him in the courage and resilience, the will to create, which made him go on with life rather than give in. And the conclusion of the novel represents the victory of those qualities in him over the elements in his nature which come from his father and which make him want to avoid discomfort and difficulty as Morel constantly tries to do. Far from embodying 'Paul's ultimate rejection of his mother' and his 'repudiation of what she stands for' in a 'decisive act of self-liberation'[12] as H M Daleski argues, his turning from the 'drift toward death' at the end of the novel is an affirmation of his mother's values and example. Daleski's case depends on the assumption that Mrs Morel's life is destructively self-sacrificial and is therefore 'the embodiment of a principle which Lawrence fought against all his life'; in refusing to join her in the darkness, Paul is 'refusing to sacrifice himself to her' and so repudiating 'a great deal of what she stands for'.[13] But the idea that Mrs Morel's life is unnaturally self-sacrificing involves a confusion about the different roles Lawrence considered appropriate for men and women. In her relationship with Paul and William, Gertrude Morel does not so much sacrifice herself as act on a 'natural' feminine impulse to find indirect fulfilment through masculine achievement. Normally this would be realized through her relationship with her husband, but Morel's failure to develop forces her to find the creative contact she needs in her sons. For Lawrence, as for Nietzsche, contemporary feminist demands that women should have direct access to traditionally male spheres of activity were an abberation, a consequence of the breaking down of established patterns of authority and demarcation of responsibilities. Neither felt that such demands could be resisted in the short term, but each believed that women's experience of kinds of activity for which they were essentially unfitted would lead them in time to retreat back into their traditional roles. Such demands for emancipation are, anyhow, characteristic of the younger liberated women in Lawrence's fiction, those who belong to Ursula's or Gudrun's generation, and are not felt or made by Mrs Morel and her contemporaries.

Gertrude Morel is disappointed by her husband's failure, but finds real satisfaction in the achievements of her sons and particularly in Paul's artistic successes. It is the sense that she has contributed to his work that gives her her greatest satisfaction and both mother and son are at their happiest when Paul is painting with his mother near—

> They were both very happy so, and both unconscious of it. These times, that meant so much and which were real living, they almost ignored.
>
> (SL p 196)

The division of labour here; the man strenuously active, the woman apparently passive, but providing stimulus and support for the creative male is that which Lawrence—following Nietzsche—regarded as ideal, because appropriate to the different degrees of strength possessed by each sex. In such a balanced relationship, both men and women find their highest fulfilment. The passage, and others like it, also help to demolish the caricature of Mrs Morel offered by some critics, who have presented her as a selfish, manipulating and shallow snob, whose aspirations are exclusively social and who sees success entirely in terms of her son's 'promotion' into the middle class.

After his mother's death, Paul realises how dependent he has been on her and feels he will be unable to meet the challenge of living fully and creatively unless he can find the same kind of support from someone else:

> Paul felt crumpled up and lonely. His mother had really supported his life. He had loved her; they two had, in fact, faced the world together. Now she was gone, and forever behind him was the gap in life, the tear in the veil, through which his life seemed to drift slowly, as if he was drawn towards death. He wanted someone of their own free initiative to help him.
>
> (SL p 495)

The role is too demanding for Clara, and she returns to her husband in a reconciliation engineered by Paul who has realised that she 'could not stand for him to hold on to' because in his present state he 'would be too much trouble to her'. Even in his own extremity, he feels he cannot subject Clara to an experience which might seriously damage her. Later, when his first attempt to take up his painting again has failed making him feel that only the less demanding creative life of marriage and family is left, he seeks out Miriam thinking that perhaps she will be able to 'take him and relieve him of the responsibility of himself'. But her decadent self-mistrust and fear of the unknown in him prevent her from taking any initiative and Paul, on his side, will not settle for a relationship based on her sacrifice of herself to his needs, so they agree to part. After their last, abortive meeting, Paul takes her back to her cousin's house where she is staying and turns away feeling that 'the last hold for him had gone'. For the first time, Paul finds himself facing the formidable challenges of living fully and creatively not only without any sustaining relationship but without even the prospect of one. And although he has felt till now that he cannot cope with life without help, he *is* able to face the challenge of a world of change and process and despite his momentary (and understandable) lapse of resolution, go on to make the affirmative movement with which the novels ends. It is a conclusion which suggests that Paul has not only recovered his vitality, but has added to it; the difficulty and suffering he has experienced have increased his strength. What is explicit here, as in many other places in Lawrence's work, is the Nietzschean emphasis on the value of conflict and pain, most economically summed up in the famous phrase from *Twilight of the Idols*—'Whatever does not kill me makes me stronger'.[14] His mother's death has exposed Paul to what Nietzsche calls 'The discipline ... of great suffering, ... That tension of the soul in misfortune, which cultivates its strength'.[15]

Our full realisation of our potential for growth depends on the continuing engagement with and assimilation of new and therefore challenging experience. For Nietzsche the ideal pattern is one of advance, followed by a period of consolidation before a fresh initiative. For human beings the greatest risks and challenges—and therefore the greatest stimulus to growth—are to be found in their close relationships with others; because those we are intimate with are, if they are vital individuals, constantly developing and changing, there is a constant challenge in our association with them. But what draws us into close relationship with others is not 'love' in the conventional sense of the term; we are impelled towards particular individuals because we intuitively recognise the significance they represent for our own growth and the realisation of our own self-hood. It is because Rupert Birkin has come to realise this through his experience of love in the conventional sense that he rejects that feeling as the basis for the new kind of relationship he wants to create with Ursula. He has come to see the notions of selflessness and service, of meeting and mingling and worship, traditionally associated with romantic love, as things which restrict rather than encourage individual development. These are to be repudiated because, as he says to Ursula,

> At the very last, one is alone, beyond the influence of love. There is a real impersonal one, that is beyond love, beyond any emotional relationship. So it is with you. But we want to delude ourselves that love is the root. It isn't. It is only the branches. The root is beyond love, a naked kind of isolation, an isolated me, that does *not* meet and mingle, and never can.
>
> (**WL** pp 161–2)

Any profound attraction depends then on the recognition by the unconscious self that the person we are attracted to has a crucial part to play in *our* growth.

The 'new' basis for relationship could be seen as merely egoistic—'purely selfish' as Ursula calls it when Birkin tries to explain his ideas in the early stages of their association, but such terms, as Birkin points out, belong to the realm of deliberate action and can hardly be applied to impulses which are as he says, 'impersonal', coming from beyond the conscious, responsible self. On the unconscious level, such a recognition and the impulsion that accompanies and is part of it, must struggle with opposing forces, with the inertia accumulated in steady engagement with familiar experience and it is this kind of conflict which is reflected in the rhythmic alternations, the advances and retreats of feeling experienced by those of Lawrence's characters who are capable of real growth, as they strive to create and maintain their central relationships.

In healthy individuals, these fluctuations of feeling cannot be deliberately orchestrated and so the creating and maintaining of relationship in Lawrence's fiction is constantly marked by failures of contact, by misunderstandings, or even tensions, which are created by the fact that even in individuals who are very close to one another, the affective rhythms, the involuntary flow and recoil of feeling, can become out of phase, as it were, and no deliberate act of will can restore mutual harmony. In the striking episode from *The Rainbow* where the young Anna and Will stack sheaves of corn in the moonlight, this complex interplay of individual psychic rhythms is given physical expression in the movements of the couple as they work. Beginning out of phase, their feelings, like their motion, become steadily more synchronous as the scene progresses. Appropriately for an episode which takes place beneath the moon, the passage is pervaded by imagery of sea and tides with the motion of the characters often described in terms of ebbing and flowing water.

At first the pair are radically out of step in the rhythm of their movements; gathering sheaves from opposite side of the field, they fail to meet in the centre—'The rhythm of the work carried him away again as she was coming near' so that 'always, she was gone before he came. She seems, in a phrase which suggests the sea, to 'stand off from him', although there is no suggestion that she is deliberately avoiding a meeting. On the contrary, her movements seem determined by forces outside herself—the moon shines down on her 'making her drift and ebb like a wave'. Lawrence is involving the traditional associations of the moon here to suggest that Anna is impelled in a specifically feminine kind of motion which is naturally different from and even resistant to masculine rhythms: the real association between the lunar cycle and menstruation links inner and outer experience. It is Will who brings their movements into harmony, through the exercise of his will, but the kind of willing involved is clearly not conscious and deliberate; it is 'a low, deep-sounding will in him [which] vibrated to her, tried to set her in accord'. In the description of its action, images of musical rhythm, moving water and darkness combine, all signalling its unconscious origins—

His will drummed persistently, darkly, it drowned everything else.

(**R** p 123)

The emphasis in the musical image is on rhythm rather than melody—and the 'sound' is linked with the directly physical appeal of beating drums which seem to compel movement in the hearer. Music is, of course, of central importance in Nietzsche's early philosophy because he took over and modified Schopenhauer's idea that it is through music that we are brought closest to the unconscious flow of things, the metaphysical Will, which is the hidden basis of the ordinary phenomenal world. For Nietzsche, music was the most direct expression of those processes which lie below the conscious level of the psyche. It is through the rhythm of his actions, which evoke a response at a similar deep physical and instictive level in Anna, that Will brings her into harmony with him and not through any attempt to persuade her into assent through words:

> Into the rhythm of his work there came a pulse and a steadied purpose . . . Ever with increasing closeness he lifted the sheaves and swung striding to the centre with them, ever he drove her more nearly to the meeting . . . And ever the splash of his sheaves broke swifter, beating up to hers, and ever the splash of her sheaves recurred monotonously, unchanging, and ever the splash of his sheaves beat nearer.
>
> (**R** p 123)

But because Anna is a separate individual with feelings and desires that do not necessarily coincide with these of Will, the harmony between them cannot be permanent and as their relationship continues through courtship and marriage, misunderstanding and frustration are inevitable as they are in any living relationship. And since the movements of feeling in each follow the alternating pattern determined below conscious level, which characterises Lawrences developing characters, their fluctuations of feeling have their own particular periodicity and cannot be brought to coincide in the interests of marital harmony by the exercise of conscious will.

The progress of the quarrel which follows Anna's carelessness with her husband's wood-carving books follows the same kind of pattern. In it, the discordant rhythms of feeling in each only gradually come into harmony again. At first—as with the alternations of desire and indifference which Lydia, in particular, experiences at the beginning of her relationship with Tom—the positive movements made by each partner fail to coincide. When Will comes home from work on the day after the dispute, he feels contrite and assumes that Anna will feel the same way:

> . . . when he came home at night, his heart relenting and growing hot for love of her, when he was just ready to feel he had been wrong, and when he was expecting her to feel the same, there she sat at the sewing-machine, the whole house was covered with clipped calico, the kettle was not even on the fire.
>     She started up, affecting concern.
>     'Is it so late?' she cried.
> But his face had gone stiff with rage. He walked through to the parlour, then he walked back and out of the house again. Her heart sank.
>
> (**R** p 164)

His abrupt departure makes Anna feel guilty, and she hurries to get things ready, hoping that he will return soon; however, as her wait lengthens, her renewed and intensified feeling of love for him and dependence on him is punctuated by periods when she reacts into asserting her own singleness and separateness:

> Anna had started guiltily when he left the house. She had hastened preparing the tea, hoping he would come back. She had made some toast and got all ready. Then he didn't come. She cried with vexation and disappointment. Why had he gone? Why couldn't he come back now? Why was it such a battle between them? She loved him—she did love him—why couldn't he be kinder to her, nicer to her?
>
> She waited in distress—then her mood grew harder. He passed out of her thoughts. She had considered indignantly, what right had he to interfere with her sewing? She had indignantly refuted his right to interfere with her at all. She was not to be interfered with. Was she not herself, and he the outsider?
>
> Yet a quiver of fear went through her. If he should leave her? She sat conjuring fears and sufferings, till she wept with self-pity. She did not know what she would do if he left her, or if he turned against her. The thought of it chilled her, made her desolate and hard.
>
> (**R** p 165)

In *Women in Love* such involuntary reversals of feeling both complicate the developing relationship between Ursula and Birkin and are largely responsible for the fact that the potentially fruitful contact between Birkin and Gerald Crich never gets beyond the initial stages. At the end of the 'Water-Party' chapter, Ursula has realised that she is 'deeply and passionately in love' with Birkin and waits impatiently for him to visit her on the day after the party—

> She stayed indoors all day, waiting for him to knock at the door. Every minute, she glanced at the window.
>
> (**WL** p 213)

Her excitement is understandable because she has become increasingly dissatisfied with her work and is finding life at home with her parents more and more constricting; Birkin seems to promise a freer and more rewarding kind of life. But as she waits her feelings change direction and the desire to move forward into a new kind of relationship gives way to an opposite impulse to retreat into separateness and rejection. It is clear from the narrative that this is not the kind of change we might expect under the circumstances, in which rationality and prudence reassert themselves after passion has died down, but an inexplicable reversal in feeling itself, which comes unbidden and over which, as a conscious, reasoning being, Ursula has no control:

> As the day wore on, the life blood seemed to ebb away from Ursula ... Her passion seemed to bleed to death ...
>
> (**WL** p 214)

By the time Birkin arrives, expecting her to be welcoming and responsive, the movement of feeling has taken her to a point where she feels separate from him again and even hostile; after his departure the hostility steadily intensifies into a positive and powerful—but inexplicable—'hatred'. A little later 'he had lost his significance, he scarcely mattered in her world' and Ursula turns 'back to the old ways with zest, away from him'. But her revulsion from the 'old ways' reasserts itself a little later with greater force and makes her more responsive to Birkin and what he represents when they meet again in the 'Moony' chapter—

> After his illness Birkin went to the South of France for a time. He did not write, nobody heard anything of him. Ursula, left alone, felt as if everything were lapsing out. There seemed to be no hope in the world. One was a tiny little rock with the tide of nothingness rising higher and higher. She herself was real, and only herself—just like a rock in a wash of flood-water.
>
> (**WL** p 275)

Complicating her development is a simultaneous, but uncreative, alternation between a conventional desire for 'pure love' and its obverse 'a luminousness of supreme repudiation', but this pattern is finally transcended when she realises that 'If fate would carry off in death or downfall all those who were timed to go, why need she trouble, why repudiate any further?'; as a result she becomes free of corrupt contemporary reality and can now 'seek a new union elsewhere'. It is in this state that she comes upon Birkin again.

In the central incident of the chapter, she sets out late in the evening for the mill at Willey Green where Birkin lives—though without making any conscious decision to go and see him and indeed without knowing that he has come back from France. The reader however is aware that her journey is connected with her sense that she can now seek a 'new union'. Walking on the bank above the mill-pond, she is aware of a figure near the water and realises that Birkin has returned unannounced. Unobserved, she watches him throw stones at the image of the moon reflected on the pond, in a mysteriously powerful scene reminiscent both of the episode in *The Rainbow* where Will and Anna stack sheaves of corn and of the later incident when Ursula and Shrebensky make love by moonlight on the sand-dunes. Birkin tries with increasing desperation to destroy the reflection; at first, he uses a single stone but despite breaking up the reflection into scattered flakes of light, he fails to shatter the centre, the 'heart of it all' which remains still 'vivid, incandescent ... not quite destroyed ... not even now broken open ...' It is as if this surviving centre possesses some power to reconstitute the complete image— 'It seemed to be drawing itself together with stange, violent pangs, in blind effort'. Birkin waits till the water has almost settled and the reflection 'almost serene' until he attacks it again, now with several stones in succession. This time there is 'no moon, only a battlefield of broken lights and shadows', but then, if more slowly this time, the moon '[regathers] itself insidiously', the 'heart of the rose ... calling back the scattered fragments' only to be attacked again, more vigorously as Birkin hurls even larger stones reducing the 'white-burning centre of the moon' till 'only a few broken flakes tangled and glittering broadcast in the darkness, without aim or meaning' remain. In the lengthy descriptions of the movement of light and water, there is a consistent emphasis on the wave-like pattern of ebb and flow which is the characteristic pattern of psychic change; like many similarly powerful scenes in both *The Rainbow* and *Women in Love*, the episode is both a detailed and convincing presentation of external reality and an objectification of psychic processes of which the characters themselves are only dimly aware. Birkin's actions spring from the difficulties and frustrations in his relationships with women in general and with Ursula in particular, something which is suggested by his angry reference to Cybele, although he himself is by no means fully aware of the reasons for his strange behaviour.

As is often the case in Lawrence's writing, physical actions reveal more about the character's fundamental being than anything which they say, or even think, about what is going on in them. Birkin associates the moon with these ancient religions in which the prominent deity was female and therefore with a conception of love between the sexes in which women are dominant. It is this conception of love which is characteristic of the society depicted in the novel although it takes different forms, ranging from the openly domineering attitude of Hermione who sees herself as the Magna Mater to the more subtle—and unconscious—assertion of primacy that Ursula makes, through her willingness to serve and sacrifice herself. The imagery used to describe the disintegrated reflection of the moon after Birkin's first attack on it links the scene with the earlier 'Water-Party' chapter in which female dominance the the destructive power women can exert over men is a central theme. When Birkin throws the stone Ursula is 'aware of the bright moon leaping and swaying, all distorted in her eyes' so that 'It seemed to shoot out arms of fire like a cuttlefish, like a luminous polyp, palpitating strongly before her'. In the later episode, the serene image of the moon reminds Birkin subliminally of the 'overweening assumption of female primacy' he has met in the women he has been closely involved with and he is provoked to a kind of symbolic reenactment of his efforts to challenge that assumption. The scene reflects the way in which he has been able to disturb Ursula's attachment to the conventional notion of love, but it also suggests that getting her to accept his new basis for relationship will be a difficult and prolonged process, determined on her side by movements of feeling in her which are beyond his—and even her— conscious control. The pattern suggested is not relevant just to changes in the relationship between men and women, of course, but to any sort of new initiative, which comes from the creative darkness of the unconscious and has to struggle with old feelings and impulses which are, however, still powerful, and resist its progress. The outcome is a struggle—in the imagery of the passage—between 'waves of darkness' and 'waves of light', the new creative impulse and the old confining one. So the dominant symbol in the scene, the moon itself, stands for more than just feminine dominance and destructiveness; more generally, it represents feelings, values, ideals which have become fixed, known, conscious. Shining as it does with reflected light the moon is an appropriate symbol for the Nietzschean conception of consciousness as a reflecting medium, mirroring in a dim, partial and often distorted way, the more extensive and creative unconscious area of the self, the 'dark sun' which illuminates the 'moon'.

In 'Water-Party' the two couples row back from the island in the lake on which the Brangwen sisters have landed earlier; night has fallen and they find their way by the light of four large, spherical Chinese lanterns, each of which has a striking scene painted on it. These scenes become visible when the lanterns are lit and their nature, and the way the characters react to them, are described in considerable detail. The fact that the glowing spheres resemble the moon (when the first is lit, it is described as a 'great blue moon of light') provides one link with 'Moony', but a more significant connection is established by the picture on Gudrun's second lantern which shows a beautiful, but sinister, underwater scene:

> It was of a lovely deep blue colour, with a red floor, and a great white cuttle-fish flowing in soft streams all over it. The cuttle-fish had a face that stared straight from the heart of the light, very fixed and coldly intent.
>
> (**WL** p 196)

Gudrun reacts with intense—and unexpected—horror to her lantern; indeed her feelings are so strong that it is clear that the image has some deep, though scarcely understood, significance for her. Her revulsion suggests, in fact, that the picture reveals something fundamental about her own nature which she is reluctant to expose and confront: it is one example of general dislike in her of being 'exposed' or of 'giving herself away' which Birkin recognises and comments on to Gerald, and which springs from her dim recognition of the destructiveness which lies in the depths of her psyche. The cuttle-fish is an image of this destructiveness, standing for a kind of power which is both predatory and at the same time soft, enveloping and insidious—the kind of subtly destructive power developed by those who lack straightforward physical strength—notably women. Such subtle power is not necessarily destructive, of course, and the cuttle-fish image is used in a more neutral way in connection with the wrestling match between Birkin and Gerald in 'Gladiatorial'. Before their tussle starts, Birkin says that he once learned some ju-jitsu from a Japanese he knew who was

> very quick and slippery and full of electric fire. It is a remarkable thing what a curious sort of fluid force they seem to have in them, those people—not like a human grip—like a polyp.
>
> (**WL** p 303)

And in the fight itself there is a 'strange, octopus-like knotting and flashing of limbs.'

Physically slighter than Europeans, the Japanese have developed a mode of fighting which depends on a fluid and subtle deployment of force, in which the more straightforward kinds of strength are used against themselves; the technique is appropriate to the comparatively frail Birkin in his contest with a larger and heavier opponent and although he does not claim to be much good at it, his knowledge of ju-jitsu allows him to do rather more than hold his own against the stronger man. In fact, this kind of subtle strength is in the end more effective than main force because, while the exercise of cruder kinds of power only compels a temporary and external submission, finer kinds of force have a more inward and lasting effect. Birkin's 'fine, sublimated energy' works with an 'uncanny force', seeming to 'penetrate into Gerald's more solid, more diffuse bulk, to interfuse his body through the body of the other as if to bring it subtly in to subjection' and spreading 'a fine net, a prison, through the muscles into the very depths of Gerald's physical being'.

The link between the sinister image of the cuttle-fish on the lantern and Gudrun's unacknowledged impulses is not directly made, but is subtly suggested both by her reaction to the painted scene and by the way in which, earlier in the same chapter, her curious 'shuddering and waving and drifting' dance before the bullocks is described. Dressed in white, she moves towards them with sinuous movements as if borne along by the tide—

> ... she drifted imperceptibly nearer, an uncanny white figure, towards them, carried away in its own rapt trance, ebbing in strange fluctuations.
>
> (**WL** p 187)

The description points forward to that of the white cuttlefish 'flowing in white, soft, streams'. Gudrun is not consciously aware of the resemblance of course and is unable to understand why she is so horrified by the lantern; her dancing is not the expression of a conscious impulse but arises, as the narrative emphasises, from the unconscious depths of her psyche.

As is usually the case in Lawrence's fiction, art, especially of a spontaneous and unrehearsed kind like Gudrun's dancing, reveals aspects of being which the characters are not only unaware of on a conscious level, but which they actively, if unconsciously, resist bringing to light in normal circumstances. Gudrun's dancing, which is improvised and not something learned, expresses her deepest needs and longings and links up with her response to art in her reaction to the painting on the lantern; both have considerable diagnostic significance, laying bare the nature of her fundamental impulses. Because Gudrun's dancing springs from and expresses her unconscious self in this way, it speaks to Ursula at a similar fundamental level—although on the surface she is amused by her sister's odd behaviour, she nevertheless recognises something of its true significance. Her eyes laugh 'as if she thought it was a great joke, but a yellow light [flashed] up in them, as she caught some of the unconscious ritualistic suggestion of the complex shuddering and waving and drifting of her sister's white form'.

To begin with, Gudrun's movements communicate a feeling of being held in bondage, 'as if some invisible chain weighed on her hands and feet', but as she becomes more absorbed and her unconscious begins to assert itself, the inhibitions and concealments which are such a marked feature of her ordinary behaviour are shed and her fundamental impulses come to light. The appearance of a group of Highland cattle seems to give Gudrun the stimulus she needs to abandon herself fully to her 'rapt trance'; although nervous of the cattle, she sees them as a challenge to some 'secret power' she feels herself endowed with and longs to exercise and her dancing is, if unconsciously, intended to frighten them and make them retreat in panic. Since the cattle are bullocks, the dance reveals her unconscious desire to torment and humiliate natural maleness and her treatment of Gerald when he appears and remonstrates with her offers further evidence of this. Still in the grip of her deep, subconscious impulses, she is—despite being his guest and lacking any sort of ordinary pretext for her behaviour—threatening and hostile towards him, slapping his face and feeling 'in her soul an unconquerable desire for deep violence against him'.

The way in which dancing can express aspects of being deeper than those usually displayed is also illustrated earlier in the novel in the dance drama of Naomi and her daughters which is performed by some of the woman guests in Hermione's house-party at Breadalby. As the story is acted out, the deepest impulses of those involved are revealed, even though they themselves are not aware of what they are bringing to light. What is—involuntarily— communicated is understood by the watchers not on a conscious level, but in a more intimate and intuitive way. So Hermione loves to watch and is aware of the subtle and subterranean things being expressed:

> She could see the Contessa's rapid, stoat-like sensationalism, Gudrun's ultimate but treacherous cleaving to the woman in her sister, Ursula's dangerous helplessness, as if she were helplessly weighted and unreleased.
>
> (**WL** p 102)

Ursula's state of 'helplessness' here resembles the 'imprisonment' expressed in her sister's dance before the bullocks although, of course, the impulses which are held captive in her by outworn cultural forms are of a different, even opposite, kind. But Hermione is frustrated in her 'knowing' here because it does not depend on the conscious awareness which is the only kind of knowledge she recognises and values; she '[writhes] in her soul, knowing what she could not know'—intuitive understanding cannot be translated into conscious 'knowledge'. In the same way, Gerald's awareness of Gudrun's 'subterranean recklessness and mockery' is something which '[penetrates] his blood' and he is excited by the possibility of unconventional kinds of relationship suggested by this knowledge. At the same time, we are made aware of the unconscious emotional duplicity in Gudrun's feelings for her sister— something neither sister is aware of at this point—and the combination of 'clinging' and 'subtle malevolence' Gudrun displays towards Ursula points forward to the nature of her relationship with Gerald. Birkin's interest is focussed on Ursula and through her dancing he registers both her present frustration and her potential for life and growth in the same unconscious fashion:

And Birkin, watching like a hermit crab from its hole, had seen the brilliant
frustration and helplessness of Ursula. She was like a strange unconscious bud
of powerful womanhood. He was unconsciously drawn to her.

(**WL** p 102)

The men also reveal their deepest selves in the dancing which follows:
Gerald feels the exhilaration of motion but cannot get quite free of conventional, learned movements and respond in an individual way to the music.
Birkin is also inhibited by the atmosphere, but can on occasion free himself
and dance 'rapidly and with real gaiety' in a way which reveals his
changeable, mobile nature—looking at him, the Contessa remarks that he is
'a chameleon, a creature of change'. The sensual, improvisatory dance
Birkin performs at Breadalby is one of the things which links the earlier with
the later 'Water-Party' chapter—just as the frustration expressed in Ursula's
dancing anticipates the sense of being in bondage conveyed by Gudrun's later
dance on the island. On the first occasion he performs it, it is Hermione who
reacts most strongly to what it conveys, seeing it as an unworthy expression
of the 'merely' physical. Her reaction is violent because simply by dancing,
Birkin seems to be challenging—or even repudiating—both her view of him
and her general view of what is important in human experience. Birkin dances
a second time on the island, this time in front of Ursula who, although less
committed than Hermione to the 'ideal' and 'spiritual' is still influenced
enough by conventional values to be uneasy when she sees 'a man who talked
as a rule so very seriously' abandom himself to the rhythms of the jazz-dance.
Conditioned to regard the spiritual and the physical as mutually antithetical
principles, on a conscious level Ursula disapproves of this 'lowering' of
himself since it is not consistent with his seriousness and spiritual worth. Yet,
at the same time, at a deeper level, she responds strongly

... somewhere inside her she was fascinated by the sight of his loose, vibrating
body, perfectly abandoned to its own dropping and swinging ...

(**WL** p 189)

It is a response which suggests that, with help from Birkin, she will be able
to move beyond the debilitating and false antithesis which conventional
idealism proposes.

The whole future of the relationship between Gudrun and Gerald is
summed up in the exchange which follows the slap in 'Water Party'. Light
though the blow is, it has a profound effect on Gerald and it is some time
before he is able to speak:

'You have struck the first blow,' he said at last, forcing the words from his
lungs, in a voice so soft and low, it sounded like a dream within her, not spoken
in the outer air.

'And I shall strike the last,' she retorted involuntarily, with confident
assurance.

(**WL** p. 191)

It is at this point that Gerald says he is in love with her, but on Gudrun's side, the exchange is more like a declaration of war than a declaration of love; their association will be a contest, a struggle for power of a destructive kind, which Gudrun is confident she will win. And her assertion that she will strike the last blow as she has struck the first is made 'involuntarily', indicating that like the impulse to violence itself, her consciousness of her own superior strength comes from the deepest level of her psyche. At the same time, the lack of consonance between conscious and unconscious is underlined by Gudrun's own realisation, on the conscious level, that she is behaving in an 'impossible and ridiculous fashion'. But because her conscious self has not reassumed full control at this point, this awareness is not strong enough to disguise or conceal her desire for violence against Gerald. Her confidence in ultimate victory is an expression of an intuitive awareness that her kind of strength, more subtle and developed than Gerald's, represents a much greater *degree* of strength.

Such subtle and perceptive power is often associated with women who, as members of the physically weaker sex, have needed to develop oblique kinds of strength: characteristically, it attains its goal through apparent submission and the creation of dependence in the other party to the relationship. It is this strategy which Gudrun instinctively employs when she becomes Gerald's mistress; in doing so, she creates a powerful need in him which ensures that she retains real control in their relationship whatever may seem to be the case on the surface. The 'old way of love', the traditional romantic love which Birkin constantly attacks, is the most pervasive and destructive form of this feminine strategy of dominance through submission.

The underwater world and its sinister denizens, with which Gudrun is linked through the imagery in 'Water-Party', is one of the major symbols of the book, standing for a fluid, inchoate realm in which the form-creating capacity of the will-to-power has lapsed. Lawrence does not leave things on the metaphorical level however—he illustrates them in a direct and concrete way through incidents like the death of Diana Crich and her lover. On the face of it, this is no more than a tragic accident—a spoilt, wilful girl persists in dancing on the roof of one of the launches, falls into the lake and drowns along with her lover who has tried to rescue her—but the narrative makes it clear that is is not a chance event but falls instead into that category of 'accidentally-on-purpose' happenings which is so important in the novel. As with other events of the same kind, notably Gerald's 'accidental' shooting of his brother, the lack of any consciously destructive motive does not imply that the act is motiveless or unintended in a deeper sense. Like her brother, Diana has a powerful unconscious urge to destruction (and self-destruction) which manifests itself in her 'accident'. Aware of such an impulse in himself, Gerald recognises it in his sister and it is this which explains his unexpected response when the bodies of the drowned couple are finally found—instead of seeing the death of the young doctor who had attempted a rescue as a tragic but natural result of the drowning girl's panic, he feels that her action was deliberate, commenting bitterly that 'She killed him'. What he is implying is supported by the position of the bodies—'Diana had her arms tight round the neck of the young man, choking him.' The relation between feminine destructiveness and romantic love, a connection which preoccupies Birkin, is suggested by the way in which the drowned pair are discovered locked in what seems like a deathly parody of a passionate embrace.

Both Gerald and Gudrun feel a kind of fascination with and affinity for the inchoate, watery realm in which the couple have disappeared. When Gerald comes to the surface during his attempts to find them, Gudrun sees him as being like some large aquatic animal, as if water rather than land were his natural element. And the question he asks Gudrun on one of his reappearances—'Why come to life again? There's room under that water for thousands'—reveals that he feels he belongs there himself and shares his sisters' death-wish. Gudrun too is both fascinated and repelled by the realisation that she is, literally as well as metaphorically, 'suspended on the surface of the insidious reality until such time as she also should disappear beneath it'.

Rupert Birkin's reaction to the girl's death is characteristically unconventional; for him it is a good thing, cutting short a 'fretful and negated' life and sparing the young man in the case a prolonged, painful and damaging relationship. Had they remained alive the couple, like most of their contemporaries, would have lived the 'life which belongs to death' which even Birkin himself is still largely held by. His epitaph on Diana and her lover, together with the way in which both Gerald and Gudrun are linked with the circumstances of the drowning has ironic implications for the future of the couple, suggesting that they are doomed to live out the prolonged, disintegrative relationship which the dead pair have—luckily—escaped.

Birkin employs the same metaphor of rebirth for the hoped-for transition from the 'life that belongs to death' to the 'life that isn't death' as Lawrence had used in connection with Lydia Lensky's development in *The Rainbow*. In each case the conscious, willing element in the psyche is in abeyance, and the character is seen as passive, impelled into a new phase of being by forces which are far more powerful and mysterious than any they are consciously aware of and which are beyond any conscious attempt at control, or even understanding. And the kind of development implied in both cases is an alternating, to-and-fro progress rather than a steady movement in one direction. Because neither the pace nor the outcome of this process can be influenced by the conscious will, Birkin—in common with other characters undergoing this kind of change—frequently feels helpless and frustrated:

> One is tired of the life that belongs to death—our kind of life. But whether it is finished, God knows.
>
> **(WL** p 208)

His strong desire to escape his present existence is not enough to bring about the change:

> ... I *do* want to die from this life—and yet it is more than life itself. One is delivered over like a naked infant from the womb, all the old defences, and the old body gone, and new air around one, that has never been breathed before.
>
> **(WL** p 208)

Lawrence's major metaphors for human development—birth and rebirth—together with the related ideas of death and resurrection and the flowing and ebbing of the tides, all suggest that the forces which determine our lives come from outside the conscious self and move us, by a process of alternate advance and retreat, toward new experience. Together with the rest of his characteristic images these also illustrate other aspects of Lawrence's view of the psyche—of the nature and relationship of the different areas, levels and processes within it. The unconscious part of the self is often associated with extensive and untamed natural settings, with the sea, for example, or with primaeval forest or jungle. Such comparisons emphasise both the sheer extent of the unconscious element in our natures and also link the powers active in human nature with those which work in the world at large. This kind of psychic landscape also allows Lawrence to suggest the awesome power of the forces emanating from that part of the self which he often calls (in a deliberately provocative way) the 'soul'. These forces appear as elemental energies like wind or tide, or as denizens of the wilderness; wild animals, angels or dark, chthonic gods, In such a symbolic landscape too, the objective insignificance of the conscious self can be vividly and concretely conveyed by representing it as a small cleared or lighted space amidst a vast, circumambient darkness.

Lawrence's view of the nature of the psyche and particularly of the relation between the conscious and the unconscious elements in it is summarised most succinctly in the Benjamin Franklin essay from *Studies in Classic American Literature*. There he attacks Franklin's rationalistic assimilation of the soul to the known part of the self, an identification which he sees as part of that 'absurd overestimation of consciousness' typical of the Western intellectual tradition:

> ... man has a soul, though you can't locate it either in his purse or his pocket-book or his heart or his stomach or his head. The wholeness of a man is his soul. Not merely that nice little comfortable bit which Benjamin makes out.
>
> It's a queer thing is a man's soul. It is the whole of him. Which means it is the unknown him, as well as the known. It seems to me just funny, professors and Benjamins fixing the functions of the soul. Why, the soul of man is a vast forest, and all Benjamin intended was a neat back garden. And we've got to fit into his kitchen garden scheme of things ...
>
> The soul of man is a dark forest. The Hercynian Wood that scared the Romans so, and out of which came the white-skinned hordes of the next civilisation.
>
> Who knows what will come out of the soul of man? The soul of man is a dark vast forest, with wild life in it.[16]

Later in the same essay, Lawrence sets out his own alternative creed:

> *That I am I.*
> *That my soul is a dark forest.*
> *That my known self will never be more than a little clearing in the forest.*
> *That gods, strange gods, come forth from the forest into the clearing of my known self, and then go back.*

> That I must have the courage to let them come and go.
> That I will never let mankind put anything over me, but that I will try always
> to recognise and submit to the gods in me and the gods in other men and
> women.[17]

The contrast between this twentieth century credo and the eighteenth century
rationalist one which provoked it is a measure of the intellectual revolution
which had taken place in the intervening period. Lawrence's beliefs illustrate
Nietzsche's claim that nineteenth century developments have forced us
radically to alter our view of human nature, so that we have now entered 'the
phase of modesty of consciousness'.

The view of the self which Lawrence outlines in his Franklin essay is clearly
related to Nietzschean ideas about the shallowness of conscious awareness.
Since, in Nietzsche's view, 'consciousness' is essentially an internal mirroring
process which does not reflect fully and accurately the decisive forces and
events in the 'soul', it follows that the 'self' must remain mysterious to the
introspecting subject. And since Nietzsche also sees the self as something
essentially dynamic, as an arena for contending forces, we are likely to find
our own development perpetually taking unexpected and even contradictory
directions. So, near the end of *The Rainbow*, when Ursula Brangwen looks
back on her life hitherto, she is struck by how much she has changed in the
various stages of her development and this makes her aware that her own
identity is a mystery, even to herself:

> In every phase she was so different. Yet she was always Ursula Brangwen. But
> what did it mean, Ursula Brangwen? She did not know what she was.
>
> (**R** p 437)

Through her awareness of her own self as a creative mystery, Ursula begins
to see the limitations of the rationalism which dominates modern living and
which she has accepted as reflecting the whole truth of things despite occasional intuitions of a different kind:

> This world in which she lived was like a circle lighted by a lamp. This lighted
> area, lit up by man's completest consciousness, she thought was all the world:
> that here all was disclosed for ever. Yet all the time, within the darkness she
> had been aware of points of light, like the eyes of wild beasts, gleaming,
> penetrating, vanishing.
>    She could see the glimmer of dark movement just out of range, she saw the
> eyes of the wild beast gleaming from the darkness, watching the vanity of the
> camp fire and the sleepers; she felt the strange, foolish vanity of the camp,
> which said 'Beyond our light and our order there is nothing', turning their faces
> always inward towards the sinking fire of illuminating consciousness, which
> comprised sun and stars, and the Creator, and the System of Righteousness,
> ignoring always the vast darkness that wheeled round about, with half-revealed
> shapes lurking on the edge.
>    Yea, and no man dared even throw a firebrand into the darkness. For if he
> did he was jeered to death by the others, who cried 'Fool, anti-social knave,
> why would you disturb us with bogeys? There *is* no darkness. We move and

live and have our being within the light, and unto us is given the eternal light of knowledge, we comprise and comprehend the innermost core and issue of knowledge. Fool and knave, how dare you belittle us with the darkness?

Nevertheless the darkness wheeled round about, with grey shadow-shapes of wild beasts, and also with dark shadow-shapes of the angels, whom the light fenced out, as it fenced out the more familiar beasts of darkness. And some, having for a moment seen the darkness, saw it bristling with the tufts of the hyena and the wolf; and some, having given up their vanity of the light, having died in their own conceit, saw the gleam in the eyes of the wolf and the hyena, that it was the flash of the sword of angels, flashing at the door to come in, that the angels in the darkness were lordly and terrible and not to be denied, like the flash of fangs.

(**R** p 438)

Ursula sees that even the majority, who think of themselves as wholly rational and social beings are driven by forces from the darkness which they refuse to recognise and, in herself, she mocks their sham existence:

She could see, beneath their pale, wooden pretence of composure and civic purposefulness, the dark stream that contained them all. They were like little paper ships in their motion. But in reality each one was a dark, blind, eager wave urging blindly forward, dark with the same homogeneous desire.

(**R** p 448)

The image of physical, instinctive life as a stream on which the conscious self helplessly floats echoes a passage from *The Will to Power* in which Nietzsche describes the human body as something 'in which the most distant and most recent past of all organic development again becomes living and corporeal, through which and over which and beyond which a tremendous inaudible stream seems to flow'.[18] The conscious self is a mere instrument of this more powerful force:

The animal functions are, as a matter of principle, a million times more important than all our beautiful moods and heights of consciousness: the latter are a surplus, except when they have to serve as tools of these animal functions. The entire *conscious* life, the spirit along with the soul, the heart, goodness, and virtue—in whose service do they labour? In the service of the greatest possible perfection of the means (means of nourishment, means of enhancement) of the basic animal functions: above all, the enhancement of life.[19]

Nietzsche argues, too, that the role of consciousness in the activity of the self as a whole is often to conceal the real nature of the forces at work in us, to assist our 'urges' to assume their various 'flattering disguises' with the result that we generally have a quite inaccurate conception of our deepest motives and interests. It is only when we employ 'external phenomenology' that we arrive at a more accurate picture:

In the tremendous multiplicity of events within an organism, the part which becomes conscious to us is a mere means: and the little bit of 'virtue', 'selflessness', and similar fictions are refuted radically by the total balance of events. We should study our organism in all its immorality.[21]

So Ursula sees the conscious personality—civilised, socially responsible, rational—as a kind of 'dress', as something which conceals, but does not alter the 'body', the instinctual self underneath:

> 'They assume selves as they assume suits of clothing,' she said to herself, looking in mocking contempt at the stiffened, neutralized men. 'They think it better to be clerks or professors than to be the dark, fertile beings that exist in the potential darkness. What do you think you are?' her soul asked the professor as she sat opposite him in class. 'What do you think you are, as you sit there in your gown and your spectacles? You are a lurking, blood-sniffing creature with eyes peering out of the jungle darkness, snuffing for your desires. That is what you *are*, though nobody would believe it, and you would be the very last to allow it.
>
> (**R** p 448)

Here the conventional self is associated with what is human, moral and social, while the real self is pictured as a solitary, predatory jungle creature, an image which links the unconscious with the wild and primitive vitality of the native American landscape or the Hercynian Forest in the Franklin essay. Such associations reflect the Nietzschean idea that instinct is a kind of re-enactment of the past in the present, that the physical side of life is part of, in Nietzsche's own phrase, an 'inaudible stream', a prolonged evolutionary process in which we are involved. The power and persistence in us of our 'animal functions' is a reminder that these things we tend to think of as characteristically and distinguishingly 'human' have developed relatively late in the history of the species; it is our 'animal' traits which are oldest and which have therefore been reinforced most strongly.

CHAPTER 6

# Body and Spirit

Nietzsche constantly insists on the dominance of the physical and instinctive and on the derivative and instrumental character of whatever is conscious. Nevertheless, he did believe that under certain circumstances, consciousness could come to dominate and subvert instinctive being. Because it has grown up comparatively recently in the history of mankind, consciousness often tends to be incompletely integrated in to the psychic economy as a whole and its 'stupidity' can endanger it:

> What one used to call 'body' and 'flesh' is of such unspeakably greater importance: the remainder is a small accessory. The task of spinning on the chain of life, and in such a way that the thread grows ever more powerful—that is the task.
>
> But consider how heart, soul, virtue, spirit practically conspire together to subvert this systematic task—as if *they* were the end in view!—The degeneration of life is conditioned essentially by the extraordinary proneness to error of consciousness: it is held in check by instinct least of all and therefore blunders the longest and most thoroughly.[1]

This unnatural and damaging dominance of consciousness over instinct is particularly important in the modern, developed societies in which most of Lawrence's characters live their lives, because Lawrence, like Nietzsche, believes that such societies are governed by value-systems in which the most important element is some variety of 'herd-morality'. This kind of morality represents the outlook of the unexceptional majority who are timid and gregarious—consequently, its highest virtues are those which are reassuring and socially useful. Its ideal is the 'good citizen', sober, punctual, reliable, peaceable and largely identified with his social function. In the Western moral tradition, the influence of 'herd' values is combined with elements of the Christian code, a different, though related, moral outlook, which Nietzsche classifies as a 'slave morality' and which he sees as a product of the resentment felt by the inferior and ill-constituted for their vital superiors. Both of these dominant ingredients in the composite moral tradition we have inherited is an example of an absolute moral code, a code that is which claims to be invariant as to persons, times and circumstances, which is binding for everyone at all times whatever conditions they find themselves in. A moral code of this kind

> claims absolute uniformity of form: it does not offer different ideals for different types of life but insists that a single pattern, a single rule, obtains for all ... Its content consists in absolute antitheses: certain qualities are utterly good, others utterly evil ... These qualities belong to conscious motives for which we are morally responsible; if our motives are guilty we suffer remorse and deserve retributive punishment. Finally, the good qualities are self-denial and pity, the evil ones selfishness and will to power[2]

Absolute codes of this kind are the creations of the conscious part of the self; their origins can be detected not only in their emphasis on the causal importance of conscious intention, but also in their simplifying, schematising tendency, which denies the distinctiveness and changeableness of the individual psyche and attempts to impose on spontaneous being a consistency false to its intrinsic nature. Under the influence of absolute morality, life becomes mechanical and repetitive instead of having organic shape and fluidity. In *The Rainbow*, both Ursula and Skrebensky are aware of the dominance of the social, 'herd' element over the individual in most of the people around them, who have assumed a 'civic uniform'. Ursula's conclusion that those around her are 'dummies' acting out a 'pale wooden pretence of composure and civic purposefulness' is echoed by Skrebensky who, with 'no civic self to maintain', watches them

> as a lion or a tiger may lie with narrowed eyes watching the people passing before its cage, the kaleidoscopic unreality of people, or a leopard lie blinking, watching the incomprehensible feats of the keepers. He despised it all—it was non-existent. Their good professors, their good clergyman, their good political speakers, their good, earnest women—all the time he felt his soul was grinning, grinning at the sight of them. So many performing puppets, all wood and rag for the performance.
> He watched the citizen, a pillar of society, a model, saw the stiff goat's legs, which had become almost stiffened to wood in the desire to make them puppet in their action, he saw the trousers formed to the puppet action: man's legs, but man's legs become rigid and deformed, ugly, mechanical.
>
> (**R** p 449)

But the fact that each sees man's animal nature as surviving, if distorted and obscured by the superficial 'social self', helps to justify the optimism of Ursula's vision at the end of the novel. The point is that the physical, instinctive side of our being, and the qualities associated with it is, in the end, more fundamental and powerful than the conscious, rational, social element—and it is so because it has been more strongly reinforced because, as the novel suggests, man has lived for most of his history in close contact with the land and the rest of nature and his being has been decisively shaped by that experience.

If the physical life lived by the Brangwens at the beginning of *The Rainbow* is described in biblical language and biblical cadences, this is not simply because Lawrence wants us to feel reverence for 'blood intimacy'; he also wants to emphasise its antiquity—to stress the fundamental continuity between life at the Marsh Farm and ancient patterns of existence. Despite the changes in life on the land—some of which might be seen as revolutionary—Lawrence wants to suggest that the historical phase which begins with the coming of industrialism represents a far more radical break with the past than anything which has happened before.

The traits appropriate to life on the land have become assimilated and now constitute our dominant instincts. Urban, industrial conditions, on the other hand, have developed fairly recently and the attitudes and habits appropriate to them—attitudes and habits largely opposite to those evolved in contact with nature—have not been so thoroughly assimilated and so remain relatively superficial. The hard, mechanical appearance of industrial man is no more than a shell, a carapace, covering the spontaneous life below, rather as the garb of the 'good citizen' conceals the 'lurking, blood-sniffing creature' which is the real self. And the mechanical shell is 'brittle' in relation to the power of the forces working underneath. The 'confident note of pro-phetic hope' at the conclusion of *The Rainbow* is not mere wish-fulfilment, 'wholly unprepared and unsupported, defying the previous pages',[3] but a vision of renewal firmly grounded in Lawrence's view of man's development through the ages. The imagery of that final vision makes it clear that at this point at least. Lawrence saw the hardness and mechanical movement of con-temporary civilized man as a surface phenomenon, as something which con-ceals but has not contaminated the instinctive life underneath, and which will be sloughed off as inexorably as the husk is outgrown and shed in vegetative life:

> She knew that the sordid people who crept hard-scaled and separate on the face of the world's corruption were living still, that the rainbow was arched in their blood and would quiver to life in their spirit, that they would cast off their horny covering of disintegration, that new, clean, naked bodies would issue to a new germination, to a new growth, rising to the light and the wind and the clean rain of heaven. She saw in the rainbow the earth's new architecture, the old, brittle corruption of houses and factories swept away, the world built up in a living fabric of Truth, fitting to the over-arching heaven.
>
> (**R** pp 495–6)

But despite the reference to 'clean, naked bodies', the transformation Ursula imagines is not simply a reversion to the more primitive, largely sensuous existence her forebears have led. The future is associated with two images which, in Lawrence's work, always stand for the integration of sense and spirit, body and soul: one is the germinating plant which will ultimately blossom, the other that tradition symbol of the reconciliation of heaven and earth, of 'higher' and 'lower', the rainbow. Both images are linked with the Nietzschean idea of spiritualisation outlined in 'Discipline', in which spirit develops out of vivid, instinctive being as the flower grows from the strong roots grappling in the darkness; both images challenge by implication the notion of a fundamental opposition between body and spirit, instinct and soul, which Lawrence and Nietzsche saw as characteristic of the Western tradition.

Evidently Ursula's attitudes have changed from the time when, disillusioned by her contact with intellectual life at College she had reacted against the general reverence for consciousness and intellect and persuaded herself that only the 'sensual darkness' was real and that physical satisfaction alone could be the basis for a fulfilled life. She had come to feel like that partly through the influence of Skrebensky who, just back from service in the Boer War, was still under the spell of the darkly sensual native life:

> He was to her a voice out of the darkness. He talked to her all the while, in low tones, about Africa, conveying something strange and sensual to her: the negro, with his loose, soft passion that could envelop one like a bath. Gradually he transferred to her the hot, fecund darkness that possessed his own blood.
>
> (R p 446)

Like him, she becomes a denizen of the 'universal night', seeing the ordinary, day-time social world as unreal—

> dark and soft and incontestable, their bodies walked untouched by the lights, darkness supreme and arrogant.
> 'The stupid lights,' Ursula said to herself, in her dark sensual arrogance.
> 'The stupid, artificial, exaggerated town, fuming its lights. It does not exist really, it rests upon the unlimited darkness, like a gleam of coloured oil on dark water, but what is it?—nothing, just nothing.
>
> (R p 447)

In touch with the Dionysian darkness which is the source of all being, Ursula had believed at that point that she possessed everything real and important—

> She was free as a leopard that sends up its raucous cry in the night. She had the potent, dark stream of her own blood, she had the glittering core of fecundity, she had her mate, her complement, her sharer in fruition. So she had all, everything.
>
> (R p 449)

But we are told that this view of things grows out of 'arrogance', suggesting that it is partial and over-confident.

From the moment their relationship is resumed, Ursula is disturbed by the lack of courage and individuality Skrebensky displays in his social attitudes and by his willingness to become an imperial administrator, devoting his energies to the development of India rather than to the proper—and more difficult task—of self-creation. His ambition to be 'lord and master of a clumsier civilisation than his own' involves an evasion of the really significant challenge. Like Nietzsche, Lawrence tended to see political ambition, the desire for authority over others, as an avoidance of the fundamental human task of 'self-overcoming', the creation of the self from the raw material of being. Ursula can see that in pursuing a career in the colonies, Skrebensky will be 'always side-tracking, always side-tracking his own soul'. So although 'she loved him, the body of him, whatever his decisions might be', she comes to realise that the physical cannot be 'all, everything' to her and that the physical satisfaction which marriage to him might bring would not be enough—she needs 'spiritual' fulfilment as well.

Unlike Anthony Schofield, who is a wholly physical being and so can only arouse a nostalgic longing for a kind of existence Ursula knows she can never recover, Skrebensky is a conscious, intellectual being and so attracts her more strongly. At the same time she is aware from the moment she meets him again that their relationship is a temporary alliance of opposites, that 'they were enemies come together in a truce'. For all his physical vitality, Skrebensky is intellectually and spiritually undeveloped, made up of 'a set of habitual actions and decisions'. In fact, Skrebensky is in many ways like a secular version of her father Will, acception the authority of the state as he accepts the authority of the church, the change reflecting Nietzsche's belief that in modern societies devotion to the state has taken the place of religious obedience. And both men are also alike in recognising that the authority to which they submit has no real validity: Will's faith is undermined by his wife's skepticism while Skrebensky sees the social world as a mere 'puppet-show'—but neither is morally courageous enough to abandon conventional ideas and set about creating his own distinctive values. Both Will and Skrebensky have the vigorous sensual being on which intellectual and spiritual creativity depend, but neither has the resolution to begin on the difficult task of organising and controlling the 'animal functions' so that they issue in some genuinely individual expression of spirit. In each the 'soul'—the spiritual dimension of the self—remains 'wavering, vague'.

Ursula cannot form a lasting relation with Skrebensky because their association only offers partial fulfilment and the urge in her towards a more complete kind of satisfaction—an urge which begins in Tom, her grandfather, and increases in force from generation to generation—cannot, in her, be denied. The affair with Skrebensky represents an instinctive, but temporary reaction against the shallow intellectuality of college life; the physical satisfaction she finds with him is needed to restore a psychic balance which has been upset. But the position she adopts when the liaison begins is an extreme and untenable one and her assertion that only the sensual is real and valuable is merely the obverse of the rationalism dominant in society at large. Her claim that the social and cultural are unreal represents, in other words, the same kind of rebellion against the dominant orthodoxy as Annable's dismissal of culture in *The White Peacock*. Both react against the current overvaluation of intellect and consciousness into a primitivism which Nietzsche sees as common and understandable—in the modern age. But for both Nietzsche and Lawrence, such an attitude is finally unsatisfactory because it does not represent any really new departure; as the simple negation of idealism it remains bound to what it denies.

In *The White Peacock*, the reaction into primitivism was provoked by the 'decadent' element in the prevailing value-system in which nature and culture were seen as antithetical. It is the idealism of his refined, aristocratic wife that drives Annable to rebellion. But the keeper lacks the strength and resilience to go beyond mere negation, whereas Birkin, who is driven, though his involvement with Hermione and her world, to an equally emphatic repudiation of contemporary humanity and its values, is able to move forward—if tentatively and with occasional lapses back into rejection—towards new kinds of commitment. In Birkin's case, the nihilistic vision espoused by Annable, of a natural world purged of corrupt humanity, is just a phase, though an important one, in his continuing development; in the 'Island' chapter of *Women in Love* he can wish for man to be 'swept off the face of the earth', even accepting his own death if 'the earth would really be cleaned of all the people' but the chapters that follow trace his growing involvement with Ursula and their mutual search for a new and more satisfactory basis for the relation between the sexes.

Both Lawrence and Nietzsche see the belief in a fundamental and necessary opposition between body and spirit as having survived the contemporary decline in Christian belief, but each also emphasises the growing importance in modern developed societies of the 'herd-morality' which is one of the major elements in our ethical inheritance. Historically, 'herd' and 'ascetic' moralities have been allies each striving, though for different reasons, to repress the 'animal' in man: it is this goal which leads Nietzsche and Lawrence to condemn both. Their hostility springs from a fear they share that in weakening or repressing the physical, instinctive elements in us, our moral tradition may make us in the end incapable of genuine culture or true spirituality, which have their roots in the animal side of being. Through Zarathustra's rehabilitation of the 'three evil things', sensuality, selfishness and lust for power, Nietzsche emphasises how much of what man has admired most has arisen from the very things in him often regarded as base, immoral or anti-social. For Nietzsche, 'civilisation' and 'culture' are opposite concepts; the elimination of the dark, dangerous, asocial elements in humanity will produce 'civilised' man, a being completely adjusted to social living, the ideal servant of an order which will be wholly mechanical, materialistic and uncreative, since the forces from which true creativity springs will have been destroyed:

> The high points of culture and civilisation do not coincide: one should not be deceived about the fundamental antagonism of culture and civilisation. The great moments of culture were always, morally speaking, times of corruption; and conversely, the periods when the taming of the human animal ('civilisation') was desired and enforced were times of intolerance against the boldest and most spiritual natures. Civilisation has aims different from those of culture—perhaps they are even opposite.[4]

The issue of 'Culture contra civilisation' (as Nietzsche puts it) is an urgent one, because Nietzsche and Lawrence alike see the pressures making for conformity in the modern state as far stronger than they have been in any previous age.

One of the main symptoms of this increasing pressure is the growing influence of democratic social and political ideals. In *Women in Love* democratizing tendencies have gone much further than in *The Rainbow*: although their father is only a school handicrafts instructor, the Brangwen sisters can mix freely in aristocratic circles, while for their forebears among the Brangwen women at the beginning of *The Rainbow* even the vicar inhabits 'worlds beyond' their own, while the lady of the Hall is a distant figure with more than human glamour, a heroine whose 'life was the epic that inspired their lives'. But in the later novel, we see another side to this breakdown of traditional hierarchies and social distinctions in the pressure to be—or to seem, at least—ordinary, average, unexceptional. It is this 'tyranny of the majority' which Gudrun and Ursula find the most irritating feature of contemporary life; as Gudrun says, in contemporary society 'the really chic thing is to be absolutely ordinary, so perfectly commonplace and like the person in the street ...' Aware that they are attractive and talented, the sisters are in open revolt against the levelling tendencies of the age; Gudrun wants to be 'high-flown and make speeches like Corneille', while Ursula would like to 'strut, to be a swan among geese'. Each takes the aristocratic view that the self is something distinctive to be developed and asserted.

Their mutual defiance of contemporary standards is evident above all in the startlingly individual way in which they dress and their almost aggressively distinctive appearance provokes hostility on a number of occasions. At the very beginning of *Women in Love* when they make their way through the poorer part of Beldover they have to pass through a group of collier's wives. As they do so, the sisters become aware that they are being stared at and that there is a strong current of hostility among the women which finds its expression in a mocking shout of 'What price the stockings' (Gudrun is wearing green silk stockings). What is interesting about the incident is the sense it conveys that what is at issue is not so much the '(natural) resentment of the poor against the well-to-do as the dislike of the gregarious for the defiantly individual spirit. Later, at the beginning of 'Water-Party' the sisters accompany their parents to the Crich estate and their flamboyantly individual outfits embarrass and annoy their father because they make the group conspicuous. For Ursula and Gudrun, this is exactly the point: their clothes make a statement, throw down a challenge to the conformist pressures of the time:

> Gudrun looked handsome and brilliant, and she wore her clothes in pure defiance. When people stared at her, and giggled after her, she made a point of saying loudly, to Ursula:
> 'Regard, regarde ces gens la! Ne sont-ils pas des hiboux incroyables?'
> 'No, really, it's impossible!' Ursula would reply distinctly. And so the two girls took it out of their universal enemy.
>
> (**WL** p 174)

The industrial system of production in developed societies is both a consequence of this weakening of individuality, and also something which accelerates it. In his working life in such a system, the individual tends to become simply instrumental; he is increasingly identified with his economic function and his humanity is suppressed in the interests of the efficient working of the whole. This process is not yet complete in the society described in *Women in Love*, but Gerald's reorganization of the mines and his elimination of anything which does not have a strictly economic justification, is the beginning of its final phase. Gerald's motive is not so much the maximisation of profits as the maximisation of efficiency; his aim is to create the perfect machine, with human and mechanical elements in perfect, frictionless interaction. For Gerald it is production itself, the struggle of man with nature in activities like mining which alone brings men together now that the 'old social state' has been destroyed. The productive mechanism reaches its greatest efficiency when men and women in their working lives are wholly identified with their functions in it; in such circumstances, the fluid and unmechanical (but not random or disorganised) rhythms natural to man have been replaced by the metronomic, repetitive rhythms of the machine. In places like Germany, where the process of regimentation has gone further, individuals already tend to be identified with their economic position in this way and instead of being known by their personal names, go by the names of their jobs instead. In one of the conversations on social matters which take place during the sisters' visit to Breadalby, Hermione's country house, Gudrun predicts that such a loss of personal identity will follow from Gerald's idea that society is no more than a productive mechanism—

> 'Oh!' cried Gudrun. 'Then we shan't have names any more—we shall be like the Germans, nothing but Herr Obermeister and Herr Untermeister. I can imagine it—"I am Mrs Colliery-Manager Crich—I am Mrs Member-of-Parliament Roddice. I am Miss Art-Teacher Brangwen". Very pretty that.'
> 'Things would work very much better, Miss Art-Teacher Brangwen,' said Gerald.
>
> (**WL** pp 114)

Gerald's success in rationalising the mines after some initial, but superficial, resistance demonstrates that such instrumentality is, at the deepest level, what is actually desired by the majority of people in modern, industrial societies. It is tempting, but misleading, to see the social change involved in quasi-Marxist terms, as involving something akin to the Marxian notion of proletarianisation. In fact, the loss of full humanity and of any genuine sense of community is not something imposed by employers or workers; Gerald himself is as much dehumanised by the measures he takes as any of his employees and at *every* level, the triumph of efficiency and economic rationality is reducing men to machines, if of different levels of complexity. In the nihilistic vision of the future of industrial society at the end of the novel—a vision which points ironically back to the very different future envisioned by the young Ursula at the end of *The Rainbow*—Gudrun foresees the virtually universal transformation of the human into the mechanical:

Let them turn into mechanisms, let them. Let them become instruments, pure wills, that work like clockwork, in perpetual repetition ... Let Gerald manage his firm. There he would be satisfied, as satisfied as a wheel-barrow that goes backwards and forwards along a plank all day—she had seen it.

The wheel-barrow—the one humble wheel—the unit of the firm. Then the cart, with two wheels; then the truck, with four; then the donkey-engine, with eight, then the winding engine, with sixteen, and so on, till it came to the miner, with a thousand wheels, and then the electrician, with three thousand, and the underground manager, with twenty thousand, and the general manager with a hundred thousand little wheels working away to complete his make-up, and then Gerald, with a million wheels and cogs and axles.

(**WL** pp 524–5)

By the time he came to write *Women in Love*, Lawrence saw this kind of outcome—in Nietzschean terms, the triumph of 'civilization'—as much more likely than the renewal of 'culture' foreseen by Ursula in the earlier novel. Lawrence shared Nietzsche's apocalyptic sense that modern man is faced with a portentous existential choice which will determine whether mankind as a whole will continue to develop creatively towards some higher, fuller state of being or lapse back into a static, merely repetitive kind of life; both men begin by being relatively optimistic but become increasingly gloomy as contemporary developments seem to dash their hopes of human renewal. Nietzsche feels increasingly that the man of the future will be the 'last man', the good citizen, timid, gregarious and identified with his social function rather than the 'superman' individual and creative; for Lawrence, in *Women in Love*, the future lies with the 'children of men', rather than with the 'sons of God'.

Nietzsche's human ideal has often been misunderstood and his 'superman' dismissed as no more than an embodiment of ruthless egoism, but in fact the superman is the individual in whom the 'animal' qualities have been retained and strengthened and serve as the basis for intellectual and spiritual capacities far greater than those possessed of less powerful impulses; Lawrence's 'sons of God' are those with the same completeness of being, or the capacity for developing such completeness. At the end of *The Rainbow*, Ursula realises that Skrebensky with his sensual vitality but 'vague' soul cannot be such a man and so, moving beyond the simple reaction into primitivism which drew her back to him, she rejects her lover and determines to wait for someone more complete who will be able to offer a more fulfilling relationship:

She repudiated him. He was as he was. It was good that he was as he was. Who was she to have a man according to her own desire? It was not for her to create, but to recognise a man created by God. The man should come from the Infinite and she should hail him. She was glad she could not create her man. She was glad she had nothing to do with this creation. She was glad that this lay within the scope of that vaster power in which she rested at last. The man would come out of Eternity to which she herself belonged.

(**R** p 494)

Skrebensky is reputiated, not because he is too sensual, but because he is only sensual. He represents something which is valuable and which is the necessary basis for the 'higher' human qualities but which does not, in itself, represent the full realization of human possibilities.

In Zarathustra's discourse 'Of the Three Evil Things', Nietzsche emphasises that egoism, cunning and violence are fundamental forces in human nature and that, paradoxically, they are the source of these attributes which have traditionally been praised as good and creative. Lawrence's characteristic images for the unconscious and the forces within it—the sea, the primeval forest, the lurking jungle predator—reflect the same view of human nature and the same conception of how the threateningly powerful forces on which it is founded are related to what is conventionally regarded as the opposite, spiritual side of man. Like Nietzsche, Lawrence believes that these apparently inhospitable conditions are the fertile soil out of which, alone, true culture develops. So when Lou Witt and her mother discuss the intellectual poverty of contemporary society in *St Mawr*, the younger woman disagrees with the suggestion that men have become too 'animal' to be intellectually creative; she insists, on the contrary, that they are uncreative because the 'animal' element in them has become weakened or perverted:

> You say they are too animal. But they're not, mother. It's the animal in them has gone perverse, or cringing, or humble, or domesticated, like dogs. I don't know one single man who is a proud living animal. I know they've left off really thinking. But then men always do leave off really thinking, when the last bit of wild animal dies in them.
>
> (**CSN** p 321)

At the end of *The Rainbow*, Ursula had seen the physical, animal energies as surviving, overlaid but unimpaired, in all those around her. Her vision had suggested that [to employ the Nietzschean contrast] 'culture', a wholeness of sense and spirit symbolized by the rainbow itself and the blossoming plant, will succeed contemporary, mechanical 'civilisation'. But by *St Mawr*, Lawrence's perspective had changed radically: the combined influence of herd and decadence moralities is now seen as having destroyed the vitality and creative potential of most of the race. Man's animal self has either been perverted by ascetic values or 'tamed', so as to conform to the herd ideal of the 'good citizen'. By and large, only two kinds of men survive—those like Rico, who retain their animal 'wildness', but in a corrupt form and those in whom it has been completely destroyed and replaced by obedience to social convention and public opinion:

> ... in men like Rico, the animal has gone queer and wrong. And in those nice, clean boys you liked so much in the war, there is no wild animal left in them. They're all tame dogs, even when they're brave and well-bred. They're all tame dogs, mother, with human masters. There's no mystery in them.
>
> (**CSN** p 322)

The idea of 'taming' is an important one for Nietzsche in connection with his contrast between 'culture' and 'civilisation'. He opposes it to 'training' in his analysis of the different ways of dealing with the instinctive side of man's nature. While taming involves the weakening or elimination of instinctive energies and gives rise to 'civilisation', training—which involves both the strengthening of the instincts and their disciplining and transformation—creates 'culture'. In repressing or eliminating the dangerous qualities in man, taming produces a kind of society which is barren and uncreative; one in which, for example, intellectual activity ceases to be a means of discovering new truths—which is what 'real thinking' involves—and becomes, instead, simply the rearrangement, in new patterns, of what is already known. In *St Mawr*, both Lou and her mother agree that the clever men of the age lack genuine intellectual originality, that they are simply 'old women, knitting the same pattern over and over again'. 'Real mind' survives only in a few uneducated individuals from outside the cultural mainstream, like Lewis the Welsh groom and Phoenix, the Indian, both of whom have partly escaped the 'taming' process.

Since the weakening or destruction of the 'wild' element in human nature makes 'real thinking' impossible, the cultural life of modern man tends to be parasitic on the achievements of the past. Incapable of expressing his own spirit, he studies bygone cultures. For Nietzsche, the most obvious symptom of this atrophy of creative energy is the overemphasis on historical studies in contemporary education; Lawrence too, feels that the era is an Alexandrian one, in which we are 'living off old fuel'. In *The Rainbow*, after the initial glamour of college life has worn off, Ursula comes to see most of her studies as outdated and irrelevant:

> During this year the glamour began to depart from College. The professors were not priests, initiated into the deep mysteries of life and knowledge. After all, they were only middle-aged men handling works they had become so accustomed to that they were oblivious of them. What was Latin?—So much dry goods of knowledge. What was the Latin class altogether but a sort of second-hand curio shop, where one bought curios and learned the market value of curios; dull curios too, on the whole. She was bored by the Latin curiosities as she was by the Chinese and Japanese curiosities in the antique shops. 'Antiques'—the very word made her soul fall flat and dead.
>
> (**R** p 434)

Watching his fellow guests at Breadalby in *Women in Love*, Birkin has a sudden intuition of the true nature of their social and intellectual lives—like Ursula and the two women in *St Mawr* he comes to see the apparent variety and vitality of modern existence as an illusion concealing the fact that what is involved is merely the creation of new permutations of old elements; though the counters are moved around, the game remains the same.

If we are to free ourselves from such repetitive and outmoded patterns of existence and enter into a full and creative kind of living, we must be continually attentive to promptings from the unconscious and have the courage to allow its emissaries, angels and dark gods, to act in and through us.

This submission is described most memorably in 'The Song of a Man Who

Has Come Through, which employs both 'elemental' and religious images in its depiction of the unconscious—

> Not I, not I, but the wind that blows through me!
> A fine wind is blowing the new direction of Time.
> If only I let it bear me, carry me, if only it carry me!
> If only I am sensitive, subtle, oh, delicate, a winged gift!
> If only, most lovely of all, I yield myself and am borrowed by the fine, fine wind that takes its course through the chaos of the world
> Like a fine, an exquisite chisel, a wedge-blade inserted;
> If only I am keen and hard like the sheer tip of a wedge
> Driven by invisible blows,
> The rock will split, we shall come at the wonder, we shall find the Hesperides.
>
> Oh, for the wonder that bubbles in my soul,
> I would be a good fountain, a good well-head,
> Would blur no whisper, spoil no expression.
>
> What is that knocking?
> What is that knocking at the door in the night?
> It is somebody wants to do us harm.
>
> No, no, it is the three strange angels.
> Admit them, admit them.[5]

Here the 'I' which is denied is the conscious self, the 'ego', which must not be allowed to control development but must be 'carried' by the invisible but powerful wind, symbol of the promptings from the unknown portion of the psyche. Responsiveness to such promptings can enable the individual to break out of the prison of dead conventions and arrive at the freedom and fulfilment suggested by the Gardens of the Hesperides. The spring fed from an unseen source is another, less violent image for the emergence of unconscious forces into consciousness and the poet's desire to be a 'good well-head' again emphasises the need for the conscious self to respond sensitively to the unconsciously determined flow of feeling, if creative selfhood is to be reached. Such images suggest the influence of the Romantics, who often use natural forces to symbolise the relation of the artist to the creative spirit which finds expression through him, but the fact that fear is the first response aroused by the 'knocking' and the reference to 'the three *strange* angels' suggest that the view of the self and of the sources of creativity expressed in the poem is Nietzschean rather than directly romantic. The 'three strange angels' are, in fact, the 'three evil things' which, for Zarathustra, are the roots of everthing valuable. In other words they represent powers which are 'strange' not only in the sense that they are unfamiliar to the conscious self, but also because they are wholly unexpected sources for the 'spiritual'. The fear with which the knocking is first greeted shows the influence of the traditional valuation of such impulses as anarchic and destructive; it is this attitude which makes some of those who are aware of the existence of the darkness in *The Rainbow* see it merely as the haunt of animal ferocity 'bristling with the tufts of the hyena and the wolf'. Both Nietzsche and Lawrence strive to alter this hostility to what has been accounted 'evil': each tries to persuade us to die in our ego-bound conceit and recognise in the 'gleam in the eye of the wolf and the hyena' the 'flash of the sword of angels, flashing at the door to come in'.

For Nietzsche, it is the experience of being moved by forces which do not originate in the known part of the self which gives birth to religion. In his account of the psychological origins of religious belief in *The Will to Power*, he argues that at an earlier, more psychologiclly naive stage of human development, any unusually vivid or passionate state of being was interpreted by the person experiencing it as a kind of possession, as an 'obsession and enchantment by the power of a person':

> Among intelligent, strong and vigorous races it is mainly the epileptic who inspires the conviction that a strange power is here at work; but every related condition of subjection, e.g., that of the inspired man, of the poet, of the great criminal, of passions such as love and revenge, also leads to the invention of extra-human powers. A condition is made concrete in a person, and when it overtakes us is thought to be effected by that person. In other words: In the psychological concept of God, a condition, in order to appear as effect, is personified as cause.[6]

Nietzsche goes on to explain that the 'psychological logic' of this attribution to supernatural entities of forces which belong to our own natures depends on the limitations of conscious awareness. Since we are unaware of the magnitude of the powers in the unknown part of the self, we are unable to accept that their activity belongs to us and conclude that some more potent being must be acting through us:

> When a man is suddenly and overwhelming suffused with the *feeling of power*—and this is what happens with all great affects—it raises in him a doubt about his own person: he does not dare to think himself the cause of this astonishing feeling—and so he posits a stronger person, a divinity, to account for it.[7]

And because he 'has not dared to credit himself with all his strong and surprising impulses', man has thereby diminished his own stature:

> in so far as everything great and strong in man has been conceived as superhuman and external, man has belittled himself—he has separated the two sides of himself, one very paltry and weak, one very strong and astonishing, into two spheres, and called the former 'man', the latter 'God' ...
>
> Religion has debased the concept 'man'; its ultimate consequence is that everything good, great, true is superhuman and bestowed only through an act of grace.[8]

Lawrence's frequent use of religious language to describe psychological events testifies to the influence of this Nietzschean account of the genesis of religion. The awesome forces from the unconscious are personified as 'angels' or 'gods' and feelings of unusual fulness or power are thought of as visitations by such supernatural beings. He retains an idiom born of error because in this way he can express his reverence for the 'flesh', the unconscious self, as the source of all and emphasise the comparative insignificance of reason, intellect and all that is conscious. Implicit in his idiosyncratic use of religious terms is a challenge to dominant Christian idealism, which sees spirit as primary and creative, flesh and the material as derivative and therefore less valuable. The challenge is made explicit in his provocative revision of the fourth Gospel

> John, the beloved disciple, says, 'The Word was made Flesh'. But why should he turn things round? The women simply go on bearing talkative sons, as an answer. 'The Flesh was made Word.'[9]

Lawrence goes on to personify the 'flesh' as the uncreated creator, God the Father, the 'word' as Christ, begotten of the Father, and to develop the association of flesh with woman and spirit with man. Although intended as a Preface for *Sons and Lovers*, Lawrence's commentary on St John was written after the completion of that novel, at a time when he was already working on what was to become *The Rainbow*, and, in fact, has more in common, in theme and idiom, with the later novel. In *The Rainbow* the validity of the traditional view of the relations between sense and spirit is a major issue, particularly in the marriage between Will and Anna.

Will's mysticism involves an idealistic inversion of the real order of things: he accepts the traditional view that spirit is primary, that it is the 'Word' which is creative and gives rise to the 'Flesh'. The result is that for him the ordinary world has significance largely because the things in it can serve as symbols of a 'higher' spiritual realm, which possesses a superior degree of reality and value. Through the power of such symbols, Will can escape from the 'confinement' of ordinary existence and gain admittance to a world of space, clarity and stability. So, looking at the pictures of the statues in Bamberg Cathedral he feels that 'the world around was only an enclosure, a room' from which he is transported by the figures 'to a marvellous finely-wrought universe'. His attitude to ordinary experience is radically different from that of his wife; Anna sometimes feels the power of the religious symbols which move her husband, but her strongest instinct is to affirm the intrinsic reality and worth of the natural world against his instrumental view of it. In the early years of their marriage, this difference in outlook often leads to disputes like that over the lamb with the flag in the window of the local church. Although Anna sometimes sees the lamb as symbolic and is awed by what it represents, she is more often amused by its lack of realism, which makes her associate it not with a real animal but with 'the little wooly lambs on green legs that the children carried home from the fair each year'. For Will, the unconvincingness of the portrayal is irrelevant, or even justifiable, since the object is not to depict the merely physical but to convey a more important spiritual truth. So he answers his wife's mockery by stressing that the lamb is 'the symbol of Christ, of His innocence and sacrifice' and that the composition as a whole 'means the triumph of the Resurrection'. His defence provokes Anna to retort that 'Whatever it means, it's a lamb! And I like lambs too much to treat them as if they had to mean something'.

Because, for Lawrence, women tend to be more closely associated with the 'Flesh' and men with the 'Word', the question of which is primary is not just a matter of abstract speculative interest, but has important implications for the proper pattern of relations between the sexes. Will's belief in the supremacy of spirit underlies the conception of these relations symbolically expressed in the panel of the creation of Eve which he begins just before his marriage (artistic rather than intellectual, he naturally expresses his values and aspirations in images rather than words). It is significant that in the carving he does not try to create a new image which would be the articulation of his own distinctive being and of the unique possibilities latent in the relationship with Anna, but instead takes as his subject a scriptural story which embodies traditional attitudes. The legend from Genesis expresses the idealism characteristic of the Judaeo-Christian tradition in which pure spirit (God) is regarded as the original creative principle which then gives rise to the hierarchy of created being. In this hierarchy of created things, spiritual status declines with increasing distance from godhead. In such a system, the fact that men are more closely associated with the 'Word', with spiritual activity, than women, gives them a superior status. In the Hebrew myth, Eve is created after and out of Adam, indicating that woman is less than man and exists for him—a sexual inequality reflected in Will's panel by the fact that the figure of Adam is much larger than that of Eve. Will's efforts to assert his supremacy in the marriage and thus give practical effect to the ideas expressed in the carving are vigorously resisted by Anna who is instinctively committed to the opposite view of things and asserts the primacy of the feminine principle of the 'Flesh' in terms similar to those used by Lawrence in the *Sons and Lovers* preface. Aware of what the panel implies, she is critical of it:

> She jeered at the Eve, saying 'She is like a little marionette. Why is she so small? It is impudence to say that Woman was made out of Man's body,' she continued, 'when every man is born of woman. What impudence men have, what arrogance!'

> (**R** p 174)

The psychological roots of Will's idealism lie in the difficulty he finds in coping with the flux and change which are the basic characteristics both of the world and of human nature. The visionary realm, to which religious symbols offer access, is essentially a negation of the real world in which—as in Lincoln Cathedral—time and change seem revealed as illusions and the suffering which contact with them brings is temporarily relieved. It is this compensatory imaginary world which the idealist comes to consider real and he rejects the natural world as illusory. Will's attempt, at the beginning of his marriage, to assume the traditional role of the dominant husband and so control the shape and direction of the relationship is—as his wife realises—a symptom of this relative weakness. Challenging his claims, Anna compares him disparagingly with Tom:

> He asserted himself on his rights, he arrogated the old position of master of the house.
> 'You've a right to do as I want,' he cried.
> 'Fool!' she answered. 'Fool!'
> 'I'll let you know who's master,' he cried.
> 'Fool!' she answered. 'Fool! I've known my own father, who could put a dozen of you in his pipe and push them down with finger-end. Don't I know what a fool you are!'
>
> (**R** p 173)

Anna's point is that those who are genuinely strong and confident, like her father, do not need to assert themselves: Tom illustrates Nietzsche's idea that the greatest power is to be found 'in simple, gentle and obliging men without the least inclination to domineer' and even Will recognises this—'He knew, with shame, how her father had been a man without arrogating any authority'. In the same passage, Nietzsche goes on to say that 'conversely, the inclination to domineer has often appeared to me an inner sign of weakness'[10]—so it is when Anna fights him off, oppressed by his lack of intellectuality that Will, 'frantic in sensual fear', retaliates by claiming domestic authority.

Will's political ambitions are confined to the domestic sphere, but like Skrebensky's desire to administer India, his demand that he should be master of the house is essentially an evasion of the more challenging task of self-mastery. In Will's case this side-tracking' of the soul is related to his idealism; just as he is unable to accept and affirm the changeable natural world, so he is unable to confront and use the forces in his own nature in the creation of the higher self. The result is that the urge for power, the desire for 'mastery' which he feels, does not find expression in a struggle towards wholeness of being, but emerges first in his attempt to become the dominant partner in his marriage. Will abandons that attempt, aware that his wife's mockery is justified, but the interest in 'some form of mastery' which is intrinsic to his maleness, remains strong:

> There was something he wanted, nevertheless, some form of mastery. Ever and anon, after his collapses into the petty and the shameful, he rose up again, and, stubborn in spirit, strong in his power to start afresh, set out once more in his male pride of being to fulfil the hidden passion of his spirit.
>
> (**R** p 174)

Although he has quickly realised the unsatisfactoriness of his 'master-of-the-house' ambitions, Will has no positive idea of how he can fulfil 'the hidden passion of his spirit' and so receive from Anna the respect for which he craves. She, on her side, although aware that all the reasons he gives for deserving her respect are the wrong ones, cannot herself suggest how he might come to merit it. At the same time, the fact that she asks him several times why he has not returned to his wood-carving indicates that she feels instinctively that it is *that* kind of masculine activity which will offer him satisfaction and arouse her admiration. Her question is significant because self-fulfilment and art are closely related in Nietzsche's philosophy because of the fact that artistic creation is one of the more developed manifestations of that outflow of power which accompanies fulness of being. Our degree of vitality decisively, if unconsciously, shapes the way in which we experience the world and the artist is someone who is able to communicate his vitality to others by conveying to them his particular vision of the world. Nietzsche argues that those with a high degree of vitality, the 'well-constituted' in whom the wasteful chaos of warring impulses has evolved into an integrated self, are able to accept and affirm reality in all its changeableness.

Such vitality finds expression in an art which treats the natural world realistically rather than symbolically—and therefore, like Paul Morel's painting, depicts it as dynamic rather than static—but which, unlike simple naturalism, also glorifies it, despite the wastefulness and suffering inseparable from its constant creativity. Such art, the 'real realism' praised by Lettie in *The White Peacock*, has a tonic effect on the spectator who, in responding participates in the artist's affirmative vision: the implicit contrast in Lawrence's first novel is with the 'false' realism of naturalists like Gorky or Zola, whose work is depressing rather than enlivening. While Anna feels an instinctive interest in her husband's artistic potential, she is unimpressed by the carving of Adam and Eve, which is his only significant work so far because she is intuitively aware that, in both subject and technique, it reflects that depreciation of the natural which is a symptom of his relative weakness. In other words, the panel is not an example of that life-enhancing 'real realism' which would indicate that Will had succeeded in organising and disciplining the forces in his own nature. Healthy art is linked with the 'mastery' Will seeks because it springs from what might be termed 'intrinsic' power, the power over the self which Nietzsche sees as representing a higher kind of strength than the 'extrinsic' power which is exercised over the natural world or other people. But Nietzsche does not regard the contrast between the two kinds of power as an absolute one—he argues that 'intrinsic power seeks outward influence, if often in subtle and indirect fashion' and art illustrates this connection in its capacity to communicate the vitality of the artist to his audience. And while the cruder and more overt ways of exerting influence are ineffective and wasteful because likely to alienate those who are subjected to them, rather as Will's attempt to make himself master arouses the determined opposition of his wife, the subtler, more developed forms of the will to power are more persuasive:

> Every living thing reaches about itself with its force to grasp as far as it can, and subjugates the weaker to itself ... The *increasing 'humanization'* in this tendency consists in this, that one feels more and more *delicately* how difficult it is really to assimilate the other: how crude injury indeed shows our power over him, but at the same time *estranges* his will from us still more—so makes him less conquerable.[11]

The 'respect' which Will craves depends, then, on the proper exercise of his urge for 'mastery', because it is the spontaneous response to the considerateness, the concern for the individuality of others, which accompany the highest degrees of strength. Secure in themselves, the strong are able to accept the fluid and unpredictable mystery of the being of others, just as they are able to accept the fluidity of nature as a whole. And the attainment of mastery over the self, the realisation of the possibilities latent in our nature through the unconscious organising will, involves an outflow of power on to the world around, of which art is one particular manifestation. This outgoing phase of being when a maximum of development has been reached is the 'Word' of the Preface and the 'utterance' which the main characters in *The Rainbow* struggle towards. The 'Word' depends on and grows out of the 'Flesh' in the sense that the 'higher' self is simply the 'lower' self disciplined and refined—indeed, as Ursula suggests in her meditation on the mystery of life, it is only when the organising process has been accomplished that 'selfhood' in any real sense comes into being. So long as the 'self' remains a simple flux of elementary urges, there cannot be any sharply defined individual identity and both Will and Anna, who continue to live largely on the sensual level, lack individuality for that reason—'They were neither of them quite personal, quite defined as individuals, so much were they pervaded by the physical heat of breeding and rearing their young'.

Since 'utterance' is the expression of achieved individuality, Will's attempt to resume artistic activity is only a partial success. After twenty years doing the mechanical work of a draughtsman and working to restore the church at Cossethay 'Now he wanted again to carve things that were utterances of himself'. But, although he has rejected the idealism of his early years and has come to accept the natural world he finds that even his most successful work remains derivative:

> He saw the puerility of his young conceptions, he saw the unreal world in which they had been conceived. He now had a new strength in his sense of reality. He felt as if he were real, as if he handled real things ... Now he wanted again to carve things that were utterances of himself. But he could not quite hitch on—always he was too busy, too uncertain, confused. Wavering, he began to study modelling. To his surpise he found he could do it. Modelling in clay, in plaster, he produced beautiful reproductions, really beautiful. Then he set-to to make a head of Ursula, in high relief, in the Donatello manner. In his first passion, he got a beautiful suggestion of his desire. But the pitch of concentration would not come. With a little ash in his mouth he gave up.
>
> (R p 355)

The portrait of Ursula is his nearest approach to 'individual expression and individual form' but its style is not completely original, and even with the dependence on Donatello, Will's nature is not developed and disciplined enough to allow him to maintain the initial level of inspiration. His attempts at applied art show the same pattern of initial excitement and achievement followed by a falling off into imitation. But despite the fact that they are only partially successful, Will's new artistic ventures do reveal how much his attitudes have changed in the years since his last serious attempt to express himself through his art. Unlike his Adam and Eve panel, his head of Ursula and his water-colours take their subjects from nature and treat them realistically, while his decorative work involves the creation of things which at one time he would have puritanically dismissed as frivolities.

His abandonment of his early mysticism and of the artistic ideals which grew out of it is a lengthy, complex and often painful process, in which his deepest values are steadily eroded by his wife's destructive common-sense. At the beginning of their marriage, he is able to escape from the discomfort to which his intense feelings often expose him by retreating into a more congenial world of the imagination, a world which he sees as simpler—and realer—than that of ordinary experience. Nietzsche argues that this impulse to escape is the basis of all idealist or supernaturalist world-views; it has its roots in the coexistence of powerful desires with an inability to find direct satisfaction. The individual in such a predicament either escapes into a subconsciously created fantasy realm from which the intractable elements in the ordinary world are excluded, or else resorts to some mode of 'intoxication' which offers a momentary access of strength. Finding himself unable to defy convention and actively woo the socially superior Lettie, George Saxton takes to 'dreaming fulfilments', while Tom Brangwen, suffering a similar kind of impasse, takes to drink.

Will's difficulties in the early stages of his marriage have a different source from those of the other two characters: they arise from the necessarily ungraspable and unpredictable 'otherness' of his wife. Because Anna is a separate individual, with feelings and desires that do not necessarily coincide with those of her husband, misunderstanding and frustration are inevitable in their relationship as they are in any marriage. And the tension between the pair in the early stages of their life together is particularly acute, because marriage makes Will aware of the intensity of his physical desire for his wife and his proportionate dependence on her.

The events which follow their quarrel over Anna's careless treatment of her husband's wood-carving tools illustrate the connection between Will's difficulties with ordinary experience and the corresponding importance to him of a consolatory ideal 'reality' which offers him a refuge from it. When his attempt at reconciliation fails, Will walks out on Anna and goes off, furiously angry, to Nottingham where he paces the streets 'with a mad restlessness, as if he were running amok'. However, the chance discovery of a book on Bamberg Cathedral brings a sudden and radical change of mood:

> He lit up with thrills of bliss as he turned from picture to picture. He had found something at last, in these carvings. His soul had great satisfaction. Had he not come out to seek, and had he not found! He was in a passion of fulfilment.
> (**R** p 164)

He is elated because he sees the pictures as a means of escape from the real world which has become, for the moment, intolerable to him:

The book lay in his hands like a door-way. The world around was only an enclosure, a room. But he was going away. He lingered over the lovely statues of women. A marvellous, finely-wrought universe crystallized out around him as he looked again, at the crowns, the twining hair, the woman-faces.

(**R** p 165)

This visionary universe and its inhabitants are soothing and satisfying because they are 'crystalline'—lucid, stable, firm in outline—while the ordinary world is fluid and changeable and therefore disturbing.

The fact that it is the statues of women which fascinate him most of all indicates, that Will's 'spiritual' experience has its roots in the physical, impulsive side of his nature. His response to the world suggested by the pictures involves that unconscious transmutation of the sensual into the spiritual which Anna has recognised in one of his earlier exalted moods when, sitting beside him in church she had 'felt he was conveying to strange, secret places the love that sprang in him for her'. She herself is aware of the interdependence of 'self' and 'soul' in her own nature and recognises the primacy of the former, while Will does not see that they are connected and ignores his 'self' because he regards it as unimportant. So, for Anna, 'The thought of her soul was intimately mixed up with the thought of her own self' to the extent that 'her soul and her own self were one and the same in her', whereas 'he seemed simply to ignore the fact of his own self, almost to refute it'.

As a woman, Anna is temperamentally alive to the importance of the 'flesh', but at first her view is more balanced that that of her husband in that she accepts both levels of being. However his extremism, his virtual rejection of the 'self', quickly provokes her into the opposite assertion that *only* the physical and sensual are real and valuable. Like Annable or Ursula or Mrs Crich, all of whom react—temporarily or permanently—against idealism in various forms, the extremism with which she comes into contact leads her to espouse a kind of militant primitivism which is its antithesis—a pattern of behaviour which illustrates Nietzsche's contention that 'Extreme positions are not succeeded by moderate ones but by extreme positions of the opposite kind'. So, in seeking to destroy Will's mysticism, Anna comes to disregard the real appeal that his exalted beliefs have for her. Will's 'idealism', his belief in a realer, more satifying world beyond the limited area of ordinary existence and his related tendency to see the natural as important only because it can symbolise or suggest that higher reality is steadily eroded by Anna's criticism; she constantly insists on the substantiality of material things and the illusory character of the 'supernatural'. But this conflict between them, which continues intermittently through the early years of their marriage is not simply the consequence of irreconcilable intellectual differences: its sources lie much deeper, in the fundamental perspectives of each partner, so that what is involved is an instinctive antagonism which is related to the contrast between the temperamental bias of women and that of men which Lawrence outlines in his Preface to *Sons and Lovers*. In the words of the narrative 'They fought an unknown battle, unconsciously'.

Anna's final victory in the engagement is evident in things like the change in the significance of the 'doorway' image which first appears in connection with Will's response to the pictures of Bamberg Cathedral. At that point it had conveyed the power which religious symbols possessed to transport him to another, 'transcendant' area of experience. The ordinary world, which is his starting point, is seen as confused, limited and uncomfortable and the movement is towards a greater feeling of space, light and freedom. He escapes from an 'enclosure' into a crystalline 'universe'. But by the time the couple visit Lincoln Cathedral, Will's attitude to his beloved symbols has undergone a radical change and the 'doorway' between ordinary and spiritual experience now seems to separate the wider, fuller, lighter natural world from a narrower, obscurer realm, the 'jewelled gloom' of the kind of religious feeling which the Cathedral represents:

> He had felt, before, that could he but go though the great door and look down the gloom towards the far-off, concluding wonder of the altar, that then, with the windows suspended around like tablets of jewels emanating their own glory, then he had arrived. Here the satisfaction he had yearned after came near, towards this, the porch of the great Unknown, all reality gathered, and there, the altar was the mystic door, through which all and everything must move on to eternity.
>
> But now, somehow, sadly and disillusioned, he realised that the doorway was no doorway. It was too narrow, it was false. Outside the cathedral were many flying spirits that could never be sifted through the jewelled gloom. He had lost his absolute.
>
> He listened to the thrushes in the gardens and heard a note which the cathedrals did not include: something free and careless and joyous. He crossed a field that was all yellow with dandelions, on his way to work, and the bath of yellow glowing was something at once so sumptuous and so fresh, that he was glad he was away from his shadowy cathedral.
>
> (R pp 205–6)

Before his meeting with Anna, Will's religion has been the most important thing in his existence; marriage brings out the intense sensuality latent in his nature and his passion for his wife becomes an equally important source of fulfilment. Together these two things come to represent the only elements in his experience to which Will attaches real significance:

> He did not attach any vital importance to his life in the drafting office, or his life among men. That was just merely the margin to the text. The verity was his connexion with Anna and his connexion with the Church, his real being lay in his dark emotional experience of the Infinite, of the Absolute.
>
> (R pp 159–60)

The religious absolute gradually crumbles under his wife's attacks until, by the time of the visit to Lincoln, Will has abandoned it altogether. As its hold weakens, Will naturally comes to depend more and more on his love for Anna, which becomes the only source of fulfilment remaining to him. As his dependence on his wife grows, so too does his feeling that he must dominate in their relationship and thus free himself from the insecurity and uncertainty which her independence creates. In other words it is Anna's success in undermining his religious beliefs which precipitates his attempts at domination: it is significant that she first becomes aware that he is 'trying to gain power over her, without knowing her' soon after their argument over the lamb with the flag, for that clash has 'broken a little of something in him'. Anna responds to his 'bullying' by attacking her husband's idealistic beliefs even more fiercely and instead of undermining them only 'a little' these later assaults have more dramatic effects on his attitudes, leaving him 'dark and destroyed, his soul running its blood'. Will now feels 'frantic in sensual fear' and as a result his efforts to asert himself become more determined—he openly demands that he should be recognised as 'master of the house'. That claim is abandoned in the face of Anna's mockery, but Will's suffering continues and is even intensified when he learns of his wife's pregnancy. She now seems 'fulfilled and separate and sufficient in her half of the world', independent of him and therefore unresponsive to his needs. Because his sense of isolation and incompleteness has become even greater than before, it gives rise to an effort to dominate which is far more sustained and radical than his earlier demand to be master. This time, he tries to reduce Anna to a mere function of his own being and the struggle between them is, as a consequence, more intense and prolonged than the earlier dispute. But this second attempt to impose his will is less crude and overt, and Anna only gradually recognises the significance of the continuous, subtle pressure she feels:

> She found that, in all her outgoings and her incomings, he prevented her. Gradually she realized that she was being borne down by him, borne down by the clinging, heavy weight of him, that he was pulling her down as a leopard clings to a wild cow and exhausts her and pulls her down.
> Gradually she realised that her life, her freedom, was sinking under the silent grip of his physical will. He wanted her in his power. He wanted to devour her at leisure, to have her.
>
> (R p 185)

When she has become aware of what Will is trying to do, Anna sees immediately that his need to dominate grows out of his feelings of weakness and dependence. Despite this, she does not try to relieve his suffering by offering comfort or sympathy; instead she becomes hard, even hostile and intensifies her husband's pain by insisting, for example, that they should sleep in different rooms:

> He depended on her. If she were taken away, he would collapse as a house from which the central pillar is removed.
> And she hated him, because he depended on her so utterly. He was horrible to her. She wanted to thrust him off, to set him apart. It was horrible that he should cleave to her, so close, so close, like a leopard that had leapt on her, and fastened.
>
> (R p 186)

Despite it's apparent callousness, Anna's instinctive recoil from him is Will's salvation as well as Anna's, because the suffering he endures compels him to develop greater strength. As a result, at the end of this struggle between them he is able, for the first time since his marriage, to stand alone:

> He could sleep with her, and let her be. He could be alone now. He had just learned what it was to be able to be alone. It was right and peaceful. She had given him a new, deeper freedom. The world might be a welter of uncertainty, but he was himself now. He had come into his own existence.
>
> **(R p 190)**

Like Paul Morel at the end of *Sons and Lovers*, or Birkin after Hermione's attack and his serious illness, Will illustrates the Lamarkian conception of development which Lawrence took from Nietzsche; each is stronger because of his suffering and to a degree proportionate to the intensity of his ordeal. Their cases show how continuing growth is dependent on challenge and difficulty and bring out the implications of this belief for human relationships. It was Nietzsche's conviction that suffering is fruitful which lies behind his constant attacks on sympathy, compassion and related emotions; such feelings—he argues—are either self-indulgent in that they really express the feeling of strength and superiority of the sympathiser, or, if genuinely felt, uselessly increase the sum of human unhappiness. And so far as pity is actually effective in relieving suffering, it tends to inhibit growth and far from conferring a benefit on the recipient, actually holds back his development. In *The Rainbow*, Will realises after the conflict with Anna that he owes his new freedom and strength to her hardness, but when his suffering was at its greatest, her behaviour seemed simply cruel and destructive: in 'rejecting' him, 'she seemed to him inconceivable, a monster, the principle of cruelty'.

The idea that antagonism and conflict play a crucial role in the development of creative relationships is linked with Nietzsche's rejection of 'love' as something admirable. Though it is usually considered the proper basis for the most valuable kinds of relationship, Nietzsche sees love, in the traditional sense, as belonging to the decadent values of Christianity, its decadent origins evident in its association with sympathy, self-sacrifice and submissiveness. It is this Nietzschean rejection of love, as traditionally conceived, which lies behind Birkin's attempts in *Women in Love* to find a new basis for lasting relationships between men and women and his ultimately successful struggle against Ursula's wish to found their relationship on 'love'. Nietzsche goes to the classical, pre-Christian world for his positive ideal of relationship, arguing that the unparalleled cultural achievements of the Greeks grew out of the *agon*, the competitive conception of friendship which dominated Greek life. Like Nietzsche, Lawrence rejects conventional 'love' as a basis for vital relationships and the importance of male friendships in many of his novels suggests that he was influenced by the celebration of the *agon* in Nietzsche's works, where it represents the highest and most creative kind of human association. In a competitive relation between two men, the approximate equality of contending forces prevents either partner from establishing a final dominance and since the element of contest is virtually continuous, the stimulus to further growth is always present: as a result the vital potential of the participants is maximised. Although particular women may be as strong as, or stronger than, particular men, the fact that the two sexes are, in general, unequal in strength, means that this kind of balance of power with its creative benefits is less likely in a relationship between a man and woman.

Although 'idealism' is usually associated with an inability to face up to and affirm the flowing, changing natural world, the intense emotion aroused in Will by the pictures of the statues at Bamberg brings in its wake a temporary access of strength which allows him to affirm reality for the moment:

> Did not Bamberg Cathedral make the world his own? He celebrated his trium-
> phant strength and life and verity, and embraced the vast riches he was
> inheriting.
>
> (R p 165)

This apparently paradoxical association of an idealistic flight from the world with a vigorous affirmation of it is linked with Will's indifference to the ethical side of Christianity. His profound religious feelings are aroused, not by doctrines, but by religious art and architecture and sometimes, as in the case of the Bamberg sculptures, such art is essentially realistic and world-affirming for all its apparently ascetic and other-worldly affiliations. Like the priest or the idealist philosopher, the artist creates an imaginery world, but there is a crucial difference in its character:

> To divide the world into a 'real' and an 'apparent' world ... is only ... a
> symptom of declining life ... That the artist places a higher value on appearance
> than on reality constitutes no objection to this proposition. For 'appearance'
> here signifies reality *once more*, only selected, strengthened, corrected.[12]

For Nietzsche, even the tragic artist is '*not* a pessimist—it is precisely he who *affirms* all that is questionable and terrible in existence ...'

Before his mother's death, Paul Morel's abundant vitality had allowed him to accept and affirm reality as process and his vision had been reflected in his theory and practice as an artist. Early in their relationship he had explained to Miriam that his aim was to portray the flow and change of being rather than to strive for accuracy of form. Trying to explain why she finds one of his pictures appealing he says

> 'It's because—it's because there is scarcely any shadow in it; it's more shim-
> mery, as if I'd painted the shimmering protoplasm in the leaves and
> everywhere, and not the stiffness of the shape. That seems dead to me. Only
> this shimmeriness is the real living. The shape is a dead crust. The shimmer is
> inside, really.'
>
> (SL p 189)

The contrast between the values of the artist and those of the Christian is reflected in the fear with which Miriam responds to Paul's dynamic vision of reality. On a later occasion when he compares some pine-trees he has been painting to 'God's burning bush', she feels that if he helps her to see the world more distinctly and vividly, reality also becomes more frightening in his company:

> Another day she sat at sunset whilst he was painting some pine-trees which caught the red glare from the west. He had been quiet.
> 'There you are!' he said suddenly. 'I wanted that. Now, look at them and tell me, are they pine-trunks or are they red coals, standing-up pieces of fire in that darkness? There's God's burning bush for you, that burned not away.'
> Miriam looked, and was frightened. But the pine-trunks were wonderful to her, and distinct.
>
> (SL p 189)

As Miriam's mystical beliefs suggest, she lacks the strength for the consistent affirmation of a reality which is constantly flowing and changing and as a result life for her involves constant suffering. The relation between idealism and suffering is summed up by Nietzsche in *The Anti-Christ*:

> Once the concept 'nature' had been devised as the concept antithetical to 'God', 'natural' had to be the word for 'reprehensible'—this entire fictional world had its roots in *hatred* of the natural . . . , it is the expression of a profound discontent with the actual . . . *But that explains everything*. Who alone has reason to *lie himself out* of actuality? He who *suffers* from it. But to suffer from actuality means to be an abortive actuality . . . The preponderance of feelings of displeasure over feelings of pleasure in the *cause* of a fictitious morality and religion: such a preponderance, however, provides the *formula* for *decadence* . . .[13]

Aware of the ambivalence of Miriam's response to the pine-trees, Paul links it with the sadness which he sees as always present in her:

> 'Why are you always sad?' he asked her.
> 'Sad!' she exclaimed, looking up at him with startled, wonderful brown eyes.
> 'Yes,' he replied. 'You are always, always sad.'
> 'I am not—oh, not a bit!' she cried.
> 'But even your joy is like a flame coming off of sadness,' he persisted. 'You're never jolly, or even just all right.'
> 'No,' she pondered. 'I wonder—why.'
>
> (SL pp 189–90)

The vision of reality involved here originates with Paul and is different in character from the way he had seen things under Miriam's influence earlier in their relationship. She is 'anthropomorphic' and had 'stimulated him into appreciating things thus' so that, mediated by him, 'then they lived for her'. Mark Spilka suggests that Paul first joins with Miriam in her 'bloodless communions' with nature and takes pride in vivifying it for her, then, in scenes like that in which they contemplate the rose tree, reacts against her demand that he should bring the roses 'into her soul' for their 'anthropomorphic slaughter'. In fact, the pattern of influences in the relationship is more complex than this suggests. Miriam's anthropomorphism is related to her relative weakness because, like Helena's fancifulness in *The Trespasser*, it is a way of seeing nature which makes it familiar and comprehensible rather than alien and therefore frightening: it is a denial of the otherness of the natural world. But if, early in their friendship, Paul collaborates with this habit of Miriam's, it seems clear the the later vision which he embodies in his paintings and struggles to articulate to Miriam, is of a different, unanthropomorphic kind which, while it does still make experience more vivid for the girl, is less reassuring and more disturbing than the earlier translation of the natural into the human. Significantly it is at this point in their relationship that Paul helps Miriam to overcome or reduce some of her physical inhibitions; in the same way he is able, through his art and his 'struggling, abstract speeches', to help her to accept the natural world without any anthropomorphic disguise. And her ability to respond to his more challenging vision of reality suggests that she is not wholly identified with decadent values.

Contrasting 'romantic' with 'dithyrambic' art in *The Will to Power*, Nietzsche argues that 'religious' art does not necessarily belong to the former category. Raphael's paintings, for instance, *seem* to express the Christian view of things but, in reality, celebrate nature and the world rather than negating them—

> Is art a consequence of *dissatisfaction with reality*? Or an expression of *gratitude for happiness enjoyed*? In the former case *romanticism*; in the latter, aureole and dithyramb (in short, art of apotheosis): Raphael, too, belongs here; he merely had the falsity to deify what looked like the Christian interpretation of the world.[14]

The Bamberg sculptures, like Raphael's paintings, are ambiguous, but their true significance is apparent in their effect on Will. The 'art of apotheosis' has its psychological roots in the artist's experience of a condition of 'plenitude and increased energy'.[15] In such a state, the world around seems transformed and it is this transfigured 'reality' which is embodied in the work of art. The work, in turn, arouses in the spectator, the state of overflowing vitality which brought about its creation so that by looking at the Bamberg sculptures, Will comes to share the strength and fulness of being experienced by the Medieval craftsman. Since the most important cause of such exceptional states is sexual feeling, sexuality is, for Nietzsche, the crucial force for the production of art. Discussing the 'genesis of art' in *The Will to Power*, Nietzsche derives artistic vision from 'That making perfect, seeing as perfect, which characterises the cerebral system bursting with sexual energy'.[15] And because 'healthy' art embodies a way of seeing the world which is characteristic of those in a state of erotic excitement, it reminds the spectator of the condition which produced it and arouses in him a similar state:

> ... everything perfect and beautiful works as an unconscious reminder of that enamored condition and its way of seeing—every perfection, all the beauty of things, revives through contiguity this aphrodisiac bliss ... The demand for art

and beauty is an indirect demand for the ecstasies of sexuality communicated to the brain.[17]

Of course, neither artist nor spectator is usually aware of the antecendents of their aesthetic experiences: sexual energy only appears in art in sublimated form. So, while the narrative brings out the erotic element in Will's response to the Bamberg pictures by stressing the fact that he is particularly fascinated by the female figures, he himself is not aware of the ultimate source of his excitement. Will's reaction, then, illustrates the close links between religious and erotic feeling; it is a masculine equivalent of the example of feminine 'spirituality' which Nietzsche offers in his discussion of 'The Will to Power as Art'. There, considering the effects of religious art, he asks 'What pleases all pious women, old or young?' and answers wryly '. . . a saint with beautiful legs';[17] Lawrence too thought sex 'so large and all-embracing that the religious passion itself is largely sexual ... Most "nice things" are "sublimated sex".'[18]

So as to distinguish the 'idealisation' characteristic of art from the quite different and less healthy kind of idealisation which is the basis for ascetic values, Nietzsche describes in some detail *how* sexual excitement transforms the contours of our ordinary experience. While normally things seem shapeless and confused, erotic 'rausch' endows the world with a new clarity, definiteness and glamour which finds objective expression in art:

> The artist gradually comes to love for their own sake the means that reveal a condition of intoxication: extreme subtlety and splendor of color, definiteness of line, nuances of tone: the *distinct* where otherwise, under normal conditions, distinctness is lacking. All distinct things, all nuances, to the extent that they recall these extreme enhancements of strength that intoxication produces, awaken this feeling of intoxication by association: the effect of works of art is to *excite the state that creates art*—intoxication.[19]

Nietzsche's emphasis on distinctness and on glamour suggests Will's experience with the pictures of Bamberg which transport him from the chaos and discomfort or ordinary reality to a clearer and more beautiful realm:

> A marvellous, finely-wrought universe crystallised out around him as he looked again, at the crowns, the shining hair, the woman-faces.

> **(R p 165)**

As well as suggesting that the shapely beauty of the sculptures grows out of the undifferentiated flux of being, 'crystallised' also echoes Nietzsche's account of why art arouses such intense feelings. In his view, one kind of excitement tends naturally to call up others so that:

> The most habitual affirmations of beauty excite and stimulate each other; once the aesthetic drive is at work, a whole host of other perfections, originating elsewhere, crystallize around 'the particular instance of beauty'.[20]

In all this, the Bamberg sculptures differ from the kinds of religious art which Will has admired hitherto. Before his discovery of the book of illustrations, his enthusiasm has been reserved either for the sort of symbolic art represented by the lamb with the flag or for the realism of the Pietas, which Anna dislikes so much. In the former, nature functions merely as a vehicle, standing for a higher, immaterial 'reality', and so accurate portrayal, distinctiveness of individual form, are unimportant and even to be avoided since their presence might subvert the task of the work which is to convey the ideal. The Pietas *do* use realism in the service of the ideal but, logically enough, what is realistically depicted and exalted in them is suffering and death, the things which bring 'liberation' from the physical and admittance into the realm of 'true being'. The Bamberg sculptures, in contrast, depict living fulness and beauty and because of this their effect is to encourage acceptance and affirmation of the world rather than rejection of it.

If the world seems more vivid and attractive to those in enhanced states of being, this is because in such states 'we infuse a transfiguration and fulness into things and poetize about them until they reflect back our fulness and joy in life':[21] the transformation in the world-as-perceived reflects the transformation in the perceiving subject. It follows that, for Nietzsche, the primary aesthetic spectacle is the individual 'intoxicated' by some powerful feeling. Such 'intoxication' is essentially the sensation of plenitude and increased energy' and its symptoms—subtlety, precision and grace of action—together constitute what is recognised as 'beauty'. In essence, then, the judgement that something or someone is 'beautiful' involves the instinctive awareness that what is being admired embodies a high degree of power and the attraction which beauty holds is the intuitive movement towards something felt as life-enhancing. The invigorating contact with the power embodied in beauty can be made indirectly through art, but we can also respond directly to the symptoms of overflowing strength in another individual. Like all 'healthy' art, the Bamberg figures increase the feeling of power in those who contemplate them, because they embody a way of seeing characteristic of enhanced states. The kind of vision they express depends on the projection of human strength and hence of human beauty, on to the world around and so, as a result of looking at the pictures, Will himself becomes like them. When he returns home after his discovery of the book, Anna sees him as he has seen the sculptures—'shining-faced, clear and beautiful in his movements, as if he were clarified'. His former glamour has been restored and in her eyes 'He was again a bright lord'.

Nietzsche insists that the highest degrees of power involve mastery over the self rather than others—intrinsic power, the integration and harmonisation of all the elements of the self, represents a greater degree of force than extrinsic power. But even intrinsic power tends to seek outward influence, if in subtle and oblique ways—through art, for example, rather than politics. The more sublimated, more 'spiritual' forms of strength are at the top of Nietzsche's hierarchy of power because they are most effective. While the cruder kinds of power tend, at most, to produce a temporary superficial obedience which conceals fundamental disaffection, higher degrees of power manifest themselves more considerately and so have a more profound influence on those in contact with them. So, in his transfigured state, Will shows none of the tendency to domineer which he displays in his less secure moments, but his influence is, nevertheless, far more potent than it is on these occasions where he tries to bully Anna into meeting his desires. These attempts simply alienate her and provoke her into resistance while here, her initial hostility quickly crumbles without any overt pressure from her husband:

> In spite of herself, she was compelled by him. He was strange, attractive, exerting some power over her.
> He came over to her, and touched her delicately. Her heart beat with wild passion, wild, raging passion. But she resisted as yet. It was always the unknown, always the unknown, and she clung fiercely to her known self. But the rising flood carried her away.
>
> (**R** p 167)

The sight of Will rouses Anna, rather as the pictures have previously roused Will: in both cases, contact with the symptoms of enhanced power due to sexual feeling awakens that feeling.

Both 'healthy' art and 'idealistic' religion create imaginary worlds, but, as I have already indicated, the relation of these realms to the world of ordinary experience is very different. While the ascetic negates the world to create his ideal realm, the 'apparent' world of art is simply reality 'selected, strengthened, corrected'. This 'art of apotheosis' proceeds from ' "aesthetic" states, in which the world is seen as fuller, rounder and more perfect', and it allows the spectator to go back to the real world better able to cope with it. The 'true world' of the idealist, on the other hand, is created by negating the actual and encourages the rejection of it. But, as Nietzsche's discussion of Raphel and romanticism suggests, these two radically different kinds of idealization can be confused. Thus, Will clearly thinks of the emotion called up by the figures as religious in character; he sees the sculptures as giving him access to a world of spiritual experience and he is unaware of their true relation to ordinary reality and of the part played by sexuality in both the transmission and the reception of the artist's vision. His ignorance illustrates the deficiencies of introspective awareness: Anna, relying on other kinds of evidence is aware however of the ways in which his fundamental impulses become transformed and re-emerge in apparently unrelated guises. As always in Lawrence's work, 'external phenomenology' is more reliable than the internal variety.

Because Will associates the effects of the Bamberg sculptures with the realm of 'true being' the erosion of his belief in the supernatural not only destroys the undesirable influence of 'idealistic' art but also cuts him off from life-enhancing contact with art which is superficially religious, but actually celebrates the natural world. So, as the weakening of his religious beliefs continues, he is increasingly forced to recognise that the 'apparent' world is all that really exists and, at the same time, deprived both of the means of escaping from it and of the kind of stimulus which will allow him to accept and affirm it. The result is that, after a time, his passion for Anna becomes the only source of that 'enhanced power and abundance' which he needs to transform the world and make it tolerable and his dependence on her becomes correspondingly extreme. At this point even temporary loss of contact with her plunges him into a terrifying, Dionysian world of universal flux which threatens to overwhelm him:

> What was he afraid of? Why did life, without Anna, seem to him just a horrible welter, everything jostling in a meaningless, dark, fathomless flood? Why, if Anna left him even for a week, did he seem to be clinging like a madman to the edge of reality, and slipping surely, surely into the flood of unreality that would drown him? This horrible slipping into unreality drove him mad, his soul screamed with fear and agony.
>
> (**R** p 187)

Nietzsche argues that it is the kind of world Will is aware of here, an 'absolute flow of happening',[22] an obscure, undifferentiated flux in which forces jostle in perpetual strife, which constitutes ultimate reality. The stable universe of our ordinary experience is an arranged and simplified world which man has instinctively constructed and consolidated over millenia in the interests of human survival.

In Nietzsche's view, the kind of predicament Will finds himself in is a fairly common one in contemporary life because scientific discoveries have tended to discredit the main means by which Western man has made the world habitable for himself. Science points to the conclusion that 'becoming' is the most basic characteristic of existence and, as a consequence, the Christian world-view has come to seem a psychological construct, created to make life bearable, rather than a reflection of reality. It is this realisation which precipitates the general psychic crisis which Nietzsche calls 'nihilism'—a state in which the world is seen as worthless and unreal:

> ... as soon as man finds out how that world [the 'true' world of the idealist] is fabricated solely from psychological needs, and how he has absolutely no right to it, the last form of nihilism comes into being; it includes disbelief in any metaphysical world and forbids itself any belief in a *true* world. Having reached this stand-point, one grants the reality of becoming as the *only* reality, forbids oneself every kind of clandestine access to afterworlds and false divinities—but *cannot endure this world though one does not want to deny it.*
>
> What has happened, at bottom? The feeling of valuelessness was reached with the realization that the overall character of existence may not be interpreted by means of the concept of 'aim', the concept of 'unity', or the concept of 'truth'. Existence has no goal or end; any comprehensive unity in the plurality of events is lacking: the character of existence is not 'true', is *false*.[23]

Our religious and philosophical traditions have accustomed us to thinking of valued attributes like truth and realness as inhering in that which is fixed and stable and according to such traditional criteria the fluid world described by contemporary science is 'false' and 'unreal'. This is why Will thinks of the very palpable forces which terrify and threaten to overwhelm him as being, paradoxically, a 'flood of unreality'. The image of the 'dark sea' which runs through the description of Will's psychic crisis provides another link with Nietzsche's thought. By its very nature the Nietzschean will to power tends to resist direct philosophical definition and in general to strain the resources of language, which has evolved as part of man's effort to render the world stable, intelligible and habitable. As a result, Nietzsche is compelled to use symbol, metaphor and other figurative techniques, usually met with in literary rather than philosophical contexts, in an effort to communicate something of its character. The sea is the most important of his recurrent images because its awesome force and incessant motion, together with its characteristic tidal rhythm of advance and withdrawal, make it a particularly apt image for Nietzsche's ultimate principle.

Anna's tactics force Will to face up to a world which at first seems unendurable and, as a consequence, he becomes able to cope with it. Initially, when she casts him off, he remains 'in an agony of suffering, thrown back into unreality, like a man thrown overboard into a sea, to swim till he sinks', but, after a time, he realises that although his situation is precarious, destruction is not inevitable and that the best course is to 'leave himself to the flood, to sink or live as might be'. But if he is not defeated by nihilism, Will lacks the strength to move beyond it as Paul Morel and Rupert Birkin do. He is capable of accepting that the values which make life possible are humanly created and have no objective existence, but he lacks the strength and resolution to follow this insight through to its logical conclusion and develop an individual 'perspective' which would be the expression of his own personal conditions of life and growth. Instead he clings to the empty shell of the traditional outlook, adhering to the forms of Christianity despite the fact that he has lost his faith.

Will's situation is, then, an example of a kind of inner crisis which Nietzsche saw as widespread in the modern age and this reinforces the reader's sense that the family history of the Brangwens is intended to have a representative quality, and that in *The Rainbow*, Lawrence's aim was to trace the growth of a distinctively contemporary sensibility. This is not to imply that the Brangwens are 'typical' in the sense of being ordinary. It is precisely because they are more sensitive than the majority that they respond more rapidly and fully to the forces shaping the modern experience, living through the crises of the present age and emerging from them in advance of the society as a whole, rather as Nietzsche felt that he had experienced in his own person the apocalyptic impact of nihilism and had progressed beyond it to a new affirmation, before most of his contemporaries were even aware of its onset. So, at the end of *The Rainbow*, Ursula's own spiritual escape from the dehumanised industrial world is evident in her vision of a regenerated England, but most of those around her are still encased in 'their horny covering of disintegration' and cannot see the potentialities latent in themselves and in those around them. However, the vital potential which is evident in the heroine also survives in them and, in time, will break the shell which surrounds it. Commenting on *The Wedding Ring*, an earlier version of the

Brangwen family chronicle, Lawrence himself stressed the representativeness of Ursula's experience—she is the symbol of her sex and in her development we see the evolution of modern womanhood, 'woman becoming individual, self-responsible, taking her own initiative'.[25] Clearly the development of 'woman' in this sense is closely linked with the progress of the male sex: if, in the later stages of the process of human advance chronicled in *The Rainbow* and *Woman in Love*, the main focus is on female experience this is largely because Lawrence tended to see women as initially more responsive to change. Because of their greater strength men tend to be more inert, to be less easily stimulated to new growth, although when their initial resistance is overcome they generally have the capacity to develop further.

CHAPTER 7

# How Instincts Develop and Change

*The Rainbow* ends with Ursula Brangwen's vision of the regeneration of the whole of her society, but by the time he came to write the second part of his Brangwen family chronicle, Lawrence was no longer convinced that healthy instinctive life survived in the majority of his contemporaries: *Women in Love* suggests that only a few exceptional individuals can find salvation and even they do not stay on in their own society as Ursula had done, but are compelled to flee in order to escape contamination by the general mediocrity and corruption around them. Lawrence was well aware of the sharp contrast in mood and atmosphere between the two novels and in a letter to an American enquirer, Waldo Frank, summed it up by describing *The Rainbow* as 'destructive-consummating', while *Women in Love* is 'purely destructive'. If the earlier novel does describe the destructive, dehumanising effects of industrialism, it also looks beyond contemporary industrial 'civilisation' to the 'culture' which will succeed it when intrinsic human vitality breaks its present bonds. In the later book this transformation no longer seems possible because the energies which would have made it happen now seem either warped or atrophied altogether. In his letter, Lawrence goes on to say that it was the Great War which altered his outlook so dramatically. If *The Rainbow* ends on a positive note, it is because it was completed before the war began—'I don't think the war had much to do with it—I don't think the war altered it from its prewar statement'; *Women in Love*, on the other hand, 'does contain the results in one's soul of the war'.[1]

Lawrence shared Nietzsche's tendency to explain historical events in psychological terms and for him the fundamental causes of the Great War were to be found in the human psyche rather than in large-scale political or economic forces. The war convinced him that his earlier faith in an essential human vitality, which had been overlaid but not significantly damaged by the ugly carapace of industrial life, had been misplaced; evidently the harm done to our instinctive selves was more fundamental than he had supposed. The general enthusiasm for war among the populations of all the belligerent nations showed that energies which would be good and creative in their healthy state were now directed towards disintegration and destruction. And even those who lacked spontaneous enthusiasm for the conflict nevertheless

193

allowed themselves to be drawn into the fighting by a sense of public duty; they did not share Lawrence's own instinctive aversion for the war and so the instinctive, life-affirming forces in them must either be thoroughly enfeebled or completely dead. In *St Mawr*, Lou Witt divides the majority of modern men into two categories: those like her husband Rico, in whom 'the animal has gone queer and wrong' and whose instincts, as a consequence are destructive rather than creative, and those in whom 'there is no wild animal left' like the young soldiers her mother has met, who have entered the war not out of any individual impulse at all but simply out of patriotic duty. Such men do not really exist as individuals; they have only a social self.

In a letter to Harriet Monroe, written in 1914, Lawrence discussed the responsibility of the artist in the face of events like the war and argued that he should ignore the large public and social dimensions of the conflict in order to concentrate on its real causes, which lie in the hearts of the individual combatants:

> The War is dreadful. It is the business of the artist to follow it home to the hearts of the individual fighters—not to talk in armies and nations and numbers—but to track it home—home—their war—and it's at the bottom of almost every Englishman's heart—the war—the desire of war—the *will* to war—and at the bottom of every German's.[2]

Since Lawrence believed that the instincts in their healthy state are 'intelligent'—perceptive, subtle and creative—and rejected the familiar idea that they are essentially savage and anarchic, he could not accept that the war was caused by some general failure of restraint which had unleashed naturally destructive energies. He also believed that the instincts were the sole motivating forces in human activity and so must lie behind the war; somehow the actual instincts of those civilised people who were enthusiastic about the war had become corrupt. In his 1912 letter to Edward Garnett Lawrence had outlined how he thought such damage can happen; reflecting on the events described in Garnett's play 'Jeanne d'Arc', Lawrence invoked the psychological mechanism which Nietzsche calls 'introversion' in which powerful impulses which have been repressed or frustrated re-emerge in extreme, corrupt and destructive form. It is not the freeing of instinct which is dangerous, but its suppression, which distorts it, turning something naturally healthy and creative, like sexuality, into something cruel and destructive. For Lawrence, the public enthusiasm for the war showed that this kind of degeneration of instinct had happened on a very large scale and he was forced to abandon his earlier, more optimistic view that the various distorting forces acting in our culture had done no more than conceal or obscure latent vitality.

Lawrence came to feel that the long dominance of Christian ideas was responsible for this widespread deformation of the instincts, but in his early work, up to and including *The Rainbow*, he presents Christianity as if it were almost marginal to most people's lives. H M Daleski describes the land and the church as the 'twin supports of life'[3] for the earlier generations of

Brangwens, but this exaggerates the importance to them of religion. While their involvement with the land is close and continuous, such religious awareness as they have is dim and sporadic, only felt when they lift their heads momentarily from the task in hand and see the church spire in the distance. Their sense of something above and beyond the physical life is not even spontaneous, but depends on that external stimulus:

> Whenever one of the Brangwens in the fields lifted his head from his work, he saw the church-tower at Ilkeston in the empty sky. So that as he turned again to the horizontal land, he was aware of something standing above him and beyond him in the distance.

> (**R** p 7)

For the Brangwens, the church serves largely as a focus for their embryonic aspirations towards a wider and fuller kind of life, rather than as the embodiment of particular moral and metaphysical doctrines; seeing the church tower makes them aware, from time to time, of realms of possible experience above and beyond the physical and sensuous life in which they are largely immersed. Despite his own firmly religious upbringing, Lawrence seems to have believed at this point that Christianity, as a system of beliefs, had never established a real hold over the bulk of the population: this is what he implies in *The White Peacock*, where he has his narrator suggest that established religion is rapidly declining and will shortly disappear. Speaking to Annable about the ruined hall church, Cyril sees it as epitomising the decay of religion as a whole—'The church ... is rotten. I suppose they'll stand all over the country like this, soon ...'

In a later story like *St Mawr*, on the other hand, religion is seen as a much more powerful and lasting influence. In that story, the decadent values of Christianity have corrupted Western man so thoroughly, over so many generations, that his basic energies are now devoted to destruction rather than creation, though usually the destructiveness is covert and underhand rather than open. In the contemporary European and American society described in *St Mawr*, the compassion and altruism enjoined by Christianity have led people to ignore the natural law that 'Creation destroys as it goes', so that they have attempted to 'abolish death' and 'save every parasite alive, until the accumulation of mere existence is swollen to a horror'. The 'accumulation of life and things' which results leads to general decay:

> Life must destroy life, in the unfolding of creation. We save up life at the expense of the unfolding, till all is full of rottenness.

> (**CSN** p 342)

The impulse to repudiate—or even destroy—the unliving or corrupt, whatever stands in the way of fuller and more creative life, is a natural and ultimately creative instinct which frees a space for new growth. If it is consistently frustrated by a moral tradition which compels at least a surface appearance of universal love, sympathy and fellow-feeling, it will nevertheless find expression although in radically altered form, reappearing as a subtle and subterranean but corrosive force, more extreme, less discriminating, no longer genuinely creative. The morality of compassion allows the unfortunate and ill-constituted to survive and their subtle revengefulness also pervades society, creating a situation in which a critical, disintegrative spirit is the dominant force. In her moment of revelation, Lou Witt sees, all around her 'People performing outward acts of loyalty, piety, self-sacrifice. But inwardly bent on undermining, betraying'.

For Lawrence, the major political upheavals of the time: the war, the Bolshevik revolution, the rise of Fascism, represent moments when the insidious destructiveness in the psyche of modern man has appeared openly, but even in apparently stable and settled societies, the same impulse is at work. When Gudrun and Ursula visit Hermione's house in the Breadalby chapter of *Women in Love*, Ursula is drawn to it because it seems like a refuge from the ugly, industrial present—

> There seemed a magic circle drawn about the place, shutting out the present, enclosing the delightful, precious past, trees and deer and silence, like a dream.
>
> **(WL** p 93)

But, as that last phrase warns us, this immunity from the ugly, the noisy, the mechanical, is only apparent since the people who assemble for the house-party are denizens of the contemporary world, embodying many of its most repellent aspects. In the quiet of the park, their conversation seems like 'a rattle of small artillery, always slightly sententious with a sententiousness that was only emphasised by the continual crackling of a witticism, the continual spatter of verbal jest'.

The imagery makes the conversation seem like a military engagement. These associations underline the destructive nature of what is being said; the target is the established social order, but there is no positive element in the criticism, no vision of renewal, but only demolition. The reader is reminded, subtly though effectively, of the barrages, the trenches and mud of the western front and by making this—on the face of it—extravagant connection, Lawrence is showing that the destructive spirit which caused the war is also at work here. The critical, skeptical, destructive talk of these cultivated people is a subtle, intellectual equivalent of the physical aggression and violence of the war. This linking of Hermione and her guests with the European conflict is particularly ironic since the originals of several of the guests were prominent pacifists; what they actually stand for, Lawrence suggests, is quite different from what they suppose themselves to represent.

In *The Rainbow*, Lawrence indicates that instinctive vitality has survived in the main characters by associating them with animals. This is particularly evident with Will and Anna, partly because they abandon their 'spiritual' aspirations and settle for a largely physical and sensual existence. But the fact that they—and especially Will—are constantly linked with fierce and predatory creatures suggests too that their impulses are more powerful than those of their forebears. This is reflected in the fact that their sexual activity is treated at greater length and in more detail than that of Tom and Lydia: in the younger couple, the most important of all 'urges' is more intense and various. Such strengthening and deepening of impulse gives Will and Anna (who should be considered as a single creative unit, as at least potentially, the composite 'angel' of Tom's wedding speech) more creative potential than their parents, but it also makes it harder for them to control and integrate their sensual energies. For Nietzsche, 'spiritual' potential is directly proportional to variety and intensity of impulse:

> With every increase of greatness and height in man, there is also increase in depth and terribleness: one ought not to desire the one without the other—or rather: the more radically one desires the one, the more radically one achieves the other.[4]

Although Will does not succeed as an artist he gets much further along the road to 'utterance' than his father-in-law who abandons the vaguer ambitions for spiritual fulfilment which were originally aroused by his experience of literature at school and reinforced by his later meeting with the aristocratic foreigner. At first, Tom had seen Lydia as the answer to both his major aspirations, as capable of offering him sensual and 'spiritual' fulfilment, but looking back on their relationship on the day of Anna's wedding, he feels that what they have actually achieved, although valuable, is more limited than he had hoped it might be. He sums up his marriage in an image of purely physical fulfilment as 'the long marital embrace with his wife' but his attempt to persuade himself that this is enough fails and he regrets the departure of Anna who is his last link with his other, unfulfilled ambition:

> What had he known, but the long marital embrace with his wife! Curious that this was what his life amounted to! At any rate, it was something, it was eternal. He would say so to anybody, and be proud of it ...
>
>   But the bitterness, underneath, that there still remained an unsatisfied Tom Brangwen, who suffered agony because a girl cared nothing for him. He loved his sons—he had them also. But it was the further, the creative life with the girl, he wanted as well.

(R p 129)

His sense of failure is puzzling because from the beginning of the novel it is women who show a spontaneous interest in the wider life beyond the farm. Tom's own intellectual curiosity is largely due to the influence of his mother and sisters. And if the Brangwen women are interested in social and intellectual developments even though they are very remote from the centres of such activity and hear 'the lips and the mind of the world speaking' only 'in the distance' it seems natural to assume that Lydia, who is educated and emancipated, will be even more alive to the life of the mind. But, in fact, the incompleteness of the first Brangwen marriage is Lydia's doing. The kind of relationship she creates with Tom is a consequence of her experience with her first husband, and it is in order to explain the character of her association with Brangwen that her past life is described in so much detail. Lensky, the Polish doctor who is her first husband is an idealist and for him the physical side of his relationship with Lydia has been primarily a means to an end. Looking back, rather resentfully in her old age, Lydia concludes that 'she was there for him, just to keep him in condition. She was to him one of the baser or material conditions necessary in prosecuting his ideas, of nationalism, of liberty, of science.' For Lydia, the wider world of ideas, of political action becomes associated with her husband's depreciation of the physical, personal and domestic and her revulsion from it is increased by the death of her children and Lensky's reaction to it. She is attracted to Tom precisely because she associates him with warmth and intimacy, with the physical qualities which Lensky had lacked. It is the instability and insecurity of most of her early life which lies behind her fascination with the Marsh on her first visit to it:

> She looked about the room he lived in. It had a close intimacy that fascinated and almost frightened her. The furniture was old and familiar as old people, the whole place seemed so kin to him, as if it partook of his being, that she was uneasy.
> 'It is already a long time that you have lived in this house—yes?' she asked.
> 'I've always lived here,' he said.
> 'Yes—but your people—your family?'
> 'We've been here above *two* hundred years,' he said.
>
> (**R** p 37)

What is stressed here is the close relation between the house and Tom himself, so that Lydia links the stability of his surroundings with Tom's own nature. Coming as she does from a much less secure background—she is 'the daughter of a Polish landowner' who was 'deeply in debt to the Jews'—she reacts in the same ambivalent way to these alien circumstances as the Brangwens, from the stability of their background have reacted to the life of change and widening experience ushered in by industrialism. But because of what she has gone through, the fascination with Tom and the Marsh, the desire for the peaceful, physical existence they seem to promise is stronger than her fears. Yet there is a major irony in all this: Lydia links the character of the man with the character of his circumstances and she is partly right because there are strong forces in Tom's nature holding him to the traditional kind of existence. But the reader knows that at this point Tom also wants very strongly to break with that life and we are reminded of that fact by the qualification of Lydia's view of him by 'seemed'. In other words their relationship is affected from the start by the fact that each misunderstands the other in a fairly important way.

It is mainly this failure by Lydia to detect in Tom the desire for something more than physical fulfilment which causes the tensions in the early part of their marriage. Despite his sexual satisfaction, he finds no outlet for his other desires and because of this he sometimes becomes angry and frustrated, feeling resentment against his wife because he realises more or less intuitively that she is responsible for his condition—

> Cold he called her, selfish, only caring about herself, a foreigner with a bad nature, caring really about nothing, having no proper feelings at the bottom of her, and no proper niceness. He raged and piled up accusations that had some measure of truth in them all.
>
> ( **R** p 63)

The idea that what he resents is his wife's faults has only 'some measure of truth'—for the most part the attempt to blame his discontent on her vices is a rationalisation of something he is unable to articulate.

The real source of his dissatisfaction is revealed when he visits his brother's mistress in Wirksworth and finds, to his surprise, that instead of the voluptuous young woman who might be expected to attract a middle-aged man, she is tall and white-haired. And it is clear from her surroundings that she has artistic and intellectual interests—

> She took him into a drawing-room, full of books, with a piano and a violinstand. And they talked, she simply and easily. She was full of dignity. The room was of a kind Brangwen had never known; the atmosphere seemed open and spacious, like a mountain-top to him.
>
> (**R** p 90)

Alfred's liaison is less a matter of physical infatuation than of intellectual intimacy. Clearly his relationship with the woman is both sexual and intellectual and so has a completeness which his marriage presumably lacks. The meeting makes Tom aware of the limitations of his own relationship and revives his desire for 'spiritual' fulfilment:

> ... when he got to the Marsh, he realized how fixed everything was, how the other form of life was beyond him, and he regretted for the first time that he had succeeded to the farm. He felt a prisoner, sitting safe and easy and unadventurous. He might, with risk, have done more with himself.
>
> (**R** p 91)

Then the other side of his nature reasserts itself as the atmosphere of the farm reestablishes its hold and the next day he thinks of 'the woman and her place' as having something about them which is 'cold and alien'. But even while he says this, his dissatisfaction persists and he sits 'perturbed'. Watching his wife sitting sewing he feels that 'It was too quiet for him':

> It was too peaceful. He wanted to smash the walls down, and let the night in, so that his wife should not be so secure and quiet, sitting there. He wished the air were not so close and narrow. His wife was obliterated from him, she was in her own world, quiet, secure, unnoticed, unnoticing. He was shut down by her.
>
> (**R** pp 91–2)

Tom feels that because his wife is an educated woman she *must* have an intellectual life of her own, but that she will not share it with him since she looks down on him as uncultivated. His doubts are created partly by his awareness of her aristocratic background and partly by a sense of his own inferiority. Despite what seems to Lydia his unshakeable confidence, Tom is in some ways very unsure of himself and uncertain about the worth of his own personality. His doubts go back to his boyhood and his youthful awareness that he could not live up to his mother's ambitions for him. Then he had taken his sufferings at school as inevitable 'as if he were guilty of his own nature, as if his being were wrong ...' Tom remains unsure of his own value and because of this he interprets Lydia's silence and withdrawal as aloofness and feels resentful. She, on her side, is at first unaware that he is dissatisfied because she sees him merely as the purely physical being he seems superficially to be. Her conception of his nature at this point in their relationship is such that she has no reason to initiate any intellectual interchange for the satisfaction it might offer him, and her own recent experience has disillusioned her so completely with ideas and idealism that she herself wants to avoid them as much as possible. She wants a relationship which is as simply and straightforwardly physical as it can be. But she is also withdrawn and silent because of the suffering she has gone through. Sometimes her apparent aloofness seems related to the trance-like state which she falls into after Lensky's death and like it serves as a defence against suffering. So, on the evening after Tom's visit to his brother's mistress, she seems to him at first 'quiet, secure and unnoticing': it is very much a matter of 'seeming' because the episode ends with his realisation that Lydia is, in fact, in quite a different sort of state:

> Suddenly, in a flash, he saw that she might be lonely, isolated, unsure. She had seemed to him the utterly certain, satisfied, absolute, excluding him.
>
> (**R** p 93)

So it is not because Lydia is indifferent to Tom that she had seemed withdrawn and unresponsive, but because she cares a great deal for him—and consequently does not want to reveal her need of him and dependence on him, because that would reveal her vulnerability and perhaps bring further suffering. But on this occasion, under the strain of knowing about Tom's visit to Wirksworth, her defences break down. She feels that the visit indicates that he is no longer satisfied with the relationship with her, that he would like another woman, and this possibility disturbs her so much, that, quite uncharacteristically she interrogates him about his feelings. What she says to him shows a sensitivity to the fluctuations of his emotions which surprises Tom:

> She was silent for a while.
> 'You do not want to be with me any more,' she said.
> It startled him. How did she know this truth? He thought it was his secret.
>
> (**R** p 92)

The insight startles Tom because it does not fit in with his conception of her attitude to him. If she really is aloof and detached, how could she know this about him?

He realises that if she is aware of things which he had thought hidden this must be because what he feels and does matters desperately to her, that far from being aloof and superior, she cares for him very much. It is this realisation that her apparent 'utter certainty' conceals need that leads Tom to abandon his ambitions for a more complete relationship and settle for simple physical fulfilment. The scene is a turning point in their marriage because it involves the ending of the illusions about each other which have got in the way of their happiness. It precedes the 'coming together after two years of married life' which is the real consummation of their relation and which is associated with the first appearance in the novel of the multi-valent rainbow symbol:

> Anna's soul was put at peace between them. She looked from one to the other, and she saw them established to her safety and she was free. She played between the pillar of fire and the pillar of cloud in confidence, having the assurance on her right hand and the assurance on her left. She was no longer called upon to uphold with her childish might the broken end of the arch. Her father and her mother now met to the span of the heavens, and she, the child, was free to play in the space beneath, between.
>
> (**R** p 97)

Here the rainbow is not so much a symbol of the union between flesh and spirit—although this is one of its important meanings—as a symbol of mutual understanding and the new balance in the marriage; the divided halves of the arch have come together.

Will's spiritual aspirations are much more strongly developed than those of his father and so it is much harder for Anna to influence him than it had been for Lydia to influence Tom. Nevertheless, in the end, the second marriage, like the first, becomes a largely physical relationship. At first Will is intoxicated by the sexual adventurousness which follows his abandonment of his spiritual interests, and feels fulfilled but, like Tom, he comes to feel that his marriage is too limited and his sense that because of this he has never quite realised his own individuality echoes Tom's sense at Anna's wedding that 'He was still as unsure and unfixed as when he had married himself'. Will and Anna are 'neither of them quite personal, quite defined as individuals, so much were they pervaded by the physical heat of breeding and rearing their young': like Tom and Lydia, they have remained 'uncertainties'. Like Tom, too, Will finds an outlet for his frustrated aspirations in an unusually close relationship with one of his daughters. Each man instinctively recognises that full development and creativity depend on the interaction of maleness and femaleness and failing to receive the appropriate stimulus from his wife seeks it elsewhere. Anna's marriage breaks her close bond with Tom and the fact that their estrangement is described just before we learn of the father's death in the flood suggests that the loss of contact and the drowning may be related:

Anna Brangwen had left her intimacy with her father undeveloped since the time of her marriage. At her marriage it had been abandoned. He and she had drawn a reserve between them. Anna went more to her mother.
Then suddenly the father died.

(R p 243)

Anna's departure deprives Tom of his last tenuous link with the fuller finer existence he had once wanted to enter and he responds, as he had responded to his earlier frustration, by drinking, and it is this which causes his death. Because Will's spiritual interests are stronger, they cannot be wholly satisfied in a vicarious way through Ursula and so, when at last he is freed by the 'developing rejection of old forms' in his children, he does not follow the same self-destructive course but, instead, returns to his art.

Ursula, as her name perhaps suggests, inherits the animal vitality of her forebears. The imagery used to describe the physical, sensual side of her nature links her closely with her father: after Skrebensky's return, for example, when her disillusionment with intellectual life and his enthusiasm for the 'African darkness' have made her temporarily reject the whole world of 'light', she feels 'free as a leopard that sends up its raucous cry in the night.' The same image occurs much earlier in the novel when, at the beginning of her marriage, Anna becomes aware that Will is trying to establish total dominance over her and thinks of him as being 'like a leopard that had leapt on her and fastened'. The association of father and daughter in this way indicates that both possess unusually powerful impulses and are therefore capable of significant 'spiritual' achievement.

In *Women in Love* and the works which follow it, the multiplicity of animal images used in *The Rainbow* gives way to a smaller number of recurrent animal images of which the most important is the horse. It is a particularly appropriate image for the 'animal' side of man because its usefulness depends on its being 'trained' rather than 'tamed' or 'domesticated' and so, despite its long association with man it has retained its essential otherness; its pristine being has not been contaminated by human traits as has a dog's, for example. Further the relation between horse and rider offers a useful—and traditional—analogy to that between instinct and reason. The horse first occurs in a way significant for human experience in *Sons and Lovers*. During one of their walks, Clara, Paul and Miriam meet a neighbouring farmer who is leading a stallion. The whole party, but particularly Paul, are struck by the combination of size and grace in the creature. The episode allows Lawrence to make the Nietzschean point that great strength expresses itself delicately rather than crudely, but its main importance lies in the way in which it associates the vitality evident in the animal with that in Paul himself, thereby anticipating Lawrence's later use of the horse as a symbol of the instinctive side of human nature. The link between man and animal is suggested in Miss Limb's response to Miriam's admiring comment on the stallion:

'Isn't he splendid!' said Miriam to her.
Miss Limb looked up. Her dark eyes glanced straight at Paul.

(R p 288)

Clearly she recognises Morel as the human embodiment of the overflowing vitality she responds to in the horse. Because the farm is an isolated one she has no human object for her affections but the transferring of her feelings to the stallion does not solve her problem and, as her interest in Paul shows, loneliness and frustration continue to trouble her. The fact that she appears to cope less well with their isolated situation than her brother suggests that her plight has a lesson for Clara, who is determined to do without a man for different reasons and Clara herself seems to recognise this, because when they leave, she blurts out suddenly 'I suppose she wants a man.' Women evidently need the support of male strength and tenderness if they are to remain sane and whole in the face of life's difficulties. The marked emphasis in the scene on the sensitivity, intelligence and attractiveness of the horse is related to Lawrence's conviction that the physical side of man's being, which is shared with the animals, is capable of great subtlety and delicacy despite the magnitude of the forces it contains.

The symbolic significance of the horse is more fully developed in *The Rainbow* in the episode, near the end of the novel, in which Ursula sees, or thinks she sees, some horses in a field she must cross on her way home. She has just written to Skrebensky to tell him that she is carrying his child and that she wants to marry him. As she goes on, she has to run the gauntlet of the herd, which terrifies her by galloping close to her several times. But for all the intensity of her fear, it is not clear whether the horses have any objective existence; the whole experience has a hallucinatory quality, and in describing it Lawrence continually blurs the line between external and internal events. In fact what is happening here is a psychological crisis of the kind already discussed in connection with both Siegmund and Paul Morel—the unity of the forces which constitute Ursula's self has collapsed and her psyche has disintegrated into a multitude of independently acting 'urges'. This psychic situation generates an unusual degree of consciousness of inner events, but the exact nature and full complexity of unconscious processes still does not enter conscious awareness, so the inner crisis seems to Ursula something external. This interpretation of a powerful but mysterious scene is supported by the passage in Helen Corke's autobiographical novel *Neutral Ground* which deals, in fictional form, with the author's tragic relationship with a musician (Lawrence used the same autobiographical material as the basis of *The Trespasser*) and her subsequent friendship with Lawrence himself, who appears in the book as Derrick Hamilton. *Neutral Ground* is, of course, a novel and not a memoir, but its origins in recent and painful personal experience suggest that it was written as a kind of therapy rather than from exclusively literary motives. Its fidelity to the facts is confirmed by other, more documentary evidence and so it seems legitimate to use it—cautiously—as a source of information about Lawrence's beliefs and attitudes. In the course of his effort to restore the heroine's psychic health after her lover's suicide, Derrick Hamilton argues that she is wasting her emotions. She replies that she can 'neither generate emotion or apply it in any definite direction'—

He took a lighter tone. 'No! true. You've not reached Nietzsche's standard of control and its consequent satisfactions.'

Ellis looked to him for explanation, but he waited for the demand. 'What exactly do you mean?' she asked, being obliged.

'He wanted to drive his emotions, like horses. Or rather, to ride them ... To feel them under him—sources of controlled power.'[5]

Here the horses are explicitly identified with the basic powers in the self, with the feelings or urges which constitute it and psychic health is associated with the 'trained team', with instinctive energies which are disciplined and integrated, but which are not 'driven', forced in a particular direction, but 'ridden'. Hamilton presents both idea and image as Nietzschean. The case for this kind of Nietzschean interpretation of Ursula's encounter with the horses is strengthened by the fact that it immediately precedes her final break with Skrebensky. It is as if the suffering she goes through and the challenge of her inner disintegration have, in the end, the effect of increasing her strength so that she is able to free herself completely from old ties and old values.

From *Women in Love* onwards, Lawrence felt that only a few people still possessed healthy and vigorous instincts, while in the great majority, the 'animal' has either been tamed or corrupted by the life-denying code which has dominated our culture for so long. Nietzsche argues that strict and absolute moral codes, like that of Christianity, originate with those whose instincts are extreme and ill-organised because of immaturity or decadence. For such individuals, a rigid moral discipline is a means to survival but, historically, the influence of such codes has not been confined to those who need them—indeed, they have been used by their originators as a means of seducing and corrupting those who are strong and well-constituted. Under the influence of ascetic ideas, the strong become divided against themselves: they come to feel guilty about their virtue and become persuaded that they are the spiritual inferiors of the lowly and unsuccessful. The results of this process can be seen in *Women in Love* in the character of Gerald Crich's father. Crich senior is a wealthy industrialist, a man of energy and drive endowed with the qualities which make for success in the world, yet his Christian faith makes him see his abilities and the wealth and position they have brought him, as the very things which make him the spiritual inferior of the colliers who work for him. Nietzsche argues that this kind of corruption of the strong by the weak and the guilt and repression which result can lead to the deformation of the instincts and if this happens, the very strength of impulse which gives the strong individual his creative potential becomes a danger; the powerful forces in him are now directed towards destruction. In such a situation, the 'strong' may adopt the tactics of the 'weak' and instinctively impose a rigid control on their impulses in an effort to prevent disaster. The 'deathliness' of Gerald's fundamental instincts is a natural outcome of his father's piety; in him conscious will tyranises over instinct so that the destructive forces in his psyche only emerge occasionally. The relationship between father and son has more than just a personal significance; they represent two whole successive phrases in the history of our culture. When Gerald inherits the mines from his father, it is not simply a matter of one individual succeeding another—Gerald's attitudes and the changes he makes, apparently so opposed to everything his father has stood for, are, in fact, the logical and inevitable result of what the older man represents.

Lawrence does not try to present the psychic inversion in characters like Gerald directly; instead he shows us how he reacts to the instinctive vitality embodied in other living creatures. The scene in which he forces his sensitive Arab mare to stand at a level-crossing gate while a very slow and noisy coal train passes is one vivid example of this. Terrified by the noise of the train, the animal tries to escape, but is brutally held there by Gerald, who controls it with an 'almost mechanical relentlessness'. The incident is powerful on a literal level, but has wider implications because the relationship between horse and rider also symbolises the relation between instinct and conscious will in the individual psyche and, as a result, the event becomes a potent image of the way in which the deliberate will of modern industrial man is holding him to a mode of life against which his deepest instincts revolt. Gerald's determination to control instinct arises from his conviction that it is 'stupid', a conclusion which springs from his awareness of the anarchic and destructive nature of the deepest forces in himself. His natural—though erroneous—conclusion is that the instincts can only be harnessed and made productive only if they are subject to the direction of the conscious self.

Sensing the destructiveness of his own impulses, Gerald naturally projects that destructiveness onto those around him as well. As Birkin points out to him early in *Women in Love*, his conviction that 'most other people' would like to cut our throats for us 'some time or other—' is a reflection of his own inner state rather than a truth about the world. Believing that all instincts are intrinsically like his own, Gerald naturally imagines that a harsh discipline has to be imposed on instinct as such to restrain its 'natural' disruptiveness and destructiveness, though, in fact, his Arab mare has retained the sensitivity and delicacy of response characteristic of healthy animal life. He treats himself and his fellow human beings in the mines in just the same way that he treats his mare, subordinating his own natural impulses and those of the miners to the establishment of a wholly rational, mechanised order. And the fact that his rationalisation of the mines meets with only token resistance from the work-force indicates that the change corresponds to the deepest desires of the miners themselves; the corruption of vital energies which Gerald represents is not specific to him, or even to his class, but is general in society.

Although the kind of rigid conscious control practised by Gerald is an attempt to prevent damage it tends, in the end, to aggravate the condition it is intended to relieve and to make the instincts even more perverse and destructive. Like Gerald, Gudrun is convinced that the instincts are naturally 'stupid' and her hostility to them is evident in an incident with Winifred Crich's pet rabbit, Bismark, which has affinities with what happens at the level-crossing. She responds to the creatures unpredictability with intense contempt, seeing the fluid, spontaneous, unexpected movement of instinctive life as evidence of its essential 'stupidity'. For her, it is the regular, predictable and rational which are valuable and which account for the superiority of human beings over the merely animal. It is because they feel the same contempt for the creature that she and Gerald recognise each other as kindred spirits: each despises instinct and believes in the dominance of conscious will. The fact that Gerald is in love with her, together with the erotic overtones of their exchange and the choice of a rabbit as the catalyst, all suggest that a particular kind of attitude to instinct in general is associated here with one particular instinct—that what the scene brings out is a shared attitude to sexuality. For both Gerald and Gudrun, spontaneous sexual feeling is characterised by the 'stupidity' which typifies instinctive activity as a whole and so each seeks to exploit sexuality consciously in a deliberate search for sensation. The rabbit's response to being held by Gerald parallels that of the Arab mare—it becomes violent, frenziedly trying to escape and in the course of its struggle inflicts wounds on its captors. Its behaviour illustrates how sexuality can become perverse and sadistic if consciously controlled and manipulated. Gerald and Gudrun are drawn together by the curious pleasure they both obviously get from the wounding because each subconsciously recognises in the other the sensationalist attitude to sexual experience which Lawrence deplored and each sees the possibility of a relationship in which their perverse interests would be satisfied.

The rabbit serves then as a symbol for one particular kind of impulse: later in the novel, when Lawrence wants an image for the general corruption of instinctive being, he again uses a horse. On their trip to the Alps the two pairs of lovers meet Loerke, a German sculptor. The women are attracted by him and he discusses art with them and shows them a picture of one of his works, a bronze figure of a naked girl seated on a stallion. When Ursula first looks at the picture, she is puzzled by the stiffness and stupidy of the bronze horse, feeling that Loerke has entirely failed to capture the sensitivity and delicacy of the real animal. She slowly comes to realise that the statue lacks these qualities because it is not a representation of a horse at all, but rather a symbolic depiction of Loerke's own essential being in which the instinctive forces, the 'animal', is corrupt and brutal. The sculpture is, in fact, a portrayal of the sculptor's deepest self and of the nature of his relationship with the girl who served as his model.

Significantly, Gudrun defends her fellow artist against Ursula's charge of inaccuracy, arguing that different individuals see the world differently. Ursula's answer is a Nietzschean one; she accepts that there is a subjective element in perception, so that what people think of as 'reality' differs, but she goes on to imply that the character of the individual's vision can have a diagnostic significance, that it can reveal, the state of health of the perceiving subject. Like Nietzsche, she works back from her response to art to the inner state of the artist. So she asks of Loerke:

'But why does he have this idea of a horse? ... I know it is his idea. I know it is a picture of himself, really—'

(**WL** p 484)

The sculptor reacts angrily to this suggestion arguing vehemently that art is not self-revelatory, but the very violence of his response suggests that Ursula is right:

> 'A picture of myself!' he repeated in derision ... 'It is a work of art, it is a picture of nothing, of absolutely nothing. It has nothing to do with anything but itself, it has no relation with the everyday world of this and the other, there is no connexion between them ... and to translate one into the other is worse than foolish, it is a darkening of all counsel, a making confusion everywhere. Do you see, you *must not* confuse the relative world of action with the absolute world of art.'
>
> (**WL** p 484)

His vehemence convinces Ursula that her diagnosis is accurate and she now feels confident enough simply to dismiss Loerke's aestheticism:

> 'It isn't a word of it true, of all this harangue you have made me,' she replied flatly. 'The horse is a picture of your own stock, stupid brutality, and the girl was a girl you loved and tortured and ignored' ...
>
> 'As for your world of art and your world of reality ... you have to separate the two, because you can't bear to know what you are. You can't bear to realize what a stock, stiff, hide-bound brutality you *are* really, so you say "it's the world of art". The world of art is only the truth about the real world, that's all—but you are too far gone to see it.'
>
> (**WL** p 485)

The stallion is not, then, a 'machine horse', an example of organic life 'conceptualised as stupid mechanical force'[6] as a result of Loerke's futuristic admiration for mechanism, but a representation of his own corrupted instincts. Loerke reveals his own decadence in his art although he is not aware that he is doing so and indeed, confuses inner with outer experience rather as Ursula does at the end of *The Rainbow*, thinking of the horse as objective rather than subjective.

The horse appears again as a major symbol in the novella *St Mawr*. The husband of the heroine of the tale is an aristocrat and fashionable painter who, like Gerald Crich, has powerful destructive forces in his nature over which he normally exercises rigid control. The conscious part of Rico's being, which holds these potentially anarchic impulses in check is compared to a rider on an unreliable horse which may suddenly turn vicious. The comparison provides another link with *Women in Love*, this time with Loerke, whose distorted instinctive energies are also symbolised by a horse which is vicious and brutal and lacks the sensitivity and intelligence characteristic of uncorrupted natural life. Rico is almost invariably tolerant and reasonable, but Lawrence emphasises that his outward behaviour does not accurately reflect his inner nature, that his self-control is, paradoxically, a consequence of the violence of his impulses. Thus, while he may feel angry, his anger never finds expression in action, or even in harsh words—although it is evident in involuntary things—but this restraint is due not to deference to social convention or to the inherent moderation of his nature, but to his awareness that if he once gives in to his feelings they will have radically destructive consequences:

> He got quite angry, and his handsome arched nose tilted and his upper lip lifted from his teeth, like a dog that is going to bite. Yet daren't quite bite.
> And that was Rico. He daren't quite bite. Not that he was really afraid of the others. He was afraid of himself, once he let himself go. He might rip up, in an eruption of life-long anger all this pretty-pretty picture of a charming young wife and a delightful little home and a fascinating success as a painter of fashionable and at the same time 'great' portraits ... He had composed this little *tableau vivant* with great effort. He didn't want to erupt like some suddenly wicked horse—Rico was really more like a horse than a dog, a horse that might go nasty at any moment.
>
> (**CSW** p 283)

It is an image of Rico's being which links him directly with the stallion St Mawr, the embodiment in the book of uncorrupted instinctive energies. It is essential that the stallion should be recognised as a real horse and not reduced simply to a symbol of a particular aspect of the human psyche, because one of the things Lawrence wants to emphasise through making the horse an important element in the story is that man has largely lost the qualities which the animal possesses. Only by introducing a non-human character can Lawrence adequately convey the splendour and power of pristine instinct, because those individuals who have retained some measure of psychic health, like Lewis and Phoenix, are in socially subordinate positions in a society dominated by the decadent and so they cannot be used to illustrate the full creative potential of instinctive energies. This is why Lou and her mother, who are thoroughly disillusioned with their fellow human beings, and particularly with men (who should possess the most powerful instincts) respond so strongly to the horse. St Mawr embodies qualities which they feel they need, but have sought without success in the human world.

The central incident of the story, in which the stallion injures Rico and another man is a result of the same kind of failure to recognise the 'wisdom' of instinctive responses which makes several characters in *Women in Love* dismiss instinct as 'stupid'. The horse sees a snake and responds to possible danger by shying and then rearing. Rico has not noticed the snake and seeing the behaviour of the horse as further evidence of its 'stupidity' tries viciously to bring it under control. In doing so, he pulls it over on top of himself. In some ways the incident resembles that in *Women in Love* where Gerald Crich forces his panicking mare to stand at the level-crossing; in both episodes, the rider disregards the instinctive reaction of the horse, seeing it as evidence of the creature's stupidity. But Rico is a less forceful and determined character than Crich and fails to bend the animal to his will. In its outcome, the accident in *St Mawr* resembles the 'rabbit' episode in *Women in Love*, because in both cases there is a struggle between an animal and a human being in which the latter is hurt. The injuries inflicted by the horse are much more serious of course, but both incidents illustrate the same thing—the damage done to the self as a whole if consciousness is allowed to thwart spontaneous, 'animal' impulses. The incident is given general significance by Lou Witt's vision of evil, which occurs just after it has happened. She sees the accident as epitomising the fate of mankind as a whole which has been corrupted by a morality of sympathy and altruism. As a result we ignore our instinctive recoil from things or people which are decadent or dead and even work to preserve them. And since decadents seek unconsciously to communicate their misery—in *The White Peacock* Annable had been drawn to Cyril for this reason—their survival and multiplication has resulted in the wide-spread corruption of the healthy. At the same time, the feelings which the dominant morality compels us to repress do not vanish, but survive in us, becoming corrupt and emerging either in insidiously destructive form in the 'undermining' which underlies the superficial friendliness of many societies, or in the sudden and violent 'breaks' made by countries like Russia and Germany.

Despite his insistence that 'urges' are the prime movers in human action, Nietzsche does argue that in certain circumstance consciousness can undermine and distort instinct in the way implied in Lawrence's horse and rider metaphor. His theory of 'assimilation', through the action of 'organic memory' means that attitudes, beliefs and ideas which are held for a sufficiently long time become 'embodied' and change human nature in significant ways. And, as the spread of ascetic values shows, the influence of a particular kind of belief is not necessarily confined to those who 'need' it. The decadent envies the healthy man and his will to power finds expression in the attempt to spread his sickness to him. Christianity is primarily a social expression of such feelings of 'ressentiment' and its victory over the paganism which preceded it is the victory of weakness over strength. As a result of centuries of Christian dominance, its imperatives have been built into the nature of western man just as pagan values were in the earlier phase of his development; the result is that he is now divided against himself in the most fundamental way. He is, in Nietzsche's phrase 'physiologically false'; his 'instincts' embody opposite valuations.'[7]

This inner division has particularly affected sexuality which, as the most powerful and pervasive urge acting in adult life, has been the main target of ascetic hostility; it is this which has brought about the 'physiological falsity' which is an important theme in Lawrence's first three novels. Lawrence constantly stressed the primacy of the 'flesh' and insists that under normal conditions it determines our values, so that when he emphasises the physical strength, fulness and attractiveness of Emily, Helena and Miriam he is implying that the values natural to them and appropriate for them are quite opposite to the ascetic, anti-natural attitudes that they do, in fact, display. But, as Miriam's case in particular shows, the problem is not simply one of conscious inhibition blocking instinctive response, but one which involves a conflict at the instinctive level itself, between opposing kinds of 'urges'. In these early novels, Lawrence's optimism is reflected in the belief that the physical and psychic can—with difficulty—be brought back into harmony again; that those whose essential being has been distorted by the assimilation of inappropriate and anti-natural values can be helped back to psychic health by those more developed than themselves. In *The Trespasser*, for example, the story centres on the change which takes place in the heroine, Helena, as a result of her summer holiday with her lover. In the course of their idyll, she gradually learns to accept the physical and sexual, although her initial revulsion severely damages Siegmund and leads to his suicide. The change in Helena is neither rapid nor straightforward, but follows the pattern of flow and recoil characteristic of Lawrence's view of human development. It is by no means complete at the end of the holiday, but Helena has made enough progress by then to make the first gesture of physical affection in her new relationship with Byrne, and it is on this mutedly hopeful note that the novel ends.

To begin with Helena thinks of Siegmund as having a dual nature and for her it is the tender, poetic side of him which is admirable and lovable just as, in *Sons and Lovers*, it is the 'spiritual' side of Paul Morel, his emotional intensity and intellectual gifts which, for Miriam, represent the 'real' Paul. Each woman also devalues the physical and sexual side of her lover's nature and their attitude communicates itself to the men, who come to feel as a result that there is something base and unworthy about their own sexuality. However, they are unable to suppress their sexual needs and as a result become weakened and frustrated and when the impulse can no longer be denied, the feeling which results is not one of fulfilment, but of guilt. *The Trespasser* and *Sons and Lovers* show that in undermining the physical and especially the sexual, both Helena and Miriam are also threatening the existence of those 'spiritual' qualities in their lovers which they admire. Their mistake is to see sense and spirit as antithetical whereas, in reality, they are interdependent and the physical, the 'body' or the 'flesh' is primary and the essential foundation of the 'soul' or 'spirit'.

And so it is when he is sexually fulfilled that Siegmund becomes the tender, poetic lover of Helena's dreams. After making love for the first time, they go out to look at the moon on the water—significantly, Siegmund's lyrical response to the scene excites Helena much more than his physical passion had done:

> 'I like the moon on the water,' she said.
> 'I can hardly tell one from the other,' he replied simply. 'The sea seems to be poured out of the moon, and rocking in the hands of the coast. They are all one, just as your eyes and hands and what you say, are all you.'
> 'Yes,' she answered, thrilled. This was the Siegmund of her dream, and she had created him.
>
> (Tr p 37)

On this occasion, Helena does recognise that the spiritual and the sensual are related, that somehow Siegmund's passion for her is responsible for his new state. Although she is surprised at the extent of the change in him, she does accept that both contrasting states are authentic expressions of her lover's being:

She wondered at him; he was so different from an hour ago. How could he be the same! Now he was like the sea, blue and hazy in the morning, musing by itself. Before he was burning, volcanic, as if he would destroy her.

She had given him this new soft beauty. She was the earth in which his strange flowers grew. But she herself wondered at the flowers produced of her. He was so strange to her, so different from herself.

(**Tr** p 36)

But the growth towards a healthier outlook foreshadowed here is interrupted by frequent lapses back into her dualistic idealism. Just before their departure, for example, at a point when she feels guilty and depressed about the injuries she imagines she has done to those around her, she looks for support to the poetic, the 'dream' Siegmund whose ability to 'radiate joy into his surroundings' has magically transformed the world for her in the past. She sees instead only his physical self and for the moment believes that the other side of him is an illusion, a mere projection of her own desires:

Life and hope were ash in her mouth. She shuddered with discord. Despair grated between her teeth. This dreariness was worse than her dreary, lonely life had known. She felt she could bear it no longer.

Siegmund was there. Surely he could help. He would rekindle her. But he was straying ahead, carelessly whistling the Spring Song from *Die Walküre*. She looked at him, and again shuddered with horror. Was that really Siegmund, that stooping, thick-shouldered, indifferent man? Was that the Siegmund who had seemed to radiate joy in his surroundings, the Siegmund whose coming had always changed the whole weather of her soul? Was that the Siegmund whose touch was keen with bliss for her, whose face was a panorama of passing God? She looked at him again. His radiance was gone, his aura had ceased. She saw him a stooping man, past the buoyancy of youth, walking and whistling rather stupidly ...

She suffered an agony of disillusion. Was this the real Siegmund, and her own only a projection of her soul. She took her breath sharply. Was he the real clay, and that other, her beloved, only the breathing of her soul upon this?

(**Tr** pp 99–100)

Here Helena experiences, although on a personal rather than a cosmic level, the nihilistic vision. What is real she sees as valueless, while that which she had valued now seems unreal. When she is in this state, Siegmund's attempts to comfort her only make things worse and she recoils from him. Later, trying to explain this recoil, she reveals that she has not yet shaken off her psychological dualism. She tells Siegmund that she had felt 'a crying of lives' against her and had looked to him for comfort:

'I wanted you—I saw you in front, whistling the Spring Song, but I couldn't find you—it was not you—I couldn't find you.'

(**Tr** p 105)

Her momentary fear that only the hateful and frightening physical side of her lover is real has passed and his authentic self is again identified with the tender, poetic elements in his being. Significantly, Siegmund fails to understand Helena here because his view of human identity is quite different and involves the recognition of all the elements in the self as real. So he replies, in puzzlement—

> 'No, I don't see it ... You would always be you. I could think of hating you, but you'd still be yourself.'
>
> (Tr p 106)

This fundamental difference of perspective is outlined at the beginning of the story, in a narrative passage which follows their first, unconsummated love-making. There, two different attitudes to the relation between body and spirit—Lawrence's terms are 'blood' and 'dream'—are distinguished. In Helena's case, the 'dream' is divorced from the physical and sensual, so that her attempt to compel Siegmund to live up to her ideal image of him damages him. His spirituality is of a different kind: it grows naturally out of his instinctive being, so that his 'dreams' are the 'flowers of his blood'. Something of what Lawrence means by this is evident in the way in which Siegmund's music-making—one of his 'spiritual' activities—is frequently described in erotic terms and linked with his passion for Helena:

> Grasping his violin, he seemed to have his fingers on the strings of his heart and of the heart of Helena. It was his little beloved that drank his being and turned it into music ...
>
>   It lay folded in silk in the dark, waiting. Six months before it had longed for rest; during the last nights of the season, when Siegmund's fingers had pressed too hard, when Siegmund's passion, and joy, and fear had hurt, too, the soft body of his little beloved, the violin had sickened for rest.
>
> (Tr p 12)

Helena's separation of sense and spirit is not simply a personal idiosyncracy. She represents a particular feminine type; she is one of those women in whom the rejection of the 'animal' in humanity, reinforced over many generations, has become a powerful instinctive revulsion. Helena's 'dreams' are 'detached and inhuman' because 'For centuries a certain type of woman has been rejecting the "animal" in humanity, till now her dreams are abstract, and full of fantasy, and her blood runs in bondage, and her kindness is full of cruelty.' (Tr p 30) Because this rejection of animality has been 'assimilated', Helena's own basic physical instincts have been confined or repressed—her 'blood' is in 'bondage'—and she behaves with a cruelty which masquerades as kindness, rather as the characters in *St Mawr*, victims of the same psychic introversion, act with outward friendliness but really intend to destroy.

These themes are developed later in the novel by the composer, Hampson, who is clearly a spokesman for Lawrencian views. Hampson feels a strong sense of kinship with Siegmund and has an intuitive understanding of his state which allows him to recognise the older man's subconscious desire to escape from life, even before Siegmund himself is really aware of it. Hampson's account of the death-wish he detects in Siegmund is, in essence, a poetic reformulation of the Nietzschean concept of death. He associates Siegmund's 'stare for the dark', as he puts it, with a weakening of the integrity of the self and a consequent tendency for it to break down and become assimilated to the mass of unorganised being which surrounds it. Nietzsche thinks of the organism as an association of wills to power which has evolved out of the universal flux and which is held together as a relatively stable unit by some governing will or group of wills. In the kind of universe which Nietzsche posits, consisting of a multiplicity of active, imperialistic wills, associations of this kind arise for the purpose of mutual defence, but an organised system will survive only so long as it has enough internal coherence to resist the constant pressure from outside. If this coherence is weakened, it will become vulnerable to the forces surrounding it. So for Nietzsche, the organic and the inorganic are not different in kind, but represent different states of the same basic forces and our familiar distinction between the 'living' and the 'dead' is, more accurately, a distinction between organised and unorganised will to power. To use Hampson's terms, the distinction is one between individual, identifiable 'life' with its relatively stable forms and the formless sea of being which 'washes' in perpetual flux round it. Hampson associates the encroachment of flux on form with a process of psychic 'leakage', in which vital energies seep away and leave the organism vulnerable so that

> ... the great mass of life that washes unidentified, and that we call death, creeps through the blue envelope of the day, and through our white tissue, and we can't stop it, once we've begun to leak.
>
> (Tr p 82)

Hampson goes on to link this loss of force with a craving for intense experience which is encouraged by the kind of woman whom creative men like himself and Siegmund find most 'interesting'. Such women value spiritual intensity in their men while endeavouring to suppress the physical impulses which are its source—and in those like Hampson and Siegmund who are 'as little gross as need be', who possess, in other words, precisely that degree of animal vitality needed to sustain their artistic activity, the influence of such feminine over-refinement can be disastrous. This is because artistic activities like Hampson's composing and Siegmund's violin playing are examples of the outflowing, power-spending aspect of the will to power, and the capacity to continue spending force in this way depends on its accumulation by means of another mode of activity of a more physical and sensual kind. Through their contact with 'interesting' women such men are continually encouraged to use up their vital energies in spiritual activity but largely deprived of the chance to replenish them with the result that:

> 'The best sort of women—the most interesting—are the worst for us,' Hampson resumed. 'By instinct they aim at suppressing the gross and animal in us ...'
>
> These deep, interesting women don't want us; they want the flowers of the spirit they can gather of us. We, as natural men, are more or less degrading to

them and to their love of us; therefore they destroy the natural man in us—that is, us altogether.'

(Tr p 84)

In such circumstances, the longing for 'vivid soul experience' weakens and exhausts the physical self; as Hampson says—

'A craving for intense life is nearly as deadly as any other craving. You become a *concentré*; you feed your normal flame with oxygen, and it devours your tissue. The soulful ladies of romance are always semi-transparent.'

(Tr p 83)

Physically stronger, and therefore less developed in other ways than Hampson, Siegmund is less spontaneously given to spiritual activity—he has something of the inertia which often characterises the physically powerful in Lawrence's work—and so his creativity depends more on the stimulus offered by a woman. After glancing at Siegmund's 'easy, mature figure and strong throat', Hampson concludes that he is someone 'whose flame goes nearly out, when the stimulant is lacking.' Siegmund's situation is therefore more dangerous than the other man's; his desire for intense spiritual experience can only be satisfied by prolonging the damaging contact with Helena. The composer is attracted by the same kind of woman, but has instinctively recognised the need to escape from feminine influence before his creative capacities are seriously threatened and he is evidently able to maintain his 'flame', his artistic activity, without external stimulus. Siegmund's position is made even more precarious by the fact that because he is relatively undeveloped his impulses lack the moderation which might allow him to husband his energies as Hampson does. The other man is able to deduce this from Siegmund's physical appearance, and predicts that, as a result, his 'flowering' will be intense and brief:

'You haven't much reserve. You're like a tree that'll flower till it kills itself,' the man continued. 'You'll run till you drop, and then you won't get up again. You've no dispassionate intellect to control you and economize.'

(Tr p 84)

The instinctive side of her lover is epitomised for Helena in the beating of his heart. She sees 'The secret thud, thud of his heart' as 'the very self of that animal in him she feared and hated.' The revulsion she feels at this particular point is linked with the state of desolation caused by her overwhelming sense of guilt; at other times her response to the heart-beats and what they represent is rather more ambivalent and suggests the presence in her of opposed instincts, although ascetic revulsion is by far the stronger feeling. When they lie on the beach during their first day together—

Presently she laid her head on his breast, and remained so, watching the sea, and listening to his heart-beats. The throb was strong and deep. It seemed to go through the whole island and the whole afternoon, and it fascinated her:

so deep, unheard, with its great expulsions of life. Had the world a heart? Was there also deep in the world a great God thudding out waves of life, like a great heart, unconscious? It frightened her. This was the God she knew not, as she knew not this Siegmund. It was so different from the half-shut eyes with black lashes, and the winsome, shapely nose. And the heart of the world, as she heard it, could not be the same as the curling splash of retreat of the little, sleepy waves. She listened for Siegmund's soul, but his heart overbeat all other sound, thudding powerfully.

(Tr pp 47–8)

Lawrence chooses the beating of the heart to represent instinctive activity in general, because in this way he can emphasise the fact that the most important vital processes proceed without the intervention of consciousness; we do not need to be aware of an activity before it can be orderly and purposeful. The heart is appropriate too because it has the characteristic double rhythm of the will to power, alternately drawing in and expelling blood as the will to power alternately accumulates and dissipates force. In his *Study of Thomas Hardy*, Lawrence had used the names for the different phrases of the action of the heart, 'systole' and 'diastole', for the double rhythm of vital processes. It is this unconscious, rhythmically alternating force which is the basic vital reality; Siegmund's 'soul' has no independent existence, but is simply a manifestation of his animal self and so it cannot be detected. As Hampson puts it, the 'natural man' is 'us altogether'.

At this point, Helena's fear of the physical is combined with fascination and awe and she seems to recognise the reality and importance of the instinctive forces in Siegmund's being and to realise that such forces are the ultimate reality behind everything, that 'God', the creative mystery, is a dynamic, impersonal, unconscious principle and not the personal and ideal being she believes in. At this stage of her development, such an insight remains only a novel and rather frightening possibility but the essential accuracy of her intuition is confirmed, in the narrative, through things like the constant association between the essential being of both main characters and the sea. Thinking about the fluctuations of her lover's passion, Helena concludes that 'The sea is a great deal like Siegmund' because 'the sea as it flung over her filled her with the same uncontrollable terror as did Siegmund when he sometimes grew silent and strange in a tide of passion'. Helena too is 'something like the sea' in being 'self-sufficient and careless of the rest.' These comparisons suggest that the forces which ultimately determine human conduct are impersonal and unconscious, that life flows and recoils like the tide in a way which indicates that the dialectical movement of the will to power underlies vital and natural phenomena alike.

But if the comparisons with the sea bring out the sheer power of human urges and suggest, by implication, that the conscious and personal is insignificant, Lawrence also uses them to illustrate the subtlety and delicacy with which the will to power can act. As in *Women in Love* and *St Mawr*, he wants to emphasise the sensitivity which belongs to uncorrupted instinct. Early in *The Trespasser*, the lovers come upon a light bulb which has been washed ashore unbroken on the beach. The discovery leads Helena to revise her ideas about the sea, which she has thought of as brutal and destructive:

'Isn't it remarkable!' she exclaimed joyously. 'The sea must be very, very gentle—and very kind ... I did not think it could be so fine-fingered ...'

(**Tr** p 53)

This realisation has important implications for her view of nature as a whole. Previously she has tended to respond only to the small and delicate in the natural world, just as she has tended to value only the limited, unmysterious, conscious portion of the human self, but like Miriam she is able to rid herself of at least some of her fears and accept and affirm larger areas of experience. Because the sea is associated in her mind with the passionate side of Siegmund's nature, the change of attitude to it also suggests that she will come to accept him more fully. Ultimately, experiences like this make it possible for her to be aware of his physical life and its rhythms without feeling the revulsion which things like the beating of his heart had earlier aroused in her. Lying beside him on the beach just before their departure, she can feel his breathing, and now realises that the awesome power of the basic forces in the psyche does not mean that they are brutal: on the contrary, delicacy and subtlety are the marks of great strength:

Helena leaned her head upon the breast of Siegmund, her arms clasping, under his coat, his body, which swelled and sank gently, with the quiet of great power.

(**Tr** p 125)

Siegmund, for his part, is always aware of Helena's resemblance to the sea, and in general of the fact that the human element in the self, the familiar realm or conscious thought, feeling and desire, is no more than a surface phenomenon concealing the real determining forces in being. And, in his musings on the inaccessible beach which he discovers on his second morning on the island, he links human nature with nature as a whole, identifying the sands, with their warm surface and underlying cold, with Helena. In both nature and man, the warmth and attractiveness conceal a darker and more forbidding reality:

The sand was warm to his breast, and his belly, and his arms. It was like a great body he cleaved to. Almost, he fancied, he felt it heaving under him in its breathing. Then he turned his face to the sun, and laughed. All the while, he hugged the warm body of the sea-bay beneath him. He spread his hands upon the sand; he took it in handfuls, and let it run smooth, warm, delightful, through his fingers.

'Surely', he said to himself, 'it is like Helena'; and he laid his hands again on the warm body of the shore, let them wander, discovering, gathering all the warmth, the softness, the strange wonder of smooth warm pebbles, then shrinking from the deep weight of cold his hand encountered as he burrowed under the surface, wrist-deep. In the end he found the cold mystery of the deep sand also thrilling. He pushed in his hands again and deeper, enjoying the almost hurt of the dark, heavy coldness. For the sun and the white flower of the bay were breathing and kissing him dry, were holding him in their warm concave, like a bee in a flower, like himself on the bosom of Helena, and flowing like the warmth of her breath in his hair came the sunshine, breathing near and lovingly; yet, under all, was this deep mass of cold, that the softness and warmth merely floated upon.

(Tr p 58)

There is a reminder of the pervasive sea imagery in the use of 'floated upon' in the final sentence, suggesting that the underlying reality is dynamic rather than static, and the idea that the landscape is breathing parallels the rhythmic flow and recoil of the tides. Reality here is associated with coldness and darkness and is contrasted with the welcoming warmth of the surface of things in a way which suggests Nietzsche's account of his intuition of the nature of ultimate reality in *The Will to Power*. In the concluding passage of that work, he describes it as a cold, undifferentiated realm, constantly in motion, and giving rise to the world of our ordinary experience. He conceives reality

> ... as force throughout, as a play of forces and waves of forces, at the same time one and many, increasing here and at the same time decreasing there; a sea of forces flowing and rushing together, eternally changing, eternally flooding back ... with an ebb and a flood of its forms; out of the simplest forms striving towards the most complex, out of the stillest, most rigid, coldest forms toward the hottest, most turbulent, most self-contradictory, and then again returning home to the simple out of this abundance ...[8]

Siegmund's awareness of the nature of things has led him to adopt a philosophy of life strikingly similar to that which Will Brangwen arrives at in *The Rainbow* as a result of his ordeal. Will had come to see experience as being like a sea and had learned that 'He must be able to leave himself to the flood, to sink or live as might be'. Siegmund sees the world in rather similar terms and has come to the same sort of conclusions about how best to cope with reality. He explains them to Helena in a rather flippant way:

> 'There's no reckoning with life, and no reckoning with the sea. The only way to get on with both is to be as near a vacuum as possible, and float.'

(Tr p 53)

The survival of the fragile light bulb amid vast tidal forces carries a moral lesson for man—Siegmund is suggesting that life and growth depend on submitting as far as possible to the unconscious forces in us and allowing their movements to carry us along. This apparently 'irrational' course of conduct is more likely to preserve us from destruction and ensure our vital progress than any consciously determined mode of life could do. Siegmund's remarks imply an attitude to life which is closely related to that set out in 'The Song of a Man Who Has Come Through': in both novel and poem, fulfilment depends on the ability to respond to intimations from the unknown part of the self. Helena's development is linked with the increasing sensitivity in her to such intimations which comes about through her contact with Siegmund. But the change which occurs in her is a difficult and lengthy one, since her new feelings have to make their way against opposing impulses which, initially at least, are much stronger. The beginnings of the change can be seen in her response to Siegmund's embrace just before they discover the light-bulb, in a scene which has affinities with the episode in *The Rainbow* in which Will and Anna stack the sheaves of corn:

> He clasped her close, seeming to rock her with his strong panting. She felt his body lifting into her, and sinking away. It seemed to force a rhythm, a new pulse, in her. Gradually, with a fine, keen thrilling, she melted down on him, like metal sinking on a mould. He was sea and sunlight mixed, heaving, warm, deliciously strong.
>
> **(Tr p 52)**

For the moment, Helena's revulsion from the movements of physical life is weakened, although the use of 'forced' suggests that there is still some resistance in her to the rhythms of the unconscious. Later, as the pair return to their lodgings, the clash of feeling in Helena is made explicit:

> As they went through the fir copse, listening to the birds like a family assembled and chattering at home in the evening, listening to the light swish of the wind, she let Siegmund predominate; he set the swing of their motion; she rested on him like a bird on a swaying bough.
>     They argued concerning the way. Siegmund, as usual, submitted to her. They went quite wrong. As they retraced their steps, stealthily, through a poultry farm whose fowls were standing in forlorn groups, once more dismayed by evening, Helena's pride battled with her new subjugation to Siegmund.
>
> **(Tr p 55)**

Helena's 'subjugation' is clearly far from complete and the relationship is therefore still threatened by the dangers which her kind of outlook involves—dangers which are suggested here in the fact that when Siegmund submits to her, the pair go 'quite wrong'.

The contrast between the two lovers at the start of their idyll is most clearly evident in the different ways in which they see the world in their most exalted moments. After their first real night of love, Helena feels 'destroyed', but, in the morning, lying in the shallows, she has an ecstatic vision of the essential reality which lies behind the material world:

> She lay and looked out on the shining sea. All things, it seemed, were made of sunshine more or less soiled. The cliffs rose out of the shining waves like clouds of strong, fine texture, and rocks along the shore were the dapplings of a bright dawn. The coarseness was fused out of the world, so that sunlight showed in the veins of the morning cliffs and the rocks. Yea, everything ran with sunshine, as we are full of blood, and plants are tissued from green-gold, glistening sap. Substance and solidity were shadows that the morning cast

round itself to make itself tangible: as she herself was a shadow, cast by that fragment of sunshine, her soul, over its inefficiency.

(**Tr** p 56)

This version of ultimate reality is the polar opposite of the dark Dionysian flux which Lawrence sees as the basis of all being, and, in fact, represents an idealistic negation of the real, with its roots in Helena's inability to accept the natural world and the forces active in it. Her vision of a world purged of materiality is a direct psychological consequence of the fact that she feels 'destroyed' by Siegmund's sexuality.

Her vision is 'poetic' rather than philosophical in character, but has clear affinities with the kind of perspective which Nietzsche terms the 'anaemic ideal' and which he derives from states 'in which the world is seen as emptier, paler, more diluted, in which 'spiritualisation' and nonsensuality assume the rank of perfection, in which the brutal, the animalic-direct, the proximate are most avoided.'[9] In such states, which are caused by psychic damage, both man and the physical world will tend to be seen as emanations of an immaterial principle, of a 'spirit' or 'soul'. Because this principle creates and permeates the material world, in moments of unusual receptivity, like that experienced by Helena, we think we are able to discern the ideal through the veil of ordinary reality and we conclude that freedom and fulfilment depend on escaping from the bonds of materiality to soar above the mundane:

> Now the cliffs were like wings uplifted, and the morning was coming dimly through them. She felt the wings of all the world upraised against the morning in a flashing, multitudinous flight. The world itself was flying ...
> She lay and rode the fine journey ... Her feet fluttered in the shadowy under-water. Her breast came out bright as the breast of a white bird.

(**Tr** pp 57–8)

The light symbolism central to both Christian and Platonic idealism is pervasive in the account of her vision and the idea that the world of ordinary experience and the body is related to that of 'true being', of soul and spirit, as shadow is to substance, or darkness to light, suggests the direct influence of Plato's simile of the cave in the *Republic*. There the sun symbolises the ultimate creative principle, a single, unchanging spiritual reality which gives rise to the coarser, more diverse and changeable natural world. Normally human beings are aware only of the shadows cast by this sun, but the more philosophical are able to penetrate to the reality behind, and even to escape from, the cave of shadows and look directly upon the sun. Helena too, sees a unity underlying the apparent diversity of the world; for her everything is essentially 'sunshine', a creative principle which gives rise to the coarser, more tangible realm which we inhabit.

In *Sons and Lovers*, the pain Paul experiences after he has made love to Miriam for the first time leads him to see the world in a similar way, although his 'idealism' is of a more extreme kind, which suggests that Miriam's reaction to their love-making causes him even more distress than Helena feels as a result of her sexual experience. After the consummation, although he is 'physically at rest' he realises that Miriam 'had not been with him ...', that 'her soul had stood apart in a sort of horror'. As a result he becomes 'Very dreary at heart' and in this state sees the world as a depleted, dream-like place, as the 'shadow' realm of Helena's vision:

> To him now, life seemed a shadow, day a white shadow ...
>
> (**SL** p 350)

In a way typical of the idealist, Paul now sees the process and change inherent in nature as evidence of its 'unreality' while another world, associated with the opposite qualities, with inactivity, with stillness and peace, is conjured up by his imagination and looked upon as more real and more attractive:

> ... night, and death, and stillness, and inaction, this seemed like *being*. To be alive, to be urgent and insistent—that was *not-to-be*.
>
> (**SL** p 350)

He sees the highest human felicity as the entrance, through death, into this permanent state of rest:

> The highest of all was to melt out into the darkness and sway there, identified with the great Being.
>
> (**SL** p 350)

Meanwhile, temporary happiness is sought in passivity and any suggestion of action is repugnant. So, when Miriam suggests that they should move, Paul is reluctant:

> 'It is a pity', he said.
> 'What?'
> 'To have to go. I feel so still.'
> 'Still,' she repeated.
> 'Stiller than I have ever been in my life.'

And he goes on to say how attractive it seems to him at this moment, 'To be rid of our individuality, which is our will, which is our effort—to live effortless, a kind of conscious sleep ...' (**SL** pp 350-1)

   Both Helena and Paul find the real world unbearable for the moment and both withdraw from it into a fantasy realm which lacks its disturbing and hurtful characteristics. Each illustrates Nietzsche's contention that the 'ideal', in the traditional sense, is a psychological creation, constructed by those who cannot cope with nature as it really is. But, in so far as it tends to preserve the sufferer from further discomfort and damage, such an attitude can be therapeutic and Nietzsche tends to think of mysticism and asceticism as intuitive strategies for self-preservation, arrived at by those whose instincts have retained a degree of health. Those who are thoroughly decadent tend, in contrast, to seek the very experiences which will damage them further. So, in Paul's case, the increasing sense of the remoteness and unreality of the ordinary world insulates him from the discomfort which his awareness of Miriam's suffering has caused. After their love-making 'he felt as if nothing mattered, as if his living were smeared away into the beyond, near and quite lovable.' Miriam herself becomes aware of the psychic distance which separates them:

> He was walking with his hand in hers. She pressed his fingers, feeling a slight fear. Now he seemed beyond her; she had a fear lest she should lose him.
>
> (**SL** p 351)

The initial sexual encounter between Paul and Miriam is followed by a week of regular love-making, but on each occasion the results are the same:

> He spent the week with Miriam, and wore her out with his passion before it was gone. He had always, almost wilfully, to put her out of count, and act from the brute strength of his own feelings. And he could not do it often, and there remained afterwards always the sense of failure and death.
>
> (**SL** p 354)

Paul is an artist and therefore very much involved with sense experience, instinctively committed to the reality and worth of the natural world, and the temporary but extreme asceticism which follows their love-making is most uncharacteristic of him. The narrative records that 'This strange, gentle reaching-out to death was new to him', and Miriam is surprised by it; when Paul talks about the attractions of a state without striving and effort, she remarks 'You don't usually say that.' Though not insensitive, Siegmund is less sensitive and perceptive than Paul and at first he is unaware of Helena's suffering, so that erotic experience has a quite different effect on him. In contrast to the passive, mystical, world-rejecting mood of both Paul and Helena, love-making restores in him 'the full "will to live"' and, as a result, he delights in activity, in the struggle with the sea and in the exercise of power:

> After a few moments of listening to the bees and breathing the mignonette, he said:
> 'I found a little white bay, just like you—a virgin bay. I had to swim there.'
> 'Oh!' she said, very interested in him, not the fact.
> 'It seemed just like you. Many things seem like you,' he said.
>
> (**Tr** p 60)

And he is just as uncomprehending when Helena tries to communicate her recent experience:

> 'I saw the sun through the cliffs, and the sea, and you,' she said.
> He did not understand. He looked at her searchingly. She was white and still and inscrutable. Then she looked up at him, her earnest eyes, that would not flinch, gazed straight into him. He trembled, and things all swept into a blur. After she had taken away her eyes he found himself saying:

'You know, I felt as if I were the first man to discover things: like Adam when he opened the first eyes in the world.'
'I saw the sunshine in you,' repeated Helena quietly, looking at him with her eyes heavy with meaning.
He laughed again, not understanding, but feeling she meant love.
'No, but you have altered everything,' he said.

(Tr p 60)

As their relationship continues, the characteristic attitudes and values of each partner increasingly influence the other. Helena's revulsion from the body and sexuality infects Siegmund and undermines his vitality so that, at the end of their time together, his way of looking at reality sometimes resembles hers. On their last morning, he sees the natural world around him as an ethereal poetic realm and so for the first time is able to understand and experience Helena's previously alien 'vision':

He swam towards the white rocks of the headlands; they rose before him like beautiful buttressed gates, so glistening that he half expected to see fantail pigeons puffing like white irises in the niches, and white peacocks with dark green feet stepping down the terraces, trailing a sheen of silver.
'Helena is right,' he said to himself as he swam, scarcely swimming, but moving upon the bosom of the tide; 'she is right, it is all enchanted. I have got into her magic at last.'

(Tr p 111)

This new kind of vision is associated with relative passivity; Siegmund lacks the vitality, the 'wilfull life' which allowed him to master the waves on the earlier occasion. And the 'magic' world is associated with birds in a way which links it with the bird and flight imagery of Helena's vision of transcendence. But, as in *Sons and Lovers*, the influence is not entirely in one direction. Just as Paul successfully manages to help Miriam to overcome at least some of her fears and extend her experience, so contact with Siegmund makes Helena less timid and inhibited. The change in her is illustrated in a scene which, ironically, is juxtaposed with that which shows Siegmund seeing the world in her way. Helena is 'no swimmer', preferring the 'bright and docile' rock-pools to the terror of the waves as she prefers the limited 'human' part of the self to the awesome impersonal forces of passion. On this occasion however, she leaves the bright, limited world of the rock-pools to explore a dark cave. Her brief adventure brings out her timidity, but also demonstrates her ability to face and overcome her fears. In Nietzsche's view, it is this kind of effort to meet new and therefore challenging kinds of experience which increases our strength. So, when Helena emerges from the cave, she has another moment of vision, but this time she sees the world not as insubstantial, but as fuller, richer and more intense than it usually seems—a change in her mode of perception which reflects her increased vitality. She comes, for the moment, to see the world as Siegmund had seen it after their night of love:

> She stood still in the archway, astounded. The sea was blazing with white fire, and glowing with azure as coals glow red with heat below the flames. The sea was transfused with white burning, while over it hung the blue sky in a glory, like the blue smoke of the fire of God.
>
> (Tr p 114)

In Siegmund's case it was clear that this transformation of the world had its roots in erotic feeling; the sources of Helena's vision are less obvious, but the way in which she sees Siegmund himself suggests that sexuality is also important in it. Like nature, he seems glorified:

> 'Siegmund!' she exclaimed, looking up at him with radiant eyes, as if it could not be possible that he had joined her in this rare place ...
> 'I, actually,' he said smiling.
> 'I did not expect you,' she said, still looking at him in radiant wonder. 'I could easier have expected'—she hesitated, struggled, and continued—'Eros walking by the sea. But you are like him,' she said, looking radiantly up into Siegmund's face.
>
> (Tr p 115)

The association of Siegmund with Eros, the god of physical love suggests that there has been a significant shift in Helena's values. Up to this point she has been associated with Christianity and with idealistic attitudes in general and so with the belief that the 'divine' is that which is remotest from nature. Nietzsche sees Greek paganism as the antithesis of this kind of idealism: in it, nature itself and the forces in it are regarded as the most real and valuable things and this affirmation is reflected in the character of the Greek gods, in whom human impulses are made divine. The fact that Helena refers to Eros, who is deified sexuality, shows how far she has moved towards the life-affirming pagan outlook, but her hesitation indicates that the revolution in her sensibility is not yet complete, that the clash of feelings in her is still not completely resolved. Indeed, her development towards full acceptance of nature and the senses is still not complete at the end of the novel because her progress is interrupted by Siegmund's suicide. She instinctively defends herself against the pain of his loss by adopting the sort of passive and withdrawn mode of life which Nietzsche associates with Buddhism and the resort to this strategy carries the assurance that she will ultimately recover and become able to live fully again. Her lover's suicide is, paradoxically, an example of the same kind of intuitive 'wisdom'.

Subconsciously aware that he has exhausted his vital energies—as Hampson predicted he would—Siegmund has decided, again subconsciously, that it would be better to end his life than to continue in mere uncreative existence, to 'remain as a trophy when there is nothing more to do.' Paradoxically, his suicide demonstrates that he retains some measure of psychic health, in contrast to characters like Banford in *The Fox*, whose thoroughgoing decadence is revealed in their determination to cling to what is, in Lawrencian terms, a kind of death-in-life. Such characters would be better off dead; they have no creative life left, but can prevent those who have from continuing to develop.

The relationship between Paul and Miriam in *Sons and Lovers* follows the same basic pattern as that between Siegmund and Helena. Miriam too is 'physiologically false' in that her feelings do not match her physical fulness and beauty; her natural responses have also been overlaid by ascetic feelings. Because of this, both women unconsciously encourage these things in their lovers which they regard as 'spiritual' and therefore as valuable and at the same time thwart their physical impulses. The result, for both Paul and Sieg-mund, is increasing weakness and exhaustion but while Paul, like Hampson, intuitively recognises his danger and breaks free before it is too late, Siegmund lacks the strength to do so and is destroyed. Mrs Morel hates Miriam because she can see that her son's continuing contact with the girl is undermining his vitality—her feelings are a consequence and not a cause of the distorted and destructive nature of the relationship between the pair. Aware of Paul's exceptional sensitivity and of the danger it represents for his psychic balance, his mother is disturbed by the way in which Miriam's influence makes him less able to cope with life's difficulties and it is this which leads her to try to separate them:

> With all the passion of her strong nature she hated Miriam for having in this subtle way undermined his joy. It did not matter to her that Miriam could not help it. Miriam did it and she hated her.
>
> (SL p 315)

Mrs Morel realises, as Paul himself had done earlier, that Miriam does not consciously set out to injure her son, but the fact that the destructive influence is exerted unconsciously does not alter her hostility.

But Miriam's case is more complex than Mrs Morel's attitude might suggest. Clara, who at first is less emotionally involved with Paul, and who is also unusually sensitive to physical indications of inner states, challenges the assumption that Miriam's asceticism is the only, or even the most fundamental element in her nature. She tells Paul that Miriam is not looking for 'a sort of soul union' but desires him in the ordinary way. Clara's confidence, and his own earlier success in modifying Miriam's attitudes make Paul resolve to return to his first love in order to see whether their relationship can be made more complete and balanced. The Failure of 'The Test on Miriam' does not, however, disprove Clara's claim, because it is clear that the result of Paul's experiment has as much to do with his own unusual degree of sensitivity as it has with Miriam's deep-seated revulsion from sex. Paul belongs to a generation of men who are in revolt against the crudities of their fathers' behaviour:

> A good many of the nicest men he knew were like himself, bound in by their own virginity, which they could not break out of. They were so sensitive to their women that they would go without them for ever rather than do them a hurt, an injustice. Being the sons of mothers whose husbands had blundered rather brutally through their feminine sanctities, they were themselves too diffident and shy. They could easier deny themselves than incur any reproach from a woman; for a woman was like their mother, and they were full of the sense of

their mother. They preferred themselves to suffer the misery of celibacy, rather than risk the other person.

(SL p 341)

Because of his family background, then, Paul cannot act toward Miriam with the kind of hardness Anna displays toward Will; instead he invariably suffers with her and so endangers himself. But, as the episode in *The Rainbow* suggests, a certain hardness, a willingness to expose others to suffering, may be a positive thing, because challenge and difficulty can add to strength and aid development while, conversely, sympathy usually has a bad effect on those it is meant to help. The passage quoted implied that their reaction against their father's insensitivity has carried the young men of Paul's generation too far in the opposite direction, so that they have become *too* sensitive to the feelings of their women and are unable to help them develop. If Paul were more callous and therefore better able to persevere with the relationship, Miriam's continuing exposure to certain kinds of experience might gradually develop in her the ability to cope with them. After a time, the healthy impulses latent in her being might become strong enough to overcome her ascetic revulsion.

The possibility of such an outcome is treated directly in the poem 'Last Words to Miriam', which is closely related in subject to this part of *Sons and Lovers*. The central idea in the poem is that difficulty and suffering generate strength and beauty, but that because of the girl's lack of response, the speaker has been unable to complete the task of transforming her. The Christian imagery which pervades the poem obliquely suggests the reasons for the girl's unresponsiveness, but the man is given the active role, as the craftsman struggling to shape resistant material, and so the major share of the blame must be his:

> Body to body I could not
> Love you, although I would.
> We kissed, we kissed though we should not.
> You yielded, we threw the last cast,
> And it was no good.
>
> You only endured, and it broke
> My craftsman's nerve.
> No flesh responded to my stroke;
> So I failed to give you the last
> Fine torture you did deserve.
>
> You are shapely, you are adorned
> But opaque and null in the flesh;
> Who, had I but pierced with the thorned
> Full anguish, perhaps had been cast
> In a lovely illumined mesh[10]

The pattern common to all these relationships is one which also appears in Lawrence's last novel, *Lady Chatterley's Lover*, in which Constance

Chatterley leaves her upper-class husband to find fulfilment with the game-keeper, Mellors.

In the relationships between men and women depicted in his early novels, short stories and poems, Lawrence was primarily interested in the effects of the 'physiological falsity' present and prevalent in our culture, particularly among women; in his treatment of Emily or Helena or Miriam he takes their psychic duality as given and offers little indication of how it has arisen. In *The Trespasser*, it is true, he links Helena's kind of sensibility with a long process of psychic evolution which has lasted over many generations and in the course of which feminine rejection of the physical and instinctive has itself become, quite literally, instinctive. But Lawrence's view of the relation between individual character and inheritance emerges most clearly in the treatment of Mrs Morel in *Sons and Lovers* and the processes he describes in that novel are derived from Nietzsche's account of how human characteristics develop and are transmitted.

Nietzsche held that instincts begin as relatively inexpert responses to a particular situation; if the situation remains stable, such responses evolve steadily into spontaneously acting impulses, traits of character, which come to embody a high degree of perceptiveness, economy and skill or, in a word, intelligence, over successive generations. Developed instincts therefore become independently acting forces and no longer need a stimulus from the environment to set them in motion; they become more efficient and more powerful but, at the same time, increasingly difficult to modify. This kind of psychic evolution is evident in the change which has taken place in the qualities which Mrs Morel has inherited from her puritan forebears. The 'high moral sense' of her ancestors has developed into a 'religious instinct' which leads her to continue striving with Morel long after she has realised that the effort to change him is futile; her persistence is not the result of a conscious, if irrational, determination, but something she simply cannot help:

> Nevertheless she still continued to strive with him. She still had her high moral sense, inherited from generations of Puritans. It was now a religious instinct, and she was almost a fanatic with him, because she loved him, or had loved him. If he sinned, she tortured him. If he drank and lied, was often a poltroon, sometimes a knave, she wielded the lash unmercifully.
>
> (**SL** p 25)

The violence of the language used brings out the awesome power of the wife's religious instinct, but the fact that it is an 'instinct' which drives her to act as she does effectively removes her behaviour from the moral realm. The emphasis on the many generations of unbroken Puritan inheritance in her background suggests that her freedom of action is severely constrained by an overwhelming 'weight' of inherited responses: moral judgement is inappropriate here, however difficult it may be for the reader to resist it. And we are made aware too that if Mrs Morel's treatment of her husband is harsh, her intention is not to injure but to improve him and if he is damaged, it is as much a consequence of his own weakness as of her strength.

But it is in the celebrated scene in which Mrs Morel is locked out of the house by her drunken husband that Nietzsche's ideas of 'organic memory' and 'assimilation' are most fully illustrated. The incident takes place when she is pregnant with Paul and many critics have recognised its relevance for the later relationship between mother and son. But the connection is even closer than has usually been thought, because what the scene records is the 'assimilation' of the mother's recent experiences and their transmission to the unborn child—an inheritance which is crucial for Paul's character and development. Such a claim for the direct transmission of experience from one generation to the next is not, of course, scientifically orthodox, but it is quite consistent with the Lamarkian ideas which Lawrence and Nietzsche shared. It is a process which is outlined quite explicitly in an essay entitled 'Making Love to Music' in which Lawrence says:

> It is a curious thing, but the ideas of one generation become the instincts of the next. We are all of us, largely, the embodied ideas of our grandmothers, and without knowing it we behave as such. It is odd that the grafting works so quickly, but it seems to ...

But, he continues,

> ... we do not just become the lofty or beautiful thoughts of our grandmothers ... We are the embodiment of the most potent ideas of our progenitors, and these ideas are mostly private ones, not to be admitted in public, but to be transmitted as instincts and as the dynamics of behaviour to the third and fourth generation.[11]

Nietzsche argues that the creation of a lasting 'memory' depends largely on two things: the repetition of a particular experience and the intensity with which the experience is felt. He believed that the experiences which make the biggest psychic impact are painful ones; pain, he says, is 'the most potent mnemonic'. Both these elements are stressed in Lawrence's description of the effects on Mrs Morel of the quarrel with her husband:

> For a while she could not control her consciousness; mechanically she went over the last scene, then over it again, certain phrases, certain moments coming each time like a brand red-hot down on her soul: and each time she enacted again the last hour, each time the brand came down at the same points, till the mark was burnt in and the pain burnt out, and at last she came to herself.
>
> (SL p 34)

Through repeated and painful reliving of the quarrel in her consciousness, the essentials of the experience are assimilated and become unconscious; in the process, the discomfort and the unnatural degree of conscious awareness of psychic processes which accompany it gradually diminish, while beneath the conscious level, a permanent modification has been effected in the psyche.

This kind of translation of conscious experience into unconscious embodiment, through repetition and pain, is central to Nietzsche's conception of organic memory. Such memorisation is not a passive storing, but an active process, which involves selection and change. Mrs Morel relives the whole experience, but only some parts of it ('certain phrases, certain moments') are rendered permanent. The process as Lawrence describes it is strikingly similar to Nietzsche's own account of the formation of enduring memories, even to the use of heat imagery:

> One must learn anew about memory: it is the mass of all experiences of all organic life, alive, arranging themselves, shaping each other, wrestling with one another, simplifying, compressing and changing into many unities. There must be an inner process which is like the formation of concepts from many particular cases: the stressing and ever fresh underscoring of the basic scheme, and omission of secondary features. As long as something can be recalled as a seperate fact, it is not yet melted down: the latest experiences still swim on the surface.[12]

Organic memory is important in heredity because it allows the transmission of parental experience to the child so that—as Nietzsche says in a passage which is particularly relevant to Paul's case—'The undissolved dissonances in the relation of the character and sentiments of the parents survive in the nature of the child and make up the history of its inner sufferings.'[13]

Mrs Morel's experience in the garden is important, then, because of its effect on the unborn child and it is the transmission of the tension between husband and wife to the infant Paul which causes the strange symptoms of suffering which Mrs Morel detects just after his birth. The baby's discomfort has no physical cause but the possibility that the mother's concern is simply a projection of her own guilt at not having wanted the child is ruled out by the fact that her neighbour Mrs Kirk notices the same symptoms and draws the same conclusion;

> Mrs Morel looked down at him. She had dreaded this baby like a catastrophe, because of her feeling for her husband. And now she felt strangely towards the infant. Her heart was heavy because of the child, almost as if it were unhealthy, or malformed. Yet it seemed quite well. But she noticed the peculiar knitting of the baby's brows, and the peculiar heaviness of its eyes, as if it were trying to understand something that was pain. She felt, when she looked at her child's dark, brooding pupils, as if a burden were on her heart.
>     'He looks as if he were thinking about something—quite sorrowful,' said Mrs Kirk.

> (SL p 50)

Mrs Morel puzzles over these signs of discomfort and then intuitively realises that she and her husband are in some way responsible for them:

> And at that moment she felt, in some far inner place of her soul, that she and her husband were guilty.

> (SL p 50)

The conflict between husband and wife has been, as it were, embodied in the child and it is the tension between paternal and maternal elements in his make-up that gives rise to Paul's precocious inner sufferings. It is this fact that lies behind Mrs Morel's strange conviction that the child somehow knows of the situation between her and her husband:

> Its clear, knowing eyes gave her pain and fear. Did it know all about her? When it lay under her heart, had it been listening then? Was there a reproach in the look? She felt the marrow melt in her bones, with fear and pain.
>
> (SL p 51)

These early symptoms are related to the sudden and inexplicable fits of depression which Paul suffers as a toddler; they too have their origins in internal rather than external discomfort. Mrs Morel realises that the inner tensions she has detected will create difficulties for Paul in later life and for a moment is tempted to repudiate the child and the worry he will bring, to 'give him back again whence he came', but the opposite impulse, to love him more because of his vulnerability is finally more powerful. The intense feeling for the child which overwhelms her at this point is not a symptom of some unnatural possessiveness but rather arises from her knowledge that life is going to be unusually difficult for the child, that he will need a great deal of love and care if he is to survive. The contrast between her treatment of Paul and her attitude to her other children is linked with his inner sufferings, like the fits of depression he suffers at three or four:

> These fits were not often, but they caused a shadow in Mrs Morel's heart, and her treatment of Paul was different from that of the other children.
>
> (SL p 64)

The naming of Paul is also linked with Mrs Morel's sense that there is an inner conflict in her infant son. The similarity of her character to that of her unbending father who 'drew near in sympathy only to one man, the Apostle Paul' clearly lies behind her choice of Christian name, but this does not mean that Mrs Morel is symbolically taking possession of the child. The spontaneous, unpremeditated way in which the name is arrived at links the choice with her intuitive realisation of the cause of the child's pain:

> 'I will call him "Paul",' she said suddenly; she knew not why.
>
> (SL p 51)

The point is that each part of Paul's name reflects one of the conflicting elements in his difficult dual inheritance from both Puritan Coppards and sensuous Morels. Nietzsche argues that inner conflicts of the kind which Paul inherits, although potentially destructive, are also necessary conditions for continuing growth and creativity: the more extreme the psychic opposition, the higher the creative potential of the individual involved—the great man is, in Nietzsche's words 'the bow with the great tension'.[14] This Nietzschean association between inner conflict and creativity is reflected in the contrast between the three sons. William, who is born before the situation in the home is at its worst, has some ability but lacks creative talent. Arthur, conceived at a time when the battle between the parents has temporarily ceased, is the most ordinary and unexceptional of the three. It is Paul who is the most creative and most individual because his nature was formed at a time when the antagonism between his parents was at its height; it is this which has created in him the tensions on which, in Nietzsche's view, distinction depends.

These episodes from *Sons and Lovers* illustrate the workings of organic memory and the transmission of experience from generation to generation. It is through these processes that consciously held beliefs and opinions can become assimilated and may develop, ultimately, into stable and spontaneously acting instincts. In Western culture, the prolonged influence of Christian ideas has made ascetic and idealistic attitudes instinctive in many people, with the result that nature and culture, body and spirit, are felt to be—and, indeed, experienced as, antithetical. Lawrence's work reflects this pervasive dualism, but his own view of reality is not dualistic—like Nietzsche he is, rather, a dialectical thinker. For both men, culture and spirit are not, properly speaking, the negations of nature and sense, but their sublimated products; each argues that the 'flesh' gives birth to the 'word'. Both argue too, that far from being an impediment to man's higher aspirations which should be extirpated, his instincts are the source of all that is valuable and creative in him. Human progress therefore demands on the strengthening of the impulsive side of our natures. Like Nietzsche, Lawrence takes an apocalyptic view of the prospects for humanity, arguing that the future of the species depends on our recognition that instinct and spirit are interdependent. If this fact is ignored, man will become fixed and sterile. If, on the other hand the moral and metaphysical revolution which both writers are striving to bring about is accomplished, tremendous new creative energies will be released. It is this possibility of a new and more fruitful kind of relation between sense and spirit in man which is symbolised in the entwined eagle and serpent which Zarathustra sees:

> Zarathustra ... looked enquiringly into the sky—for he heard above him the sharp cry of a bird. And behold! An eagle was sweeping through the air in wide circles, and from it was hanging a serpent, not like a prey but like a friend: for it was coiled around the eagle's neck.
> 'It is my animals!' said Zarathustra and rejoiced in his heart.
> 'The proudest animal under the sun and the wisest animal under the sun—they have come scouting.'[15]

It is significant that in the only novel in which he describes a successful revolution against the Christian-idealist tradition, Lawrence uses the same composite symbol: the chief deity of the new Mexican order in *The Plumed Serpent* is the pagan god Quetzalcoatl, half bird and half snake. With the re-establishment in Mexico of the old pagan gods, the Christian separation of sense and spirit is rejected and the foundations laid for a higher and healthier kind of culture, in which there is no destructive conflict between apparently irreconcilable principles.

The possibility of such an outcome depends—as I have tried to show—on a conception of the self which derives from Nietzsche. Nietzsche thinks of the self as something essentially complex and fluid, as a society of dynamic urges which is normally organised in a hierarchical way with a particular ruling group of urges directing the activities of the organism as a whole. But the power relationships in the self do not remain stable; there is a constant struggle among the active elements in the psyche for control, so that human development follows a characteristic pattern of advance and retreat from new values and attitudes. What ultimately determines the shape of our lives is this flow of feelings, because our feelings are instinctive judgements of what is useful and harmful for us at particular stages of our growth, and originate with those urges currently dominant in us.

Nietzsche's view of morality, as something personal and fluid, is closely related to his psychology. True morality is expressed in our spontaneous movements of feeling. Our moral judgements cannot, therefore, be valid for others and are not even relevant to our own needs, except at the time they are made. Both Lawrence and Nietzsche contrast this fluid, provisional, individual kind of morality with the 'absolute' morality imposed by Christianity, with its claim to universal validity. They argue that this kind of code was developed in the first instance by those who *needed* to impose a rigid and prolonged discipline over their impulses, but was then used as an instrument of revenge by those ill-constituted individuals and has corrupted and weakened the strong. Both thought that the continuing dominance of absolute morality and of the idealistic metaphysics associated with it threatened the vitality of mankind and both philosopher and novelist tried, in their different ways, to precipitate that 'revaluation of values' which would halt the decline of man into sterility.

In Nietzsche's view, art had a particularly important part to play in the struggle to free man from this debilitating tradition because, in its dependence on the senses and on the incessantly changing material world, art is subversive of the ideal and absolute. Nietzsche argues that this was the case even with an artist like Raphael who thought of himself as celebrating the Christian view of things; in rather the same way, Lawrence tends to attribute to writers a 'passional inspiration' which is evident in their works, and which is quite opposite to the doctrines they consciously uphold. For Lawrence, literature is the most important of the arts because of the direct part it can play in reshaping our values. Within the field of literature, he sees the novel as pre-eminent, because it is able to register more fully than any other literary form, the complex and shifting world of relationships which for him, as for Nietzsche, is the essence of reality:

> The novel is the perfect medium for revealing to us the changing rainbow of our living relationships. The novel can help us to live, as nothing else can: no didactic Scripture, anyhow.[16]

The novel can help us to live because it is capable of modifying as well as reflecting our feelings, and since those feelings are expressions of our fundamental values, by doing so it can bring about that revaluation of values which Lawrence and Nietzsche regard as an urgent necessity. Lawrence sums up the power and importance of the novel in *Lady Chatterley's Lover*:

> It is the way our sympathy flows and recoils that really determines our lives. And here lies the vast importance of the novel, properly handled. It can inform and lead into new places the flow of our sympathetic consciousness, and it can lead our sympathy away in recoil from things gone dead. Therefore, the novel, properly handled, can reveal the most secret places of life: for it is in the *passional* secret places of life, above all, that the tide of sensitive awareness needs to ebb and flow, cleansing and freshening.
>
> (**LCL** p 104)

Nietzsche's influence on Lawrence was profound, but precisely because of this it is only rarely evident in direct references or obvious borrowings. Instead it tends to appear in that more subtle and pervasive fashion which we might expect when ideas have been thoroughly assimilated and creatively used. The kind of relationship involved is admirably described by Angus Wilson in his lecture on 'Dickens and Dostoevsky'. Wilson accepts the conclusion arrived at by another critic who has examined the question, that 'the actual provable influence of Dickens upon Dostoevsky is not very important and only very limited', but he goes on to argue that:

> 'this refutation of evidence of direct influence is not all that important, for the relation between the two novelists is much more exciting than a matter of provable evidence of somebody being influenced by this particular thing or that particular thing. You see, speaking as a novelist, I am fairly sure of this, that it is only minor writers who influence you in the sense that you can say 'Yes, that little bit of my book came actually from that writer'. You would take in this way only from a minor writer. A major writer has a quite different kind of effect upon you. He affects your whole outlook, your whole vision, the whole fictional world you live in, and that isn't a matter of taking little pieces and incorporating them, however transformed.[17]

What I have been arguing is that Nietzsche had this kind of significance for Lawrence; that the German philosopher did indeed profoundly affect Lawrence's whole vision and with it, the character of the fictional world he created.

# Notes

NOTES TO CHAPTER 1 (pp 1 to 21)

1  Harry Steinhauer, 'Eros and Psyche: a Nietzschean motif in Anglo-American literature', *Modern Language Notes*, 64 (1949), pp 217–28 (p 225),

2  John Carey, 'D H Lawrence's Doctrine', in *D H Lawrence: Novelist, Poet, Prophet*, ed. Stephen Spender (London, 1973), pp 122–34 (p 133).

3  David S Thatcher, *Nietzsche in England 1890–1914* (Toronto, 1970).

4  Patrick Bridgwater, *Nietzsche in Anglosaxony: A Study of Nietzsche's Impact on English and American Literature* (Leicester, 1972).

5  Friedrich Nietzsche, *Twilight of the Idols* and *The Anti-Christ*, trans R Hollingdale (Harmondsworth, 1968), p 45.

6  D H Lawrence, review of *The Dragon of the Apocalypse*, by Frederick Carter in *Phoenix: the Posthumous Papers of D H Lawrence*, ed McDonald (London, 1961), pp 292–303 (p 298).

7  T H Huxley, *Evolution and Ethics and Other Essays* (London, 1894).

8  Daniel Gasman, *The Scientific Origins of National Socialism: Social Darwinism in Ernst Haeckel and the German Monist League* (New York, 1971), p 31.

9  Ernst Haeckel, *The Riddle of the Universe at the Close of the Nineteenth Century*, trans McCabe (London, 1900).

10 A R Orage, *Nietzsche in Outline and Aphorism* (London, 1907), p 29.

11 Arthur Schopenhauer, *Essays of Schopenhauer*, trans Dircks (London, 1897), p 174.

12 Schopenhauer, *Essays*, p 143.

13 Walter Kaufmann, *Nietzsche: Philosopher, Psychologist, Anti-Christ*, 3rd edn (Princeton, 1968), pp 87–8.

14 Schopenhauer, *Essays*, p 144.

15 Lawrence, 'Study of Thomas Hardy' in *Phoenix*, pp 398–516 (p 398).

16 George Allen Morgan, Jr, *What Nietzsche Means* (Cambridge, Mass, 1943), p 64.

17 Friedrich Nietzsche, *Beyond Good and Evil*, trans Volz (London, 1907).

18 *The Complete Works of Friedrich Nietzsche*, ed Levy, 18 vols (Edinburgh, 1909–13).

19  Graham Hough, *The Dark Sun: A Study of D H Lawrence* (Harmondsworth, 1961), p 296.
20  Kingsley Widmer, *The Art of Perversity: D H Lawrence's Shorter Fictions* (Seattle, 1969), p 240.
21  Bridgwater, *Nietzsche in Anglosaxony*, p 107.
22  Eric Bentley, *The Cult of the Superman* (London, 1947), p 212.
23  Lawrence, 'Study of Thomas Hardy', *Phoenix*, pp 490–1.
24  Lawrence, 'Study of Thomas Hardy', *Phoenix*, p 490.
25  Lawrence, *Twilight in Italy* (Harmondsworth, 1972), p 80.
26  Lawrence, *Twilight in Italy*, pp 142–3.
27  Nietzsche, *Thus Spake Zarathustra*, trans Hollingdale (Harmondsworth, 1961), p 144.
28  *The Collected Letters of D H Lawrence*, ed Moore, 2 vols (London, 1962), I, p 324 (26 Feb 1915), hereafter *Collected Letters.*
29  *Collected Letters*, I, p 327 (2 March 1915).
30  *The Letters of D H Lawrence*, ed Huxley (London, 1932), p 237 (June 1915), hereafter *Letters.*

NOTES TO CHAPTER 2 (pp 22 to 51)

1  Julian Moynahan, *The Deed of Life: the Novels and Tales of D H Lawrence* (London, 1971), p 7.
2  Moynahan, *Deed of Life*, p 10.
3  Moynahan, *Deed of Life*, p 6.
4  Stephen J. Micko, *Toward 'Women in Love'* (New Haven, 1971), p 10.
5  Frank Kermode, *Lawrence*, Fontana Modern Masters series (London, 1973), p 14.
6  Moynahan, *Deed of Life*, p 6.
7  Nietzsche, *The Will to Power*, trans Kaufmann and Hollingdale (New York 1968), p 345.
8  Nietzsche, *Will to Power*, p 274.
9  The strength of the aggressor can be measured by the opposition which he needs; every increase of growth betrays itself by a seeking out of more formidable opponents—or problems: for a philosopher who is combative challenges even problems to a duel. Section 7 p 23, *Complete Works*, ed Levy, Vol XVII, *Ecce Homo*, trans Anthony M Ludovici Foulis (Edinburgh and London, 1911).
10  Lawrence, 'Why the Novel Matters' in *Phoenix*, pp 533–8 (p 536).
11  *Nietzsche's Werke, Grossoctavausgabe*, 2nd edn, 20 vols (Leipzig, 1901–13), xiii, p 268, trans in Morgan, pp 63–4; hereafter Nietzsche, *Grossoctav.*
12  Nietzsche, *Thus Spake Zarathustra*, trans Hollingdale (Harmondsworth, 1961), p 137.
13  Nietzsche, *Will to Power*, p 346.
14  Nietzsche, *Will to Power*, p 344.
15  Morgan, *What Nietzsche Means*, p 71.

16 Nietzsche, *Grossoctav*, XIII, p 231, trans in Morgan, p 69.
17 Morgan, *What Nietzsche Means*, p 69.
18 Edward D Conklin, *Heredity and Environment in the Development of Man* (Princeton, 1922), p 45.
19 Morgan, *What Nietzsche Means*, p 70.
20 Nietzsche, *Grossoctav*, XIII, p 237, trans in Morgan, p 69.
21 Morgan, *What Nietzsche Means*, p 168.
22 Nietzsche, *Daybreak: Thoughts on the Prejudices of Morality*, trans Hollingdale (Cambridge, 1982), p 36.
23 F R Leavis, *D H Lawrence: Novelist* (Harmondsworth 1964), p 109.
24 Leavis, *D H Lawrence*, p 109.
25 Kermode, *Lawrence*, p 8.
26 Kermode, *Lawrence*, p 15.
27 H M Daleski, *The Forked Flame: a Study of D H Lawrence* (London, 1965), p 81.
28 Eliseo Vivas, *D H Lawrence: the Failure and Triumph of Art* (Evanston, 1960), p 223.
29 Marvin Mudrick, 'The Originality of *The Rainbow*', in *D H Lawrence: A Collection of Critical Essays*, ed Mark Spilka, Twentieth Century Views series (Englewood Cliffs, 1963), pp 29–49 (p 37).
30 Hough, *The Dark Sun*, p 78.
31 Nietzsche, *Grossoctav*, XIII, p 256, trans Morgan, p 101.
32 Nietzsche, *Will to Power*, p 363.
33 Robert E Gajdusek, 'A Reading of *The White Peacock*, in *A D H Lawrence Miscellany*, ed Harry T Moore (Carbondale, 1959), pp 188–203 (p 192).
34 Morgan, *What Nietzsche Means*, pp 79–80.
35 Morgan, *What Nietzsche Means*, p 80.
36 Morgan, *What Nietzsche Means*, p 81.

NOTES TO CHAPTER 3 (pp 52 to 92)

1 Morgan, *What Nietzsche Means*, p 72.
2 Morgan, *What Nietzsche Means*, p 73.
3 Nietzsche, *Grossoctav*, XII, p 105, trans Morgan, p 127.
4 Morgan, *What Nietzsche Means*, p 74.
5 Nietzsche, *Will to Power*, p 342.
6 Morgan, *What Nietzsche Means*, p 73.
7 Nietzsche, *Will to Power*, p 264.
8 Nietzsche, *Will to Power*, p 272.
9 Nietzsche, *Will to Power*, p 264.
10 Nietzsche, *Will to Power*, p 271.
11 Morgan, *What Nietzsche Means*, p 86.
12 Lawrence, review of *Georgian Poetry: 1911*-1912, in *Phoenix*, pp 304–7 (p 306).
13 Morgan, *What Nietzsche Means*, p 93.

14  Nietzsche, 'The Case of Wagner', in *Complete Works*, vol VIII, *The Case of Wagner* and *We Philologists*, trans Ludovici (Edinburgh, 1911), pp 1–51 (p 20).
15  Nietzsche, *Grossoctav*, XIV, p 327 trans Morgan, p 94.
16  Morgan, *What Nietzsche Means*, p 95.
17  Morgan, *What Nietzsche Means*, p 97.
18  Nietzsche, *Grossoctav*, X, p 191, trans Morgan, p 99.
19  Morgan, *What Nietzsche Means*, p 98.
20  Lawrence, *Collected Letters*, I, p 156 (Autumn 1912).
21  Nietzsche, *Will to Power*, p 542.
22  Nietzsche, *Will to Power*, p 543.
23  Nietzsche, *Will to Power*, p 542.
24  Nietzsche, *Will to Power*, p 10.
25  Nietzsche, *Will to Power*, p 20.
26  Nietzsche, *Will to Power*, p 18.
27  Keith Sagar, *The Art of D H Lawrence* (Cambridge, 1966), p 13.
28  R E Pritchard, *D H Lawrence: Body of Darkness* (London, 1971), p 27.
29  Gajdusek, 'A Reading of *The White Peacock*', p 189.
30  Miko, *'Women in Love'*, p 8.
31  Morgan, *What Nietzsche Means*, p 110.
32  Morgan, *What Nietzsche Means*, p 110.
33  Nietzsche, *Twilight of the Idols* in *Twilight of the Idols* and *The Anti-Christ*, trans Hollingdale (Harmondsworth, 1968), pp 21–111 (p 42); hereafter either *Twilight* or *Anti-Christ*.
34  Nietzsche, *Twilight*, p 42.
35  Nietzsche, *Twilight*, pp 55–6.
36  Nietzsche, *Twilight*, p 56.
37  Nietzsche, *Twilight*, p 57.
38  Nietzsche, *Will to Power*, p 32.
39  Nietzsche, *Will to Power*, p 466.
40  Nietzsche, *Will to Power*, p 35.
41  Morgan, *What Nietzsche Means*, p 59.
42  Nietzsche, *Grossoctav*, XII, p 149, trans Morgan, pp 99–100.
43  Nietzsche, *Will to Power*, p 349.
44  *The Complete Poems of D H Lawrence*, ed de Sola Pinto and Roberts, 2 vols (London, 1964), I, pp 92–4; hereafter *Complete Poems*.
45  *Complete Poems*, II pp 926–7.
46  Nietzsche, 'Homer's Contest', in *Complete Works*, vol II, *Early Greek Philosophy and Other Essays*, trans Mugge (Edinburgh, 1911), pp 51–62 (p 51).
47  Nietzsche, *Zarathustra*, p 64.
48  Lawrence, *Collected Letters*, I, p 281 (5 June 1914).
49  Nietzsche, *Gay Science*, p 91.
50  Nietzsche, *Will to Power*, p 207.
51  Nietzsche, *Beyond Good and Evil*, p 75.
52  Robert Lynd in the *Daily News*, 5 Oct 1915, repr in *D H Lawrence: The Critical Heritage*, ed R P Draper (London, 1970), pp 91–2 (p 91).

53  Nietzsche, *Zarathustra*, p 145.
54  Mark Spilka, *The Love Ethic of D H Lawrence* (London, 1958), p 49.


NOTES TO CHAPTER 4 (pp 93 to 128)

1   *Collected Letters*, I, p 282 (5 June 1914).
2   Nietzsche, *Will to Power*, pp 283-4.
3   *Collected Letters*, I, p 282 (5 June 1914).
4   Nietzsche, *Grossoctav*, XIII, p 280, trans Morgan, p 105.
5   Nietzsche, *Will to Power*, p 211.
6   Nietzsche, *Grossoctav*, XIII, p 33, trans Morgan, p 103.
7   Nietzsche, *Ecce Homo*, p 254.
8   Nietzsche, 'Schopenhauer as Educator', in *Complete Works*, vol V, *Thoughts out of Season II*, trans Collins (Edinburgh, 1910), pp 101-201 (pp 109-10).
9   Nietzsche, *Will to Power*, p 408.
10  Nietzsche, *Will to Power*, p 518.
11  Graham Hough, *The Dark Sun* (Harmondsworth, 1961), p 72.
12  *Collected Letters*, I, p 281 (5 June 1914).
13  *Collected Letters*, I, p 181.
14  *Collected Letters*, I, p 180 (17 January 1913).
15  Nietzsche, *Will to Power*, p 357.
16  Nietzsche, *Will to Power*, p 355.
17  Nietzsche, *Will to Power*, p 357.
18  Nietzsche, *Will to Power*, p 355.
19  Huxley, introduction to *Letters*, p XI.
20  Louis L Martz, 'Portrait of Miriam' in *Imagined Worlds, Essays in Honour of John Butt*, ed Mack and Gregor (London, 1968), pp 343-69 (p 351).
21  Nietzsche, *Gay Science*, p 297.
22  Nietzsche, *Will to Power*, p 284.
23  Nietzsche, *Will to Power*, p 284.
24  *Collected Letters*, I, p 180 (17 January 1913).
25  Nietzsche, *Will to Power*, p 264.
26  Nietzsche, *Will to Power*, p 265.
27  Nietzsche, *Gay Science*, pp 298-9.
28  Nietzsche, *Gay Science*, p 299.
29  Nietzsche, *Gay Science*, p 299.
30  Miko, *'Women in Love'*, p 95.
31  Lawrence, 'Study of Thomas Hardy' in *Phoenix*, p 446.
32  Miko, *'Women in Love'*, p 105.
33  Nietzsche, *Grossoctav*, XII, p 30, trans Morgan, p 268.
34  Nietzsche, *Grossoctav*, XIII, p 50, trans Morgan, p 277.
35  Nietzsche, *On the Genealogy of Morals*, ed Kaufmann (New York, 1969) p 155.
36  Nietzsche, *Will to Power*, p 16.

37  Nietzsche, *Genealogy*, p 155.
38  Nietzsche, *Gay Science*, p 330.


NOTES TO CHAPTER 5 (pp 129 to 160)

1   Nietzsche, *Gay Science*, p 247.
2   *Collected Letters*, I, p 282 (5 June 1914).
3   Morgan, *What Nietzsche Means*, p 194.
4   Julian Moynahan, *The Deed of Life: the Novels and Tales of D H Lawrence* (London, 1971), p 30.
5   Mark Schorer, 'Technique as Discovery', in *D H Lawrence: 'Sons and Lovers'*, ed Salgado, Macmillan Casebook Series (London, 1969), pp 106-11 (p 109).
6   Daleski, *The Forked Flame: a Study of D H Lawrence* (London, 1965), p 85.
7   Morgan, *What Nietzsche Means*, p 63.
8   Lawrence, 'Study of Thomas Hardy', *Phoenix*, p 398.
9   Lawrence, 'Study', p 401.
10  Nietzsche, *Twilight*, p 71.
11  Nietzsche, *Will to Power*, p 421.
12  Daleski, *Forked Flame*, p 57.
13  Daleski, *Forked Flame*, p 59.
14  Nietzsche, *Twilight*, p 23.
15  Nietzsche, *Beyond Good and Evil*, p 136.
16  Lawrence, *Studies in Classic American Literature* (London, 1965), p 10.
17  Lawrence, *Studies*, p 16.
18  Nietzsche, *Will to Power*, p 347.
19  Nietzsche, *Will to Power*, p 355.
20  Morgan, *What Nietzsche Means*, p 99.
21  Nietzsche, *Will to Power*, p 355.


NOTES TO CHAPTER 6 (pp 161 to 192)

1   Nietzsche, *Will to Power*, pp 355-6.
2   Morgan, *What Nietzsche Means*, p 163.
3   Leavis, *D H Lawrence: Novelist* (Harmondsworth, 1964), p 148.
4   Nietzsche, *Will to Power*, p 75.
5   *Complete Poems*, I, p 250.
6   Nietzsche, *Will to Power*, pp 85-6.
7   Nietzsche, *Will to Power*, p 86.
8   Nietzsche, *Will to Power*, pp 86-7.
9   *Letters*, pp 95-6 (January 1913).
10  Nietzsche, *Grossoctav*, XI, p 251, trans Morgan, p 122.
11  Nietzsche, *Will to Power*, pp 403-4.
12  Nietzsche, *Twilight*, p 39.

13  Nietzsche, *Anti-Christ*, pp 125–6.
14  Nietzsche, *Will to Power*, p 445.
15  Nietzsche, *Twilight*, p 72.
16  Nietzsche, *Will to Power*, p 424.
17  Nietzsche, *Will to Power*, p 424.
18  Lawrence, 'Making Love to Music', in *Phoenix*, pp 160–6 (p 161).
19  Nietzsche, *Will to Power*, p 421.
20  Nietzsche, *Will to Power*, p 434.
21  Nietzsche, *Will to Power*, pp 423–4.
22  Nietzsche, *Will to Power*, p 421.
23  Nietzsche, *Grossoctav*, XII, p 30, trans Morgan, p 268.
24  Nietzsche, *Will to Power*, p 13.
25  *Collected Letters*, I p 273 (22 April 1914).


NOTES TO CHAPTER 7 (pp 193 to 232)

1  *Collected Letters*, I, p 519 (27 July 1917).
2  *Collected Letters*, I, p 295 (17 November 1914).
3  Daleski, *The Forked Flame: a study of D H Lawrence* (London, 1965), p 82.
4  Nietzsche, *Will to Power*, p 531.
5  Helen Corke, *Neutral Ground: A Chronicle* (London, 1933), p 275.
6  Kenneth Inniss, *D H Lawrence's Bestiary: A Study of his Use of Animal Traps and Symbol* (The Hague, 1971), p 143.
7  Morgan, *What Nietzsche Means*, p 160.
8  Nietzsche, *Will to Power*, p 550.
9  Nietzsche, *Will to Power*, p 187.
10  *Complete Poems*, I, pp 111–2.
11  Lawrence, 'Making Love to Music', *Phoenix*, p 160.
12  Nietzsche, *Grossoctav*, XIII, p 237, trans Morgan, p 69.
13  Nietzsche, *Complete Works*, vol VI, *Human, All-To-Human* I, trans Zimmern (Edinburgh 1909), p 295.
14  Nietzsche, *Will to Power*, p 507.
15  Nietzsche, *Thus Spake Zarathustra*, p 53.
16  Lawrence, 'Morality and the Novel', *Phoenix*, pp 527–32 (p 532).
17  Angus Wilson, 'Dickens and Dostoevsky', in *Dickens Memorial Lectures 1970*, supplement to *The Dickensian*, September 1970, pp 41–61 (p 42).

# Index

*References to volumes are in italic, references to poems, plays, essays etc are in single quotation marks.*

241